T0323466

China's Technological Leapfrogging and Economic Catch-up

China's Technological Leapfrogging and Economic Catch-up

A Schumpeterian Perspective

KEUN LEE

OXFORD
UNIVERSITY PRESS

Great Clarendon Street, Oxford, OX2 6DP,
United Kingdom

Oxford University Press is a department of the University of Oxford.
It furthers the University's objective of excellence in research, scholarship,
and education by publishing worldwide. Oxford is a registered trade mark of
Oxford University Press in the UK and in certain other countries

First Edition published in 2021

Impression: 2

Published in the United States of America by Oxford University Press
198 Madison Avenue, New York, NY 10016, United States of America

British Library Cataloguing in Publication Data
Data available

Library of Congress Control Number: 2021940864

ISBN 978-0-19-284756-0

DOI: 10.1093/oso/9780192847560.001.0001

Printed and bound in the UK by
TJ Books Limited

Preface

I am pleased to publish my second book on China after an almost 30-year interval since the first one (*Chinese Firms and State in Transition*, 1991). That first book was an outgrowth of my doctoral thesis from the University of California, Berkeley, and dealt with China's economic system reform in the 1980s under Deng Xiaoping. This book deals with a new and significant topic for China: technological innovation, which has emerged as one of the most important factors for the current and future growth of its economy. Such a change in topic also reflects the change in the scope of my own research; I have shifted from being a scholar on economic system transition from planned economies to market economies to an innovation scholar following the Schumpeterian tradition.

Perhaps the change in my research interests reflects the actual transitions in China in the intervening decades. When China made a radical change from being a closed communist economy to becoming an open market economy in late 1978, many economists in the Western world doubted that it would succeed, and certainly not at the scale of achievement it has reached today. That pessimistic view may partly have stemmed from consideration of the possible conflict between an authoritarian political system under the communist regime and the vitality of the market economy, which was partly applicable to the case of the former Soviet Union. However, as a Korean who also lived under a form of authoritarianism known as developmental dictatorship for several decades and witnessed the remarkable East Asian miracle, I believed that China would be as successful as Korea. Thus, I decided to study China's transition as the topic of my doctorate thesis under the guidance of professors Laura Tyson, Benjamin Ward, and Gregory Grossman, who are all big names in comparative economic systems involving research on the former Soviet Union and China. Berkeley was, at the time, the best place for such research.

Following its miraculous economic growth, spurred on by the Beijing Consensus, China is now facing a slowdown. Global attention has moved to the issue of the middle-income trap, the situation in which economic growth slows down as a country reaches the middle-income stage. Several countries, such as Thailand, Turkey, and Brazil, have been caught into this trap. One of the sources of the trap identified in the literature is the difficulty of building innovation capabilities that will enable upgrades from a low-wage-based industry to a high-end goods-based one. The prevailing view is that authoritarian rule cannot be combined with innovation. This book deals with this interesting issue in the context of China. It provides an assessment of how China has made a transition from labor-intensive products to technology-intensive products, embracing innovation while remaining under communist rule. It also discusses China's limitations and future prospects, especially after the onset of a new "cold war" between China and the US, which was signaled by the tariff war initiated by the Trump administration. The discussion then moves on to the question of whether or not China will fall into another trap called the "Thucydides trap," or the conflict between the existing hegemon and a rising power, and of whether the country will face further economic slowdown due to the US policy of containing the growth of China.

This book plays around three key terms, namely, the Beijing Consensus, the middle-income trap, and the Thucydides trap, and applies a Schumpeterian approach to these concepts. Schumpeter was an economist who put forward technological innovation and big business as the core factors that determine long-term economic growth. These are also the most important factors that have affected and will affect the current and future economic changes in China, respectively. Thus, one of the unique features of this book is that it conducts a Schumpeterian analysis of the Chinese economy at multiple levels, namely, the firm, sector, and macro levels. Another feature is that it also conducts a comparative analysis that examines China from a Korean perspective based on a similar experience of growth under a developmental authoritarian state. Regarding the first aspect, I apply to China the theory and insights from my 2013 book (*Schumpeterian Analysis of Economic Catch-up: Knowledge, Path-Creation, and the Middle-Income Trap*), which earned the 2014 Schumpeter Prize. For the second aspect, I apply to China ideas and analytical tools similar to those from my 2016 book on Korea (*Economic Catch-up and Technological Leapfrogging*).

These two aspects also mean that this book examines the Chinese economy from an "economic catch-up" perspective (Abramovitz 1986; Gerschenkron 1962). Economic catch-up simply refers to the closing of the gap between the economies of a latecomer, like China, and a forerunner, like the US. However, a key insight from my 2013 book is that a catch-up starts with learning from and imitating a forerunner, but finishing the race successfully requires taking a different path. This act is also known as leapfrogging, which implies a latecomer doing something different from, and often ahead of, a forerunner. Technological leapfrogging may lead to technological catch-up, which means reducing the technological gap, and then finally to economic catch-up in living standards (per capita income) and economic size (GDP). This linkage from technological leapfrogging and catch-up to economic catch-up corresponds exactly with a similar linkage from the Beijing Consensus to escaping (or not) the middle-income and the Thucydides traps. One conclusion from this book is that China's successful rise as a global industrial power has been due to its strategy of technological leapfrogging, which has enabled the country to move beyond the middle-income trap and possibly the Thucydides trap, although at a slower speed.

One limitation of the book is that some chapters are rewriting, modifications, or updates of already published journal articles that I have co-authored with others. However, this limitation is also a mark of quality in that they have all undergone the referee process for journal publication. For example, the journal article version of Chapter 2 has been cited more than 420 times according to Google Scholar as of June 2021, and it has become a classical analysis of technological catch-up and the rise of Huawei in China. I would like to acknowledge the following articles, for which I am the corresponding author and all the necessary copyrights and permissions have been obtained from the publishers; the degree of revision, rewriting, and updating of the articles for inclusion in this book varies from chapter to chapter.

Chapter 2: Qing Mu and Keun Lee (2005), "Knowledge Diffusion, Market Segmentation and Technological Catch-up," *Research Policy*, 34(6): 759–83; Chapter 3: Keun Lee and Young Sam Kang (2010), "Business Groups in China," in: A. Colpan, T. Hikino, and J, Lincoln (Eds.), *Oxford Handbook of Business Groups;* Chapter 4: Sungho Rho, Keun Lee, and Seong Hee Kim (2015), "Limited Catch-up in China's Semiconductor Industry," *Millennial Asia*, 6(2), 147–75; Chapter 5: Keun Lee, Mansoo Jee, and Jong-hak Eun (2011), "Assessing China's Economic Catch-up at the Firm-Level and Beyond," *Industry and Innovation*, 18(5), 487–507; Chapter 6: Keun Lee, Xudong Gao, and Xibao Li (2016), "Industrial Catch-up in China," *Cambridge Journal of Regions, Economy and Society*, 10(1), 59–76; Chapter 7: Jun-Youn Kim, Tae-Young Park, and Keun Lee (2013), "Catch-up by Indigenous Firms in the Software Industry and the Role of the Government in China," *Eurasian Business Review*, 3(1): 100–20; Chapter 8: Si Hyung Joo, Chul Oh, and Keun Lee (2016), "Catch-up Strategy of an Emerging Firm in an Emerging Country," *International Journal of Technology Management*, 72(1/3): 19–42. Chapter 9 is a substantially revised and updated version of the following article: Keun Lee and Shi Li (2014), "Possibility of a Middle Income Trap in China: Assessment in Terms of the Literature on Innovation, Big Business and Inequality," *Frontiers of Economics in China*, 9(3), 370–97.

I would like to acknowledge the colleagues who provided diverse feedbacks and inputs at various stages of the research related to some parts of this book, starting from the early 2000s. I profusely thank B. Lundvall, Justin Lin, Ed Steinmuller, Dominique Foray, Eduardo Albuquerque, Young-Rok Cheong, Hwy-Chang Moon, Dong-Hoon Hahn, Young-Nam Cho, Christine Wong, Wing T. Woo, Barry Naughton, Jae-Hong Lee, Wanwen Chu, Lu Ding, Jong-hak Eun, Zhuqing Mao, and Mansoo Jee. A special thanks go to Justin Lin, who provided me with many opportunities to interact with Chinese colleagues, such as Yong Wang and Jiajun Xu, at the Institute for New Structural Economics founded by him. Similar thanks go to Jin Chen at Tsinghua University, and Xiaobo Wu and Shi Li at Zhejiang University. This work was also supported by the Laboratory Program for Korean Studies by the Ministry of Education of the

Republic of Korea and the Korean Studies Promotion Service of the Academy of Korean Studies (AKS-2018LAB-1250001). Finally, I profusely thank Adam Swallow, the editor of the Oxford University Press, for his support for this project from the beginning to the final publication, as well as the three anonymous reviewers who provided important feedback on the final version of the manuscript.

This book was completed in January 2021, in the middle of the second wave of the coronavirus crisis.

Keun Lee

Contents

PART II. ASSESSING THE CATCH-UP IN A COMPARATIVE PERSPECTIVE

PART III. PROSPECTS OF CATCH-UP AND
LEAPFROGGING

List of Figures

List of Tables

List of Abbreviations

ASIC	(chips) application-specific integrated circuit (chips)
BTM	Bell Telephone Manufacturing Company
CAD	computer-aided design
CDMA	code division multiple access, a standard in telecommunication
CEO	chief executive officer
CIT	Center for Information Technology
COCOM	Coordinating Committee for Multilateral Export Controls
CPU	central processing unit
DRAM	(chips) dynamic random access memory (chips)
DVD	digital video disk
EPO	European Patent Office
ERP	(software) enterprise resource planning (software)
FDI/DFI	foreign direct investment/direct foreign investment
FVA	(share of) foreign value added (in gross exports)
GDP	gross domestic product
GRIs	government research institutes
GVCs	global value chains
HJD-04	a name of a model of telephone switch developed by the Chinese team
IC	integrated circuits
IDM	integrated device manufacturers
IT	information technology
ITT	International Telephone and Telegram Corporation
IPRs	intellectual property rights
JV	joint venture
LSI	(chips) large-scale integrated (chips)
LTE	long-term evolution, a name of a standard in wireless telecommunications
LTEF	Luoyang Telephone Equipment Factory
M&A	merger and acquisition
MII	Ministry of Information Industry
MIT	middle-income trap
MNCs/MNEs	multinational corporations/multinational enterprises
MPT	Ministry of Posts and Telecommunications
NBS	National Bureau of Statistics of China
NIS	national innovation systems
OBM	own brand manufacturing
OEM/ODM	own equipment/design manufacturing
ODI	outward direct foreign investments
PTIC	Posts and Telecommunications Industrial Corporation

R&D	research and development
RMB	Renminbi (Chinese currency)
SAIC	State Administration for Industry and Commerce
SASAC	State Assets Supervision and Administration Commission (of China)
SMEs	small and medium size enterprises
SMIC	Semiconductor Manufacturing International Corporation
SOE(s)	state-owned enterprises
SPC	stored programmed control
SSI	sectoral systems of innovation
SUV	sport utility vehicle
TSMC	Taiwan Semiconductor Manufacturing Company
UMC	United Microelectronics Company (of Taiwan)
UREs	university-run enterprises
USPTO	United States Patent and Trademarks Office
VCR/VCD	video cassette recorder/video cassette disk
WSOEs	wholly state-owned enterprises
WTO	World Trade Organization
ZTE	Zhongxing Technology Enterprise

1

Introducing Schumpeter to China

1.1 Beijing Consensus, Middle-Income Trap, and Thucydides Trap

When China opened its door and reformed its policies in December 1978, its per capita income was less than 10 percent of the world average in terms of purchasing power parity-adjusted dollars in 2000 prices. By the early 2010s, its GDP per capita had reached over half of the world average, which made China an upper middle-income country, with its per capita income higher than 20 percent of the US level. By the late 2010s, the per capita income of China reached the 30 percent level of the US, at par with that of Brazil. This phenomenon indicated a rapid catch-up, from merely 2.5 percent of the US level in 1980 (Figure 1.1). China had successfully reduced absolute poverty; the population living under the poverty line decreased from more than 50 percent in 1980 to less than 10 percent in 2001 (Ravallion and Chen 2007; Table 10).

However, such rapid growth was accompanied by worsening income inequality for four decades, or at least until the late 2000s (Li 2018). China's sudden rise as the world's number two giant economy (from 10 percent the size of the US economy in 1980 to 70 percent in 2020) alarmed the incumbent superpower, the US, forcing it to change its former policy of engagement to containment, starting with the trade war in 2018. A simple way to understand such a remarkable achievement and the emerging challenge in China is by referring to a series of keywords, from the Beijing Consensus to the middle-income trap (MIT) and then to the Thucydides trap.

The first term, Beijing Consensus, describes the successful rise of China and its possible difference from the existing ways of economic growth, such as the Washington Consensus or East Asian model.[1] China has shown some deviation from the conventional prescription of the Washington Consensus (Williamson 1990) and the IMF or World Bank lines. However, Yao (2010) suggested that such a deviation also follows certain common policy lines of the Washington Consensus, such as openness. As a developmental state, China shares features

---

[1] The term "Beijing Consensus" has not been academically defined. Ramo (2004) defined it as a combination of emphases on innovation, sustainability, equality, and self-determination. Yao (2010) called it authoritarian growth. See Lee (2006) or Rodrik (1996) on the comparison of the Washington Consensus with the East Asian model.

China's Technological Leapfrogging and Economic Catch-up: A Schumpeterian Perspective. Keun Lee, Oxford University Press. © Keun Lee 2021. DOI: 10.1093/oso/9780192847560.003.0001

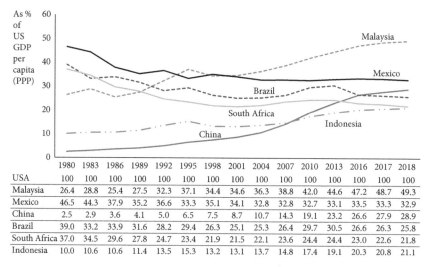

	1980	1983	1986	1989	1992	1995	1998	2001	2004	2007	2010	2013	2016	2017	2018
USA	100	100	100	100	100	100	100	100	100	100	100	100	100	100	100
Malaysia	26.4	28.8	25.4	27.5	32.3	37.1	34.4	34.6	36.3	38.8	42.0	44.6	47.2	48.7	49.3
Mexico	46.5	44.3	37.9	35.2	36.6	33.3	35.1	34.1	32.8	32.8	32.7	33.1	33.5	33.3	32.9
China	2.5	2.9	3.6	4.1	5.0	6.5	7.5	8.7	10.7	14.3	19.1	23.2	26.6	27.9	28.9
Brazil	39.0	33.2	33.9	31.6	28.2	29.4	26.3	25.1	25.3	26.4	29.7	30.5	26.6	26.3	25.8
South Africa	37.0	34.5	29.6	27.8	24.7	23.4	21.9	21.5	22.1	23.6	24.4	24.4	23.0	22.6	21.8
Indonesia	10.0	10.6	10.6	11.4	13.5	15.3	13.2	13.1	13.7	14.8	17.4	19.1	20.3	20.8	21.1

Figure 1.1 Per capita income of selected economies as percentage of that of the US: the MIT (middle income trap)

Source: Drawn using the raw data from the IMF database. Purchasing power parity-based GDP per capita is used.

such as mercantilist export orientation with the East Asian miracle model (World Bank 1993), pioneered by Japan and followed by the Asian Tigers South Korea (hereafter Korea) and Taiwan (Lee, Lin, and Chang 2005). Chapter 5 of this book presents the commonalities and differences among the three consensuses (Beijing, Washington, and East Asia).

The Beijing Consensus is now less mentioned in and out of China because the rate of economic growth peaked at 14 percent around 2008 and then continued to decline to less than 7 percent or 5 percent toward the end of 2010s (Figure 1.2). This leads to the second term, MIT, which has risen as an important issue in the Chinese economy and is extensively discussed in the literature.[2] World Bank (2012: 12) defines the MIT as a situation in which a country's per capita GDP stays within the box of 20 percent to 40 percent of the US level for several decades; many countries, including Mexico, Thailand, and Brazil, are considered stuck in the trap (Lee 2019a: 24–30). China has reached the 30 percent level of US per capita income, exactly the middle point of the box range. The question is whether China will be similar to Brazil and fall into the trap or keep growing beyond the box, as Japan and Korea did in the past. This issue is the focus of Chapter 9 of Part III of this book.

---

[2] In 2007, Naughton (2007: 5–6) observed that the challenges that China faces are shifting and increasingly resembling those faced by other middle-income developing economies than those faced by former planned economies.

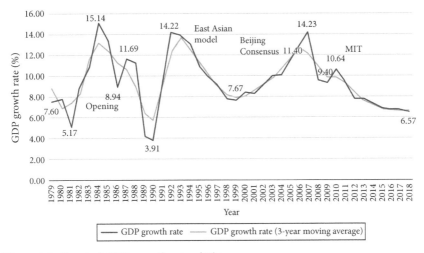

Figure 1.2 Trend of GDP growth rate of China

The Trump administration took actions (e.g., tariffs) to stop China from growing into another superpower that would threaten the American hegemony; consequently, China currently faces another trap, namely, the Thucydides trap. The
trap originally refers to a situation in which a war is almost inevitable when one
power threatens to displace another (Allison 2018). We and this book, focusing
on the impact on China, define the Thucydides trap as a situation in which the US
causes China to stop expanding as an economic power. The issue is whether
China will fall into this trap, which is dealt with in Chapter 10 of this book. The
chapter also analyzes the global value chains (GVCs) of China to show their role
in linking the MIT to the Thucydides trap.

In a way, this book is an assessment of China's economic catch-up for concepts
such as the Beijing Consensus, MIT, and Thucydides trap. The word "catch-up"
dates back to the famous work of a Russian economic historian, Gerschenkron
(1962), where he discussed the process in which latecomers in Europe in the late
nineteenth century tried to catch up with the forerunning UK. Such a concept of
catch-up was also adopted in Abramovitz's (1986) article on "catching-up, forging
ahead, or falling behind" when he compared the economic performance of
European countries during the post-World War II period. Thus, economic
catch-up has been simply defined as the narrowing of a latecomer firm's or country's gap vis-à-vis a leading country or firm (Fagerberg and Godinho 2006; Lee
and Malerba 2018). We focus on data such as per capita income levels and economic size measured by the GDP of China, US, and other countries to discuss
economic catch-up. Technological catch-up means closing the gap in technological capabilities measured qualitatively or quantitatively (e.g., patent counts and
R&D-to-GDP ratio).

The abovementioned three keywords will be running throughout the book; nevertheless, this book adopts a Schumpeterian perspective as its theoretical framework. Schumpeter is the economist who emphasized the importance of innovation (creative destruction) and big businesses as leading engines of economic change. These factors are particularly relevant when we discuss the possibility of MIT in China in Chapter 9 and of the Thucydides trap in Chapter 10. The important elements of the Beijing Consensus have also affected the emergence of large and innovative firms, which rarely happened in typical developing countries.

Considerable studies have considered MIT to occur when middle-income countries are trapped between low-wage manufacturers and high-wage innovators because their wage rates are excessively high to compete with low-wage exporters and their level of technological capability is considerably low to enable them to compete with advanced countries (Lin 2012b; Williamson 2012; Yusuf and Nabeshima 2009; World Bank 2010, 2012). That is, the MIT phenomenon is a problem of growth slowdown because of weak innovation.

The importance of large businesses in the process of economic development has long been recognized in the literature. Schumpeter emphasized in his earlier work that entrepreneurship is mostly associated with startups or SMEs. Nevertheless, his later work (Schumpeter 1934: 71–72) discussed the contribution of large businesses in generating innovation by large R&D investment and thereby enhancing the living standard of people.[3] Although the use of the criterion of large businesses in assessing MIT is relatively new, Lee et al. (2013) verified the importance of large businesses in economic growth in and beyond the middle-income stage via a rigorous econometric method. Their study determined that many middle-income countries command an insufficient number of large businesses, which is one of the reasons for their slowdown in the middle-income stage. Thus, Chapter 3 of this book discusses the origins of large businesses in China, particularly business groups.

As already mentioned, this book adopts the Schumpeterian economics of catch-up as its theoretical framework. Nelson and Winter (1982) initiated a great revival of evolutionary economics and motivated research applying Schumpeter's insights to the study of technological and economic catch-up. Such research includes a series of works, including those of Verspagen (1991), Nelson (2008a, 2008b), Fagerberg and Godinho (2005), Lee (2013, 2019a), and Mazzoleni and Nelson (2007). A distinctive feature of these works by Schumpeterians is the emphasis on innovation and technological capabilities as the enabling factors of catch-up. Fagerberg and Godinho (2005) and Mazzoleni and Nelson (2007) noted

---

[3] Schumpeter (1934: originally 1911 in German) discussed the role of entrepreneurs in economic development. This changing emphasis from entrepreneurship to large businesses is called Schumpeter marks I and II. Chandler's (1990) *Scale and Scope* also showed how large businesses in the US and Germany have contributed to these countries' economic growth.

that in the 1960s and 1970s the main factor supporting catch-up was capital accumulation. However, in the 1980s and 1990s, the accumulation of technological capabilities was more relevant than other factors. At present, only the countries that have immensely invested in the formation of skills and R&D infrastructure seem to be capable of catching up; those that did not tend to fall farther behind.[4] Lee and Kim (2009) found that secondary education and political institutions are important for low-income countries, whereas policies facilitating technological development and higher education seem to be highly effective in generating growth for upper middle- and high-income countries.

A typical sequence of catch-up by latecomers starts with learning from fore-running countries before moving into the innovation phase (Nelson 2008a, 2008b). Therefore, a successful catch-up should consider the institutions of knowledge learning and creating and the modes for access to the foreign knowledge base. Thus, our primary objective is to provide a comparative analysis of China in terms of the modes and performance of learning and building technological capabilities mostly at the hands of large businesses. Then, we aim to assess the performance and prospects of Chinese domestic firms in acquiring "indigenous innovation capabilities" to transcend the middle-income stage and overcome the Thucydides trap. Our analysis starts at the firm or sector level and continues to the national and policy dimensions.

Several unique elements of the learning and knowledge access strategies of China can be found in the Chinese catch-up model (i.e., the "Beijing Consensus"), which is different from the experience of Korea or Taiwan (Lee, Jee, and Eun 2011). These unique features include the following: (1) parallel (indirect) learning from foreign direct investment (FDI) firms to promote domestic companies in the framework of "trading markets for technologies," which is considered "forced technology transfer" in the US terminology in their negotiation with China; (2) forward engineering (the role of university spin-off firms) in contrast to reverse engineering (copycat making) adopted in Korea and Taiwan; and (3) the acquisition of foreign advanced technologies and brands through international mergers and acquisitions (M&As) and going global (*zouchuqu*) at an earlier stage of the economic development.

Chapter 5 of Part II of this book compares the Beijing Consensus with the East Asian model and Washington Consensus. Chapters 6, 7, and 8 discuss successful cases of firms and sectors in China, which represent some or all of the three elements of the Beijing Consensus defined above. In this regard, an outstanding exemplar firm leading China's catch-up is Huawei. We accordingly start by

---

[4] Such emphasis on capabilities is in line with the so-called capability triad in Best (2018), which is comprised of three factors, the business model, production capabilities, and skill formation, and their interconnections.

explaining the origins of Huawei in Chapter 2, and the process of how it caught up with the Swedish giant Ericsson is elucidated in Chapter 8.

The analyses in these chapters utilize a common framework called a Schumpeterian model of technological leapfrogging and catch-up, as elaborated in the next section.

1.2 Schumpeterian Model of Technological Leapfrogging and Catch-up

1.2.1 Schumpeterian Theory of Technological Leapfrogging and Catch-up

Although Schumpeter emphasizes innovation as a key determinant of long-run economic change, technological innovation remains exogenous or unpredictable. In neoclassical economics, innovation is still a black box or residual. Then, it is modern Schumpeterians, called neo-Schumpeterians, with their collected work in Dosi et al. (1988), who explained that innovation is unnecessarily unpredictable because innovation also happens in a relatively ordered pattern ("order in change"). A step toward this direction of endogenizing innovation is the emergence of the concept of "innovation systems" (Freeman 1987; Nelson and Winter 1982) as a key concept of neo-Schumpeterian economics.

Innovation systems can be discussed at various levels, such as national, sectoral, subnational, regional, firm, and inventor. At the national level, the concept of national innovation systems (NIS) has been proposed by Lundvall (1992) and Nelson (1993) and is defined as the various elements and relationships that interact in the production, diffusion, and adoption of new and economically useful knowledge. At the sectoral level, the concept of sectoral systems of innovations (SSI) is proposed by Malerba (2002). A Schumpeterian thesis has presented that this innovation system determines the performance of nations and firms, as verified in many empirical studies.[5] A malfunction of these systems is called "system failure," comparable with market failure in neoclassical economics. A comprehensive application of the SSI concept in many sectors was presented in a collected volume of Malerba (2004a), which dealt with sectors in advanced or European economies. A follow-up study on the sectors in the latecomer economies was undertaken by Malerba and Mani (2009) and Malerba and Nelson (2012). The application of Schumpeterian theory to the context of catch-up by latecomers has led to a recognition that latecomers' catch-up can also be well explained because it also follows certain regularities and patterns (Lee 2013).

[5] Lee and Lee (2019) developed a composite NIS index and proved the linkage of this index to economic growth in a country-panel analysis.

Economic catch-up is defined in the literature as the narrowing of a latecomer firm's or country's gap vis-à-vis a leading country or firm (Fagerberg and Godinho 2005). Nevertheless, Lee and Malerba (2018) proposed that catch-up by latecomers does not mean only the act of cloning because what is achieved by a successful catch-up invariably diverges from practices in the countries serving as benchmark models. This divergence reflects the fact that exact copying is almost impossible and that a successful catch-up involves changes and modifications to existing products and technologies.

This issue of cloning versus divergence can also be considered in terms of imitation versus innovation (Kim 1997) and is one of the most fundamental questions facing latecomers in their effort to catch up. This issue in catch-up can also be observed from the evolution of the literature. Traditional literature, such as Lall (2000); Westphal, Kim, and Dahlman (1985); and Hobday (1995), has observed that latecomers tried to catch-up with advanced countries by assimilating and adapting the incumbents' more-or-less obsolete technology. On the contrary, a new and contrasting view, such as by Lee and Lim (2001) and Lee (2013), is that latecomers do not simply follow the advanced countries' path of technological development; rather, they sometimes do something new, skip certain stages, or create a new path that is different from those of the forerunners. That is, several choices are available for a possible entry or catch-up strategy by latecomers, such as path following, stage skipping, and path creating, in which *path* means the trajectory of technologies and *stage* means the stages in the trajectories.

Following Lee and Ki (2017), Figure 1.3 shows the different trends of the productivities (the vertical axis) of technologies of different generations (with the horizontal axis representing time), which explains the three strategies mentioned above. We suppose that the current time is period 91 in the figure and that leading incumbent firms have adopted the currently most up-to-date, second-generation technology and are thus benefitting from the highest productivity. Therefore, three choices or strategies are available for a latecomer firm that intends to make a late entry.

The **first choice** is to adopt the first-generation or oldest technology with the lowest price, that is, the path-following strategy. This strategy indicates that latecomers move along the old technical trajectories of incumbents. An advantage of this strategy is that established firms are unaffected by the transfer or leakages of proprietary technologies because latecomers target and aim to purchase the oldest technologies. Such technologies are readily available at low prices, particularly during business downturns. However, given their lowest level of productivity, late-entrant firms cannot compete with incumbents with a higher productivity in the same market. Thus, these firms must try to enter a different segment (low-end segments) typically during the mature stage of a product life cycle while utilizing other advantages, such as low costs in labor. For instance, the late entry and

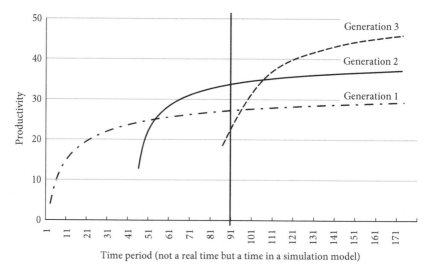

Figure 1.3 Three types of catching-up and leapfrogging
Source: Adapted from Lee and Ki (2017).
Notes: Path-following strategy: to adopt the oldest (generation 1) technology
Stage-skipping strategy: to adopt the latest (generation 2) technology
Path-creation (leapfrogging) strategy: to adopt the emerging (generation 3) technology.

gradual catch-up of the Korean steel company POSCO is a path-following strategy backed up by the government to seek its survival as a late entrant while utilizing the business downturns in the global steel industry to purchase facilities and equipment at low prices (Lee and Ki 2017).

The **second choice** is the stage-skipping strategy, which refers to the case in which latecomer firms follow the same path as that of incumbents but skip older-generation technology (Generation 1 in Figure 1.3) to adopt the most up-to-date technology (Generation 2 in Figure 1.3); this technology is of the same generation as the technology of incumbents. Thus, a fierce competition may occur between incumbents and late entrants because the latter fully utilize the advantage of latecomers to be able to adopt up-to-date technologies (Gerschenkron 1962). In addition to available financial resources to purchase up-to-date technologies, another issue is the market availability of such up-to-date technologies or the willingness of any established firm to transfer such technologies to latecomer firms. In this context, intellectual property right (IPR)-based protection of technologies may be a barrier for catch-up. If this aspect of technology transfer or acquisition is solved for the benefit of a late entrant, then this firm may emerge as a powerful rival because the late-entrant firm not only benefits from the same productivity level the incumbents have but also utilizes the probably low costs of labor or other factor conditions. The forging ahead of POSCO from Korea with its expansion of capacity with a second mill is an example of a stage-skipping strategy because it adopted up-to-date technologies and such stage skipping was facilitated by a downturn (Lee and Ki 2017).

The **third choice**, which is an ambitious and risk-taking strategy, is the path-creating strategy. This strategy refers to the case of a latecomer exploring its path of technological development by utilizing a new techno-economic paradigm or a new generation of technologies. Figure 1.3 shows that in this strategy the late entrant chooses the emerging or third-generation technology ahead of that of the incumbent or leading firms, which have adopted a second-generation technology. This strategy is consistent with the idea of leapfrogging discussed by Perez and Soete (1988), who observed that leapfrogging could happen during the shifting in generations or paradigms of technologies.

An apparent advantage of this path creating or leapfrogging is that this strategy chooses technologies with high long-term potential or productivity, as shown in Figure 1.3. However, a risk is that the emerging or new technology is neither stable nor reliable, and it has lower productivity or higher costs at its early stage than the productivity or costs associated with the current-generation technology adopted by incumbents.[6] Thus, despite the high potential of the emerging technology, a firm that adopts the technology has to endure high costs. Losses might be incurred during the initial stage in the market. Not every firm, but probably late entrants or inferior firms with productivity levels lower than those of a leading firm, has many reasons to shift rapidly and lightly to new technologies. In this sense, latecomers have a greater incentive than incumbents to take the risk of adopting new technologies. Nonetheless, even such risk-taking by latecomers usually requires initial support from the government. Without subsidies or incentives, latecomer firms would not dare to take the risk of adopting emerging technologies because they tend to face small or weak demand during the initial entry stage and thus would have a difficult time achieving the initial production volume that would enable some degree of economy of scale (Lee, Lim, and Song 2005).

Technologies have accordingly been regarded as exogenous, and firms, particularly latecomer firms, are considered to face a binary choice of either adopting new technologies or not. However, latecomers usually not only assimilate adopted technologies but also substantially improve them. On this basis, we consider two modes of path creation. One is the radical innovation-based mode, in which a new path is created by the in-house, endogenous innovation activities of a latecomer. The other is the adoption and follow-on innovation mode, in which an outside supplier-driven innovation is adopted ahead of incumbents and is further improved. An example of the latter is the so-called "secondary innovation" (Wu et al. 2009) or second-generation innovation (Breznitz and Murphree 2011), which transforms acquired foreign technologies into domestic innovations.

---

[6] Two risk types with leapfrogging strategy are discussed in Lee et al. (2005).

Another dimension of leapfrogging can be conceived in terms of inter- and intra-sectoral leapfrogging, depending on whether it occurs within the same sector or across different sectors. Inter-sectoral leapfrogging is similar to a "long jump" to a certain extent according to Hidalgo et al. (2007), who argued that late-comer economies must shift to a core product space located far away from their current or peripheral position. By contrast, intra-sectoral leapfrogging involves jumping across generations of technologies within the same sector. It is easier or less risky than the inter-sectoral long jump if latecomers have already built certain absorptive capabilities, such as manufacturing experience, in relevant industries.

Table 1.1 shows the preceding discussion on the variations in the concept of leapfrogging (Lee 2019b).

Although the path-following strategy based on the initial factor–cost advantages helps the gradual catch-up of late entrants' market shares, a sharp increase in the latecomers' market shares is likely to occur when a shift in technologies or demand conditions occurs. Such a shift is utilized by the path-creation or stage skipping of latecomers, both of which can be considered a case of leapfrogging. That is, leapfrogging is "a latecomer doing something differently from forerun-ners, often ahead of them." The leapfrogging thesis of Perez and Soete (1988) suggested that the shift in generations of technologies could be a "window of opportunity" for latecomers to forge ahead with the rapid adoption of new tech-nologies, whereas incumbents could fall into the "incumbent trap," that is, being locked in existing technologies given the superiority associated with them. A decisive investment at the opening of new windows irreversibly changes the leadership in an industry, namely, a forging ahead, which pushes old incumbents to the cliff of falling behind (Lee and Malerba 2017).

Windows are always doomed to open because generations of technologies and business cycles frequently change. Therefore, leadership change and catch-up by latecomers can be predicted to occur repeatedly. Lee and Malerba (2017) have considered three kinds of windows of opportunity. The first is, of course, the

Table 1.1 Variations of technological leapfrogging

---

(1) Compared with the path of the incumbent (Lee and Lim 2001)
    (a) Stage-skipping
    (b) Path-creating
      (cf) Path-following Catch-up
(2) Two variations of path-creating leapfrogging (Lee and Ki 2017)
    (a) Adoption and follow-on innovation-based leapfrogging
    (b) Radical innovation-based leapfrogging
(3) Inter- vs. intrasectoral leapfrogging (Lee 2019a)
    (a) Intra-sector leapfrogging
    (b) Inter-sector leapfrogging

Source: Author; Lee (2019b).

emergence of a new techno-economic paradigm or of a new generation of technology, as originally mentioned by Perez and Soete (1988). The second type of window of opportunity can be opened with changes in market demand and business cycles (especially downturns), as analyzed by Matthews (2005) for the cases of semiconductors and liquid crystal displays. The rationale is that downturns set a brake on the incumbent, and resources become cheap, reducing the cost of the late entry. Finally, a third source of opportunity can open with the change in government regulations or interventions in the industry. Ramani and Guennif (2012) analyzed how the change in the regulatory system has given a chance to Indian firms in the pharmaceutical industry. The role of the government has also been prominent in several East Asian cases of catch-up, such as China's telecom equipment industry (Mu and Lee 2005) and South Korea's and Taiwan's high-tech industries (Lee and Lim 2001; Mathews 2002b).

Along the line of thoughts discussed above, the main hypothesis we are trying to state in relation to the concept of leapfrogging is that all successfully finished catch-ups (closing the gap) in *ex post* sense tend to involve a variant of leapfrogging, which is a necessary condition in this sense, although leapfrogging involves risks and thus may not be a sufficient condition for success. Technological leapfrogging is a precondition for success in technological catch-up or in closing the gap with incumbents in terms of technological capabilities. Then, such technological catch-up in several sectors may lead to economic catch-up in terms of the growth of per capita GDP or economic power. This eventual linkage from technological leapfrogging to economic catch-up via technological catch-up is what we mean by the title of this book. We focus on this main hypothesis with the Chinese experience in this book.

1.2.2 Specifying the Model for the Chinese Context

Malerba (2004) stated that a sector is a set of activities unified by linked product groups that share common knowledge. The building blocks of SSI are as follows: (1) knowledge and technological regimes, (2) demand conditions (or market regimes), (3) actors and networks and the coordination among them, and (4) surrounding institutions, including IPRs, laws, and culture.

The first component in SSI is knowledge and technological regimes. According to Malerba and Mani (2009), knowledge and technology play important roles in innovation and production. Technology is a unique trait of firms that cannot be automatically diffused and freely shared. Knowledge and technology are absorbed—albeit at varying levels—based on the capability that firms have developed for a long time. Therefore, the pattern of entry, technology development process, and potentialities of catch-up differ according to the attributes of knowledge and technology.

Demand and market regimes comprise the second major component of SSI. In general, competitive advantage in markets is determined by three factors, namely, cost leadership, product differentiation, and first mover (Lee and Lim 2001). Cost leadership is a strategy by which customers are attracted by offering lower prices than competitors. Although it is mainly based on low production cost by improving productivity, it is often driven by low wage labors. The strategy of using low wage labors is a typical pattern of latecomers' catch-up. The difference is in the manner with which new functions or new designs are introduced to meet the varying needs of customers. Finally, the first-mover advantage is a benefit resulting from the know-how, sales and distribution channels, brand value, and market power.

Actors comprise the third major component of SSI. The most important actor is the firm, because firms are in charge of innovating, launching, and selling commodities; they are likewise the ones accumulating knowledge and technology along with their objectives, capabilities, and organization (Malerba 2002). Other actors include research institutions, the government, and even financial institutions.

Then, the SSI framework applied in the catch-up context implies that catch-up dynamics can be explained by referring to the ease and difficulty associated with the particular nature of the technological and market regimes and then by analyzing how actors, such as firms and governments, respond to exploit the potentials through deploying diverse strategies (e.g., variants of leapfrogging) while trying to overcome the limits imposed by the regimes. Such divergence reflects the heterogeneity of sectors and the responses by the actors.

Many studies have examined industrial catch-up in emerging or latecomer economies. Lee and Lim (2001) tried to link the technological regime to catch-up possibility. They focused on elements of the regime such as the frequency of innovations, fluidity of technological trajectories, and degree of access to foreign knowledge. Jung and Lee (2010) found that catch-up tends to occur in sectors with technologies in which the involved knowledge is highly explicit and easily embodied in capital equipment latecomers can import and install. Lee (2013) confirmed that technologies with a short cycle of time could lead to a high possibility of catch-up, which is consistent with the leapfrogging thesis. Mu and Lee (2005) observed that the segmentation of the Chinese market into several tiers (low to high ends) is a unique trait, and the lower end markets may serve as entry points and nurturing bases for indigenous firms. Lee, Cho, and Jin (2009) considered modularity as another determinant of the technological catch-up in China and found that indigenous firms in the cell phone and automobile sectors achieved a fast catch-up upon their entry into the market because of the high (cell phone) or increasing (automobile) modularity of the technologies.

The current study modifies the existing catch-up model to be highly suitable for the case of China. First, this study considers how the large market size and strong bargaining power of China affect access to foreign technology. Thus, we investigate the role of market segmentation as a nurturing ground for indigenous firms. The current study follows Mu and Lee (2005) and focuses on catch-up in market shares in the domestic Chinese market, whereas Lee and Lim (2001) focused on catch-up in the export market. This difference is a result of the differences in the size and degree of openness between the domestic markets in China and Korea. Chinese markets have been more open and competitive from the beginning compared with Korean ones; thus, discussing the competition of foreign versus indigenous firms in these markets is reasonable.

Second, we include the technology cycle time of sectors as an additional element in the technology regime to reflect the double-edged nature of the frequent generation change in technologies. Lee (2013) argued that short cycle technology-based sector means low entry barriers for latecomers, given their quick oblescience (getting outdated) of knowledge associated with existing technologies owned by incumbents, and, at the same time, corresponds to high growth prospects associated with frequent innovations. So, it makes sense for latecomers to target such sectors. However, such short cycle technology-based sectors could provide latecomers with a high chance to catch up only when the latecomers have accumulated a certain level of technological capability. Otherwise, frequent changes in technologies could hinder these latecomers from catching up by truncating their learning processes (Lall 2000).

Third, we explicitly separate firms from the government because of the paramount importance and complexity of the role of the government in China. The decentralized political structure of China (Xu 2011; Chung 2016) and inefficient financial systems (Fuller 2016) often lead to conflict of roles between the central and local governments and to weak growth of private firms. The divergent catch-up dynamics in China has often been attributed to the inconsistency and discoordination among the different levels of governments, which has also to do with the size of the economy divided into many country-like provinces (Thun 2006; Chu 2011).[7] Thus, interaction between national and regional innovation systems is one of the most critical dimensions in understanding the Chinese industry (Breznitz and Murphree 2012).

After learning from previous failures, for instance, in auto sectors in the early days (Lee, Qu, and Mao 2021), the central government has turned to more interventionistic and effective techno-industrial policies (Chen and Naughton 2016; Chu 2011). So, it can be said that the Chinese state has evolved to become more like East Asian-style developmental states (Johnson 1982; Amsden 1989) or state capitalism (Fuller 2016; Milanovic 2019), trying to achieve another "compressed

---

[7] A study of auto sector by Thun (2006) suggests that there are three types of development model in China, with Guangzhou and Beijing as a local laissez-faire system, Shanghai as a model of local developmental state, and Changchun and Wuhan as a model of state-owned enterprises.

development" in a slightly different context than the East Asian Tigers and Japan (Whittaker et al. 2020).[8] This factor of the government or developmental states plays a key role in the discussion of catch-up in many sectors dealt with in Chapter 6 and in information technology (IT) services in Chapter 7 in particular.

Figure 1.4 depicts the preceding discussion and presents our theoretical framework, which was introduced by Lee, Gao, and Li (2016). It first considers catch-up as increasing market shares and then reflects the idea that substantial resources should be allocated to R&D to increase market shares (catch-up) and that firms will devote abundant R&D resources only when they are sure of the linkage between high R&D expenditure and high R&D outputs (product development or innovation). Then, the new R&D outcome is combined with the firm's capabilities in manufacturing, marketing, and logistics as parts of the value chain to produce a commodity heading for a test in the market. Here, technological regime components serve as determinants of the expected chance for product development; for instance, high barrier to accessing foreign knowledge and uncertainty tends to make firms unsure of whether their R&D effort can provide tangible results. Factors such as cost edge, product differentiation, market segmentation, and first-mover advantages act as determinants of the expected competitiveness of the to-be-developed products. The framework indicates that the eventual outcome in market share catch-up emerges from the complex and delicate interaction of the technological and market regimes and the strategies of and policy interventions by firms and governments.

This framework (Figure 1.4) is applied to cases of catch-up in diverse sectors treated in this book. Each catch-up episode is explained as an outcome of the interaction of the technological and knowledge regimes and the responses by the actors, such as firms and the state. In the Chinese context, the term "catch-up" primarily refers to closing the gap between forerunning non-Chinese (or foreign) and indigenous Chinese firms in terms of their market shares in China and technological capabilities.

If we specify the main hypothesis proposed in the preceding subsection to the Chinese context, it is that China's successful catch-up in technological capabilities and market shares has been possible owing to the strategy of technological leapfrogging, although the eventual outcomes are also shaped by other factors, including interventions by the governments and broad institutions. China's successful rise in telecommunications systems and handsets, with Huawei as the leader, is associated with its stage-skipping-style leapfrogging at an early stage of its growth, as will be discussed in Chapters 2 and 6, and then with moving onto a

---

[8] D'Costa (2014) uses another term, "compressed capitalism", to refer to a system-wide account of the unfolding of global capitalism in late-industrializing countries that goes beyond industrial change.

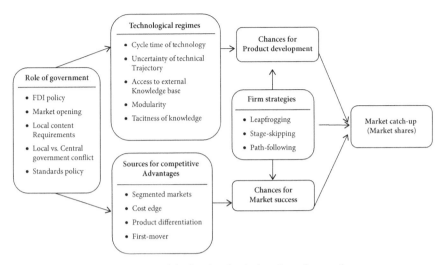

Figure 1.4 Schumpeterian model of technological and market catch-up
Source: Author; Lee, Gao, and Li (2016).

path-creation-style leapfrogging at a later stage, as will be discussed in Chapter 8 in comparison with Ericsson. By contrast, the limited catch-up in semiconductors will be explained in Chapters 4 and 6 through several factors, including the difficulty in trying leapfrogging due to the late entry (low absorption capacity), frequent changes in technology (short cycle times), and tight restriction against technology transfer to China, in addition to inconsistent industrial policy. In consideration of another factor emphasized in the catch-up model (Figure 1.4), the role of the government or industrial policy will be assessed in various sectors, such as IT services in Chapter 7 and IT manufacturing in Chapters 2 and 6, in terms of its interaction with firm-level effort to find a new path different from that of incumbents, thus mitigating the risk involved in leapfrogging.

The last part of this book discusses the national-level implications of diverse sectoral stories of technological leapfrogging and catch-up. That is, we explore the linkage from technological leapfrogging and catch-up to economic catch-up of closing the gap with the US in terms of per capita income (the MIT issue) and the size of GDP as a measure of economic power (the Thucydides trap issue).

In the subsequent section, we provide a summary of the key findings of each part and chapter. We start with Part I, which discusses the origins of technological catch-up in China, focusing on the emergence of large businesses, such as Huawei in telecommunications and semiconductors. Part II provides a comparative analysis of China's technological catch-up in consideration of the experiences in other regions, nations, and firms. Part III, the concluding part, discusses the prospect of the Chinese economy.

1.3 Main Findings from Each of the Three Parts

1.3.1 Origins of Catch-up and the Early Effort

Part I of this book deals with the origins of technological catch-up in China. In consideration of China's catch-up spearheaded by large flagship companies in IT sectors, the first chapter (Chapter 2) in this part first elaborates on the origin of Huawei, a leading company in China that is successful in telecommunications systems and handset products for domestic and global markets. Then, Chapter 3 discusses the broad origins of large businesses in China that were mostly state-owned enterprises in the early period but are presently diversifying into privately owned companies. Chapter 4 discusses the issue of why China's catch-up is limited in the semiconductor sector and searches for answers in the hard and soft institutions surrounding the sector. Summaries of the key findings of the chapters in Part I follow.

Chapter 2 examines the growth of technological capabilities in the telecommunications industry in China, with a focus on Huawei and ZTE, which have become well known due to Trump's measures against them. These companies grew rapidly by localizing the production of fixed-line telephone switches, which were earlier imported or produced by foreign joint venture (JV) companies. While the market used to be completely dominated by foreign products in the 1980s, four locally owned companies caught up with the foreign companies in market shares and became absolute leaders by the end of the 1990s. To explain this interesting and first case of catch-up, the chapter utilizes the Schumpeterian model of technological learning and catching-up proposed in the preceding section. This case can be considered a variant of technological leapfrogging because it involves the stage-skipping catch-up. In terms of the technological trajectory of telephone switches, China skipped the analog-based telephone switches but leapfrogged into digital-based telephone switches (Shen 1999; Mu and Lee 2005). Such stage-skipping was possible because the technological regime of the telephone switches was featured by a more predictable technological trajectory and lower cumulativeness, and the involved technologies were already mature ones; thus, technology transfer was not that restrictive.

The catch-up can be explained by three factors, namely, (1) the famous Chinese strategy of technology transfer called "trading market for technology," (2) the knowledge diffusion from the first foreign JV, Shanghai Bell, to the local R&D consortium and then to other locally owned companies including Huawei, and (3) the government's explicit promotion measures. Given the large market in China, access to knowledge was made possible by the strategy of "trading market for technology," which pushed the JVs to transfer their technologies to the Chinese side. The case of a JV, Shanghai Bell, shows that China took advantage of its large market size to push the foreign partner in the JV, Alcatel's Bell Telephone

Manufacturing Company, into a contract enabling technology transfer. The Chinese partner was able to acquire the related technology of manufacturing, installing, and engineering through the establishment and operation of Shanghai Bell. Public research consortium led by Center for Information Technology benefited from such technology diffusion and eventually developed the first indigenous digital automatic switch, HJD-04, in 1991. Moreover, indigenous Chinese firms were able to secure their competitive advantage due to the segmented nature of markets. The telecommunications equipment market in China is segmented, and indigenous firms differentiate their products to meet various demands in the low-end markets, such as rural markets. Finally, the initial protection and promotion by the government, such as high tariffs on imported goods and coordinated loans, provide an additional competitive advantage for indigenous firms. In summary, the key success factors include the coordinated acquisition of foreign technology by taking advantage of the bargaining power associated with market size, the regulation of JVs to allow knowledge diffusion, and the plan for domestic capability building given the initial condition of segmented markets.

Chapter 3 elaborates on the origins of large businesses, particularly business groups, which have been leading the economic catch-up in China. The Chinese government explicitly defines the business groups that must be registered with the State Administration for Industry and Commerce. Business groups that have at least five affiliated companies must be registered; their number has increased rapidly to form the backbone of the economy. A majority of firms listed on the stock markets are business groups, which are comparable to their counterparts in Japan (*keiretsu*) and Korea (*chaebols*). However, the chief differences between large business groups in China and those in Korea and Japan are that the former are less diversified and are owned by the state and not by particular families (as in Korea) or commercial banks (as in Japan). The central and provincial governments, including their diverse agencies and subsidiaries, controlled 45 percent of the business groups in 2007. The dominance of the state was more evident in terms of total revenue; the state-controlled ones accounted for 78 percent of the total revenue. However, non-government ownership is growing fast, and business groups of private and other ownership accounted for approximately 45 percent of a total of 2,856 business groups in 2007, although their share in terms of sales remained less than 20 percent. In terms of sectors, the top 30 business groups tended to be present heavily in energy, utilities, and services, whereas manufacturing was dominant in the top 500 business groups.

Chinese business groups typically maintain a vertical structure, with the core company at the first tier, closely related companies at the second tier, semi-closely related companies at the third tier, and loosely related companies at the bottom. The core firms are also called parent company or group company because they own majority equity shares of their subsidiaries and unite the business group into a single controlled structure. They are generally large industrial or commercial enterprises, whose business defines the primary business area of the group. Several large business groups have finance companies and R&D companies as affiliated companies. The performance of the business groups improves over time, but they often show inferior or comparable performance relative to stand-alone firms. Chinese business groups also have strengths (high growth) and weaknesses (lower profitability) similar to those in neighboring countries, such as *chaebols* in Korea, which is understandable because business groups in China are also known to have multitier structure, leading to asset stripping and agency costs similar to their counterparts in other countries.

Chapter 4 analyzes China's semiconductor industry from the SSI perspective. The innovation systems of China's semiconductors have been ever-evolving, with the government playing the crucial role of policy actor. However, the industry remained limited in terms of catch-up in market shares and technology. The chapter explains the reasons for the limited catch-up first in terms of the characteristics of the technology regime of the industry. In the semiconductor industry, innovations are frequent, and technologies are highly cumulative, which places the latecomer in a disadvantageous position in terms of entry possibility. Furthermore, the market for standard integrated circuit (IC) chips is not segmented but highly integrated, which implies no low-end niche market for latecomers to enter first. Therefore, latecomer firms encounter difficulty in seizing a market opportunity through differentiated marketing. The situation worsens with the continued increase of the required investment and shortening of life cycles. Furthermore, the existing practice of Western countries restricting the transfer of core technologies to Communist countries, such as China, had aggravated the difficulties faced by Chinese firms.

Although China's semiconductor industry faced many obstacles in its quest for catch-up, several promising signs emerged in the 2010s, at least before the Trump administration took measures to check the growth of Chinese firms in high-tech areas. The first is the continuing explosion of the Chinese market and its increasing importance after the global financial crisis. Second, China expects an increased flow of human capital equipped with up-to-date technology in this field by working in foreign firms and by obtaining education and training in foreign countries, although this factor had become complicated during Trump's administration in the US. As these favorable factors are combined with the consolidation of the domestic innovation system, such as R&D capabilities of domestic firms, research organizations, and universities, China's position is expected to rise, and technology catch-up may become a possibility in varying degrees. Thus, as the general absorptive capacity of actors in China increases, changes and rise of the new generation of technologies could serve as a window of opportunity for leapfrogging. However, some delay is now expected if Chinese firms are forced into increasing difficulty in terms of access to key high-technology components owing to the US–China hegemony struggle since 2018. China must find a way not to rely on foreign technologies but to allocate more resources for indigenous innovation, which means more delays in catch-up.

1.3.2 Assessing the Catch-up from a Comparative Perspective

Part II of this book assesses China's catch-up and leapfrogging from a comparative perspective. Chapter 5 provides the first comparison of China's catch-up model, namely, the Beijing Consensus, with the Washington Consensus and East Asian Model. Chapter 6 assesses its catch-up in key manufacturing sectors compared with that by Korea in the same sectors. Chapter 7 deals with the catch-up in IT services compared with that in manufacturing. Finally, Chapter 8 focuses on Huawei to show how it has been able to catch up with Swedish Ericsson in the telecommunications system sector.

Chapter 5 assesses China's catch-up model, often called the Beijing Consensus, from a comparative perspective. This chapter extend a similar comparative analysis by Lee (2006a), who compared the Washington Consensus with East Asian sequencing. The idea of sequencing originated from Rodrik (1996), who pointed out that although Latin America endorsed and simultaneously tried all 10 elements of the Washington Consensus, Korea and Taiwan adopted only the first half (i.e., macroeconomic stabilization, 1–5) but maintained microeconomic intervention by not committing to the second half (i.e., privatization, liberalization, and deregulation) until the later stages. Now, China shares several elements of the East Asian model because it also pursued the export-oriented, outward-looking growth strategies (Lee, Lin, and Chang 2005). A further commonality lies in its emphasis on the elements missing from the Washington Consensus, namely, technology policy and higher education revolution.

However, the Chinese catch-up model (i.e., the Beijing Consensus) has several unique elements that are not found in Taiwan or Korea, such as parallel learning from FDI firms, forward engineering in contrast to reverse engineering, and active international M&As. One may also say that several commonalities are observed across Chinese and neighboring Asian strategies that can be summed up as the "BeST (Beijing–Seoul–Tokyo) consensus" (Lee and Mathews 2010); the BeST consensus identifies firms and the state developmental agency as the two primary vehicles for latecomer development.

However, the specific implementation process has several distinctive Chinese flavors that are associated with its size. For instance, tremendous bargaining power associated with size is an important factor in the technology transfer strategy, and the international M&A strategy is related to the size of the cash power of large corporate sectors. The initial success of the university spin-off firms is associated to a lesser degree with the availability of a large population of educated human capital at a lower cost that can also take advantage of the agglomeration economy in college locations. These characteristics must be understood in a relative sense. However, during the early stage of their catch-up, Taiwan and Korea did not experience the emergence of university spin-offs to the extent that China experienced in the 1990s and 2000s. In terms of parallel learning from FDI firms, Taiwan also pursued this goal, although China is capable of relying on stronger bargaining power in its negotiations with MNCs for technology transfer. The sheer size of its economy and its attendant cash power enable China to utilize this strategy ("trading market for technology") on a much larger scale.

In general, these strategies help China achieve a "compressed catch-up" and avoid several of the risks involved. It avoids the risk of the "liberalization trap," where premature financial liberalization leads to macroeconomic instability, by following the East Asian sequencing rather than the Washington Consensus. In this sense, the current Beijing model seems to be a natural extension of the earlier gradual approach (Lin, Cai, and Li 1996) to system transition responsible for China's early success.

Chapter 6 assesses China's catching-up and leapfrogging in key manufacturing sectors compared with the Korean experience. In this chapter, the catch-up performance in four sectors is measured by the changes in market shares of indigenous firms. The market share trend of indigenous cell phone makers has been very volatile, which is characterized by a quick catch-up, retreat, and recent regaining of the catch-up. By contrast, the telecommunications system sector initially exhibited a slow catch-up through the path-following strategy and then has displayed a rapid catch-up through a path-creation strategy or leapfrogging. The automobile sector is characterized by a steady catch-up with medium speed, which is slower than that of the IT sector. Finally, the semiconductor sector has the most modest performance of catch-up. The chapter explains the varying records of market catch-up by referring to the diverse aspects of the technological and market regimes, such as modularity, degrees of embodied technical change, tacitness of knowledge, knowledge accessibility, and frequency of innovations.

Easy access to foreign technologies from developed countries (mobile phones versus semiconductors), high degree of modularity (mobile phones versus automobiles and semiconductors), and frequent changes in the generations of technologies or short cycle times of technologies (mobile phones and telecommunications systems versus automobiles) generally help latecomers catch up. More importantly, sectors with a high degree of tacit knowledge (e.g., automobiles) tend to show a slower speed of catch-up than the manufacturers of telecommunications equipment with a high degree of explicit knowledge. Whether markets feature segmentation (or the existence of low-end niche segments for Chinese latecomers) seems to play an important role in the market regimes. Chinese firms manage to achieve initial success from a low-end market in segmented market conditions (e.g., telecommunications equipment and mobile phones) or markets protected by the government (e.g., telecommunications equipment). Conversely, they face high entry barriers in markets with no such segmentation (e.g., memory chips), which is one of the reasons for the slow progress of Chinese firms in the memory chip sector (see also Chapter 4).

A tricky point in this condition is the double-edged nature of the technological regime featured with rapid technical change or short technical cycles. The short cycle time of technologies and frequent changes provided opportunities for latecomers in mobile phones and telecommunications equipment, whereas the frequent generation changes interfered with the Chinese effort to catch up with the ever-moving forerunners in IC manufacturing. Therefore, the difference must come from the level of initial absorptive capacity (or the initial gap) and the degree of lateness in entry by latecomers, beside the degree of market segmentation. For instance, the Chinese entry into the IC chip market is relatively behind than that into the mobile phone market. Lee (2013) clarified that short cycles provide latecomers with a good chance to catch up only when they have already accumulated certain absorption capabilities. Otherwise, the frequent changes in technologies become an additional barrier against catch-up. Therefore, sectors with short-cycle technologies require the leapfrogging strategy to target and jump to emerging or next-generation technologies, as exemplified by the TD-SCDMA standard.

The above stories of the sectors also suggest that technological regimes are not the only paramount determining factor; the outcomes are affected by the roles of actors, including firms and governments. Despite having similar regimes of rapid technical changes, the wireless telecommunications sector in China succeeded in catching up in contrast to IC manufacturing. In these comparable cases, one of the reasons for the difference is the varying roles of the government; the Chinese government has been timely and consistent in implementing its supportive role in the telecommunications sector but not in the semiconductor sector during its early days, where the government was not confident and was thus inconsistent (Chapter 4). The case of the early days of the semiconductor industry in Korea is an example of how the difficulty posed by the nature of the technological regime can be mitigated by the supportive role of the government in conducting joint R&D with private actors. The government may indeed play the role of a facilitator in the process of catch-up, but this statement does not mean that such a condition is always necessary, as shown by the case of cell phones, where a successful catch-up was achieved without much government activism.

Finally, concerning the choice among the alternative catch-up strategies (e.g., path following, stage skipping, and path creating), the path-following strategy on the basis of initial factor–cost advantages may aid the gradual catch-up of market shares. However, the implementation of this strategy alone may not be sufficient to stage a rapid catch-up or overtake the incumbents, which may require the leapfrogging (path-creating or stage-skipping) approach. In the path-following strategy, latecomers move along the existing technical trajectories of incumbents, but incumbents tend to become increasingly reluctant to provide the former with technologies if the latter emerge as competitive threats in the market. This situation indicates the need and reason for latecomers to turn to the leapfrogging approach, as observed in sectors in China and Korea. However, given the intrinsic risks in using the leapfrogging strategy (e.g., uncertainty in standard choice and (non)-existence of initial markets, identified by Lee, Lim, and Song (2005), supplementary actions are often required by governments.

Chapter 7 analyzes the market and technological catch-up of indigenous Chinese firms in two IT services sectors, namely, games and business software (enterprise resource planning (ERP) and security software) and focuses on two aspects. The first aspect is about how latecomer firms have been able to learn and access the foreign knowledge base and acquire their innovation capabilities. The second aspect is the role of the government and regulation in the process of catch-up. Indigenous firms in China have selected different learning and catch-up strategies in different technological regimes. For the online game sector, where imitation is easier and incremental innovation is more important than radical innovation, Chinese firms started with handling the publishing (or distribution) of games developed by foreign incumbents and later secured in-house game development capabilities by imitating the products of global leaders. In the business software sector, where imitation and creative innovation are difficult, Chinese firms acquired third-party technologies through M&As and then differentiated their products by taking advantage of local specificities.

In general, IPRs are critical in the business of these two segments. Despite the entry barrier effect of IPR protection by the foreign incumbents, the latecomer firms discussed in this chapter were shown to circumvent the barrier to entry and learning and to acquire their innovation capabilities. However, such learning and acquisition would not have led to commercial success without government regulation against foreign companies, such as business restrictions in online gaming and exclusive procurement for indigenous products in applied software (ERP and security software). Such restriction against foreign companies is a critical constraining factor against their market share expansion in the Chinese market. This study underscores the importance of the government and regulation in "artificially opening" windows of opportunity for latecomers, although the process often involves "unfair" business practices from the incumbent point of view. However, such intervention has led to a market structure that is more competitive than a monopoly by a few (foreign) companies, which means more economic efficiency. Thus, the policy implication is that the initial protection of domestic markets and firms may be essential in the early stage because latecomers have limited resources and need time to learn. However, after acquiring their in-house R&D capabilities, policy-makers may switch to a new institutional regime, allowing fairer competition with foreign companies. This observation implies that when access to foreign knowledge is not difficult, the necessary intervention can be merely the protection of the initial market in the form of entry limit or exclusive procurement and does not have to be in the form of sharing R&D cost or activity itself.

Chapter 8 explores the question of how Huawei has been able to emerge as the leading firm in the telecommunications system sector, overtaking the long-lasting incumbent Swedish giant, Ericsson; Huawei overtook Ericsson in terms of sales revenues in 2012. It answers this question by focusing on whether a latecomer firm trying to catch up uses technologies "similar to or different from" those of the forerunners. The study investigated the patents by Huawei and Ericsson and found that Huawei relied on Ericsson as a knowledge source in its early days but subsequently reduced this reliance and increased its self-citation ratio to become more independent. The analyses of mutual citations (direct dependence), common citations (indirect reliance), and self-citations provide strong evidence that Huawei caught up with or overtook Ericsson by taking a different technological trajectory. Compared with Ericsson, Huawei developed its technologies by relying on more recent and scientific knowledge; the analyses of citations to scientific articles and citation lags show that Huawei extensively explored basic research and maintained up-to-date technologies to accomplish its technological catch-up.

Overall, this study suggests that leapfrogging by exploring a new technological path different from that of forerunners is a possible and viable catch-up strategy for a latecomer. The higher reliance on scientific articles by a latecomer, in this case, Huawei, makes sense because articles are free from IPR protection and litigations with incumbents, which is different from patents. A higher reliance on recent patents is consistent with the idea that a latecomer should try to minimize reliance on old or existing knowledge (patents) owned by incumbents. Moreover, Huawei's case re-confirms the hypothesis that catch-up in technological capabilities tends to precede catch-up in market share, which was verified in the Samsung versus Sony case on consumer electronics by Joo and Lee (2010). Huawei overtook Ericsson in terms of quantity and quality of patents before annual sales. In summary, the results suggest that Huawei's catch-up with Ericsson in the telecommunications equipment market is owing not only to its cost advantage, the large domestic market, and the Chinese government's support but also more importantly to its technological leapfrogging based on its technological strength and independence.

1.3.3 Prospect of the Chinese Economy under the Double Traps: MIT and Thucydides

Part III of the book links the discussion of technological catch-up in the preceding parts to the issue of economic catch-up at the national level as measured by GDP size (economic power) and per capita income (living standards). Thus, this part tackles recent and broad issues, such as the MIT and Thucydides trap, but discussions extend many micro and meso analyses performed in the preceding parts.

Chapter 9 discusses the possibility of China falling into the MIT in terms of three checkpoints: innovation capability, big businesses, and inequality. The main finding is that China is performing well in terms of the first two criteria of innovation and big businesses, but some uncertainty lies in the last criterion of whether China generates Kuznets curve-type dynamics of the growth leading to better equality. Additional details are discussed in the following paragraphs.

First, China has increasingly become innovative; thus, it differs from other middle-income countries. It has strongly been pushing for considerable R&D expenditure and has been ahead of the typical middle-income countries. Its spending on R&D as a percentage of GDP, known as R&D intensity, more than doubled from 0.6 percent in 1995 to over 1.3 percent in 2003 and is now over 2 percent, which is higher than that of several high-income economies. Moreover, the number of US patents filed by China exceeded 2,500 in 2010, which exceeds that filed by other middle-income countries (less than 300 patents per year). During the 10 years from 2010 to 2019, the number increased by nearly 10 times to reach 21,726, which is more than that of Germany (21,074) and close to that of Korea (22,183), which is now ranked third after Japan.

Second, China has many world-class big businesses, which is more than its size predicts, not only in finance, energy, and trading as in the past but also increasingly in manufacturing. Thus, it differs from other middle-income countries with few globally competitive large businesses. In terms of the number of firms listed in Fortune Global 500, Japan has substantially declined since the mid-1990s from 149 in 1994 to 52 in 2018 and the US since the 2000s from 197 in 2001 to 121 in 2018. By contrast, the number for China increased from 3 in 1993 to 20 in 2005, 61 in 2010, and 119 in 2018 (almost at par with the US). China outranks Japan as second across the world in terms of the number of large firms, which is consistent with the fact that China replaced Japan as the second-largest economy in the world in 2010.

Third, China faces some uncertainty in terms of inequality. The Gini coefficient continuously increased from approximately 0.3 in 1981 to reach its peak of 0.49 or so in 2008–2009 but has decreased to roughly 0.46 to 0.47 since then. This recent decrease may be a sign that the Kuznets curve is representing China's situation. However, China is now facing new sources of inequality, such as wealth (including financial and real estate assets) and non-economic factors (including corruption). China should now pay more attention to the third aspect, that is, inequality, than the other two aspects. A more flexible approach in rural to urban migration should be one of the key policy agendas in addition to providing broader access to education at the secondary and tertiary levels.

Chapter 10 analyzes the issue of whether China would fall into the Thucydides trap, which is defined here as a situation where the US causes China to stop expanding as an economic power. The US government since the Trump administration has intended to stop China from growing into another superpower that would threaten the American hegemony. Whether the US will succeed is a vital question. China will not collapse unless the US dares to wage an all-out war by taking drastic measures across various fronts of confrontation. Further, one unexpected factor is the outbreak of Covid-19 in 2020, which hit the US badly, whereas China boasted a V-shaped recovery to record even a positive growth rate in 2020. If we use the most recent 10-year trend of catching up in terms of GDP size, or reducing 30 percent point gap within 10 years, namely, from 40 percent of the US in 2010 to 70 percent in 2020, we can expect that China will catch up with the US in GDP size by 2030, or in 10 years or so.

Before Donald Trump came to power, China was navigating steadily to grow beyond the MIT, building its China-led GVC and localizing formerly imported goods into domestic production. The Belt and Road Initiative was tried to scale up and globalize the China-led GVC. However, it suddenly faced another trap of Thucydides because of the US measures for containing the further rise of China as a superpower. The sudden emergence of this new trap disrupted the China-led GVC formed around Asia, which still relies on the West for key high-technology goods. Such disruption would have further repercussions on the prospect of China's growth beyond the MIT because it must now allocate resources not only on economic competitiveness and "Made in China 2025" but also on socio-economic stabilization and job creation, which gained importance in response to exogenous shocks and external challenges.

This rebalancing implies an additional fiscal burden, which tends to increase the fiscal deficits of the government and debts of the corporate sector. The overall national economy attained fiscal surplus in 2007, or before the global crisis, off-setting local deficits by the central surplus. However, the overall balance eventually turned into deficits, reaching 5 percent in 2018 as the deficits by local governments (higher than 10 percent of GDP) increased more than the budget surplus of the central government (5 percent or higher). Several worsening symptoms in the Chinese economy suggest that the policy response to external shock, including the trade war, by allocating resources to the problem sectors has increasingly burdened the domestic economy and government budget.

China wants to be different from its neighboring Asian economies in terms of economic system, but it still is a developmental state. Thus, it shares several weaknesses of East Asian capitalism, such as weak financial sector, vulnerability to exogenous shocks, and cronyism associated with the tension between political authoritarianism and independent and sound private sector growth. It might not necessarily have to adopt Western-style liberal democracy, but a viable alternative that is compatible with the people's rising demand for political democracy and basic human rights must be implemented. Such a demand has become increasingly visible through the Hong Kong Crisis in 2019 and the coronavirus eruption in 2020. Its Asian neighbors have gone through their path of political democratization, but China now faces the challenge of crossing this unknown territory. This situation may be a more challenging trap than the MIT and Thucydides trap. Therefore, China now faces triple traps.

1.4 Contributions and Limitations

Given the voluminous literature on the Chinese economy, this book contributes to the existing literature by taking a Schumpeterian perspective and focusing on technological innovation in the Chinese economy, which is timely and sensible because the growth engines of the Chinese economy have been moving away from FDI, low-value-added exports, and privatization to innovation and high-value-added exports.

The early success of the Chinese economy was well explained by Lin, Cai, and Li (1996) and later by Lin (2011). Lin's works took a neoclassical economics approach to structural changes in the Chinese economy, from labor-intensive to capital-intensive industrial structure, but firm- or sector-level analysis of technological innovation was not the focus. Furthermore, Lin's work analyzed China's structural transformation mostly from a low- to middle-income economy, but this book focuses on the challenge at the upper middle-income stage where innovation capability is the real binding factor for further economic growth beyond the MIT. *The Chinese Economy: Transitions and Growth* (Naughton 2018), which is the second edition of the well-known book first published in 2007, is very comprehensive as it covers and updates diverse aspects of the Chinese economy, such as demographic, macroeconomic, and institutional transitions. It also deals with industry and technology issues in agriculture, manufacturing, and foreign trade and investment. However. its approach is a broad touch. In comparison, the chapters in this book provide a more in-depth analysis of technological innovation in China, such as the role of innovation in the rise of Huawei, the MIT, and the Thucydides trap.

This book shares the same theme of innovation as that of Fu (2015), which also discussed diverse issues of innovation in China. However, this book tackles technological leapfrogging as the core concept and analyzes it at the firm and sector levels. It also differs in terms of scope from other books on China but focusing on a few sectors, such as Breznitz and Murphree (2012) on IT sector and Fuller (2016) on the IC industry. Dealing with more sectors and more dimensions of firms, sectors, and the nation as a whole, this book takes a comparative approach, in which the Chinese experience and path are compared with those of its Asian neighbors, such as Japan, Korea, and Taiwan, which all share the tradition of developmental state and industrial policy. It combines leapfrogging and comparative analyses and offers insight into the prospect of China going beyond the MIT. This feature of the book linking technological leapfrogging and catch-up to macroeconomic catch-up in income levels and economic sizes extends to the issue of the Thucydides trap, which is one of the most recent issues facing China.

In summary, the following are the new and interesting features of this book. First, it provides a consistent treatment of the three key concepts related to China, namely, Beijing Consensus, MIT, and Thucydides trap. Second, it develops a Schumpeterian model of technological leapfrogging and catch-up and applies this to analyze Chinese firms and industries. Third, it finds that China's successful rise as an industrial power has been possible owing to its strategy of technological leapfrogging, which would enable it to move beyond the MIT and probably the Thucydides trap, although at a slower speed.

The book would be more complete if a chapter is devoted to the three platform business giants of the so-called BAT (Baidu, Alibaba, and Tencent), which correspond exactly to Google, Amazon, and Facebook, in terms of business models. However, the basic principle in the growth of BAT is similar to the explanation in Chapter 7 regarding the IT services sector, that is, a combination of China-specific contents and asymmetric protection by the government. BAT represent more business model innovations adapted for the Chinese context than technological innovations (Chakravarthy and Yau 2017), although they keep evolving from the former to the latter direction and recently to a combination of both types of innovations as they keep embracing artificial intelligence in their new platform businesses (Jia et al. 2018).

Another limitation of the book relates to the fact that several chapters are rewriting, modifications, and updates of already published journal articles of the author. However, the fact that those chapters have been peer-reviewed for journal publications should attest to the quality of this book.

PART I

THE ORIGINS OF CATCH-UP
AND THE EARLY EFFORT

2

The Origins of Technological Catch-up in China

The Birth of Huawei and ZTE in the Telecom Sector[1]

2.1 Introduction

This book looks at China's rise as an economic power from a Schumpeterian perspective, with a focus on technological development. China's technological rise has been spearheaded by the growth of several leading companies. Huawei and ZTE are among those that have been highlighted during the US–China trade conflict since 2018. This chapter reveals the historical origins of these high-tech companies and discusses how they have emerged and grown rapidly during the 1980s and 1990s. Particular focus is placed on the telecommunications industry in which these firms have emerged.

The telecommunications industry in China experienced rapid growth during the 1980s and 1990s. In 1980, the number of telephone sets in China and the world were 4.18 million and 450 million, respectively (Wu 1997). By August 1997, however, the switch capacity in China amounted to more than 110 million lines, and the telephone network had become the second largest in the world (MII 1997). At the end of 2001, the number of fixed-line telephone subscribers in China was 180,390,000, again the second largest in the world (MII 2001). The number of mobile phone subscribers reached about 250,000,000 by the end of 2003, which was the largest in the world. In addition to the growth of the market and services, the growth of the technological capabilities and competitiveness of the telecommunications industry in China has been remarkable. The case of digital automatic telephone switches, which is often called the stored programmed control (SPC) switches in China, is a notable example (Li 2000; Liu 2001).

The market share of local firms' (including Sino-foreign joint ventures (JVs) and indigenous firms) products in digital automatic switches increased from less than 50 percent in the 1980s to more than 90 percent in 1996. It was only in 1981 that the first set of foreign digital automatic switches was imported and installed in China, but within 10 years, indigenous Chinese firms began developing and

---

[1] This chaper is an updated rewriting of the article, Qing Mu and Keun Lee (2005), "Knowledge Diffusion, Market Segmentation and Technological Catch-up," *Research Policy*, 34(6): 759–83.

China's Technological Leapfrogging and Economic Catch-up: A Schumpeterian Perspective. Keun Lee, Oxford University Press. © Keun Lee 2021. DOI: 10.1093/oso/9780192847560.003.0002

producing digital automatic switches themselves. Apart from Sino-foreign JVs such as Shanghai Bell, many digital switches were manufactured by indigenous (or non-foreign direct investment (non-FDI) local) firms. In 1998, 98 percent of the newly added digital automatic switches in China were made by local firms, and since then, non-FDI-based indigenous firms such as Great Dragon, ZTE, and Huawei have been exporting to foreign countries. This means that the Chinese-made digital switches have become internationally competitive. This chapter aims to provide a systemic explanation of the process of technological catch-up in the telecommunications equipment industry in China.

There are several studies on the telecommunications industry in China from diverse perspectives but with less focus on technological development.[2] There is also some research focusing on technological development in China.[3] Liu and White (2001) and Gu (1999) focus on the concept of national innovation systems and make comparisons between before and after the reforms. Four studies more closely related to the theme of this chapter are those of Shen (1999), Fan (2006), Kwak (2000), and Zhang and Igel (2001).[4]

This chapter adopts the Schumpeterian model of technological leapfrogging and catch-up proposed in Section 1.2.2 (Figure 1.4) in Chapter 1. It is a modification of a model by Lee and Lim (2001) but takes the specificities of China into account. For example, with respect to access to foreign knowledge base, we emphasize the factor of knowledge diffusion in Sino-foreign JVs and the fact that China commanded powerful bargaining power based on its huge market size in negotiating technology transfer at favorable conditions. As regards the sources of competitive advantage of indigenous firms, we emphasize the segmented nature of the Chinese market and the fact that the initial growth of the indigenous firms was based on rural or peripheral markets where there was less presence of multinational corporations (MNCs).

---

[2] Zhou (1998) and Wang (1998) address the issue of monopoly break-up. Other studies focus on industrial policy by the government, centering on concepts such as "import- assimilation-improvement or innovation" (Wu 1997; Liu 2000). Yam et al. (2004) conduct regression analysis of the relationship between measures of innovation capability and firm performances in the telecommunications equipment industry.

[3] Shi (1999) compared the practices of the US, Japan, and Korea in terms of catching-up through imitative innovation (Kim 1997). Another interesting phenomenon in China is the emergence of university-run or spin-off companies, which are discussed in Lu and Lazonick (2001), Liu and Jiang (2001), and Gu (1999). Regarding the role of the government during the transition, there is a study by Wen and Kobayashi (2002) on the development of the CAD industry in China.

[4] Shen (1999) discusses the Chinese road to high technology using the case of the telephone switch. Her research focus is, however, on industry policy by the government rather than on technological innovation at the firm level, and needs to be updated. Fan (2006) discusses the history of China's telecom equipment industry with a focus on four indigenous firms but does not investigate at depth the origins of these four firms. Kwak (2000) observes the factor of organizational learning through Sino-foreign JVs but does not mention other key factors. Zhang and Igel (2001) approach the telephone switch industry from the perspective of the management of complex products and systems.

A key theme of the chapter is technological leapfrogging. Latecomers do not simply follow the path of technological trajectory of the advanced countries or firms. They often skip some stages or even create their own path that is different from the forerunners. As noted in Perez and Soete (1988), every country is a beginner in terms of the newly emerging techno-economic paradigm, which implies the possibility of leapfrogging by latecomers. According to the idea of leapfrogging, some latecomers may be able to leapfrog older vintages of technology, bypass heavy investments in previous technology system, and catch-up with advanced countries (Hobday 1995). Hence, we propose that this is a case of stage-skipping catch-up, according to Lee and Lim's (2001) typology of the concept. In terms of the technological trajectory of telephone switches, China skipped analog-based telephone switches and leapfrogged into digital-based ones (Shen 1999). This phenomenon is interesting, because we can observe other cases of leapfrogging in China.[5]

In what follows, Section 2.2 provides a brief overview of the evolution of the telecommunications equipment industry in China. Section 2.3 discusses a theoretical model of technological learning and catching-up applied to the case of the telecommunications industry in China. Section 2.4 investigates the transfer of the digital automatic switch technology through the establishment of JVs. A case study of Shanghai Bell is used to explore how China "traded market for technology" by establishing a foreign JV and absorbing the switch technology from the foreign firm. Section 2.5 investigates the R&D process of indigenous organizations and firms to develop digital automatic switches. Here, the focus is on the case of the first large-capacity central office switching system (HJD-04 system) and on how related knowledge diffused from Shanghai Bell (foreign JV) to indigenous firms and R&D organizations. Section 2.6 discusses the emergence and growth of indigenous firms such as Huawei, focusing on the origin of its knowledge base, the sources of competitive advantage, and the role of the government. Finally, Section 2.7 provides a summary and concluding remarks.

2.2 Evolution of the Telecommunications Equipment Industry in China

The evolution of the telephone switch technology can be divided into three stages: the manual switch (1880s–1920s), the electro-mechanical switch (1920s–1960s), and the electronic (SPC) switch (1965–now). The first "manual switch" stage

---

[5] In the Chinese market, there was no VCR era, as the market skipped the VCR to grab the VCD or DVD. Also in telecommunications services, even before the fixed-line telephone services were more widely installed, mobile phone service began and surpassed the fixed-line telephones in terms of penetration ratio.

Table 2.1 Evolution of the telephone switch technology

Name of switch	Time of invention	Time of commercialization	Switching pattern	Controlling pattern
Magneto telephone switchboards	1878	1880s	Jacks and plugs	Manual
Step-by-step switch	1891	1892	Step-by-step	Electro-mechanical
Crossbar switches	1917	1926 (in US); 1938 (in Sweden)	Crossbar	Electro-mechanical
Analog electronic switch	1960	1960s	Reed relay	SPC
Digital electronic switch	1970*	1970s	Digital	SPC

Source: Zhu (1993), Flood (1994), and Lee and Lee (1992).

Note: * indicates the time of installation.

includes magneto telephone switchboards and common battery exchanges. There are two types of "electro-mechanical switches." The first that appeared was the "step-by-step switches," after which the "crossbar switches" emerged. The third-stage product, the "electronic stored program control (SPC) switch," can also be divided into two phases: the analog automatic switches and the digital automatic switches (Zhu 1999; Flood 1994; Lee and Lee 1992). The evolution of the switch technology is shown in Table 2.1. As shown in the table, the switching pattern of the analog electronic switch is reed relay, and the controlling pattern is SPC. However, the switching pattern of the digital electronic switch is digital, and the controlling pattern is SPC (Mody and Sherman 1990).

After the founding of the People's Republic of China, a telecommunications administration system was established, and a communications network centered in Beijing and connecting the whole country was built (X. Zhang 2000). The first step-by-step telephone switch equipment factory, Beijing Wired Factory, was set up in 1957 with the help of former Soviet experts. In 1958, the factory began to produce JZB (47 type) step-by-step telephone switches, which replaced the imported equipment in China. Because of the disadvantages of these switches, such as slow speed, big noise, adjustment, and frequent maintenance needs, the Ministry of Posts and Telecommunications (hereafter, MPT) decided to stop their production in 1974 (Zhu 1999).

In 1966, the Tenth Research Institute of the MPT developed the first coded crossbar telephone switching system, which became widely employed in telephone networks throughout the country.[6] The major models of crossbar switches

---

[6] The Tenth Research Institute of the Ministry of Posts and Telecommunications, http://www.xdz.com/wenzhang/zlzy/kyjg/leaf/html/2290_0.html.

developed by this institute included the JT-801 switching exchange series, the HJ09 trunk-local-rural switching system, and the HJ10 terminal switching system. In 1975 a slightly improved version of crossbar switches was developed by the Academy of Telecommunications Science & Technology under the MPT and passed the MPT's approval. Until then, owing to the closed-door policy, China had not been able to absorb advanced telecommunications technology from the West, and the level of technological capability was very low. Only after the open door policy, in May 1984, a more advanced crossbar switching system with more than 10,000 ports capacity was developed and produced in Tianjin. China had not developed or produced the analog electronic switch (Zhang 1999). But fully automatic digital switches had already been widely installed in other parts of the world. In sum, in China the step-by-step switches were mainly used in the 1960s and 1970s, and the crossbar telephone switches were mainly used in the 1980s.

According to Wu, former minister of the MPT, as of 1980 China lagged 20 to 30 years behind the developed countries as the step-by-step switches comprised about 29 percent of the telephone network and the crossbar switches 33.7 percent, while analog electronic switches, imported from foreign countries, represented only 6.7 percent of the network in China (Wu 1997: 13).[7] Thus, it can be said that the telecommunications network in China was dominated by the out-of-date step-by-step and crossbar central office switches before the first digital automatic (SPC) switch made by Fujitsu (Japan) was imported and installed in the Fujian Province in 1981 (Wu 1997: 73; Xin et al. 2000: 21; Cheng 1999: 47).[8] After the first installation, all major multinational SPC switch manufacturers began to sell their switches in China.

Realizing the attractiveness of its market size and the resulting bargaining power, the Chinese government actively approached multinational suppliers for technology transfer and JV negotiations. In 1984, the first FDI was approved to establish a very large JV in China, namely, Shanghai Bell Telephone Equipment Manufacturing Corporation (hereafter, Shanghai Bell), with the Bell Telephone Manufacturing Company (hereafter, BTM), a son company of the International Telephone and Telegram Corporation (ITT) at that time and later the Alcatel, as the partner in the JV. Another JV agreement between Siemens in Germany and a factory owned by the Ministry of Electronics Industry (MEI) in Beijing was signed in October 1988 to establish the Beijing International Switching System Corporation (BISC) to produce the Electronic Worldwide Switch Digital (EWSD)

---

[7] In his original text, Wu (1997: 13) used the words "electronics telephones switches (including electronics and semi-electronic telephone switch)," which must be referring to imported analog electronic switches, since he also stated that digital switches were not installed in China until the 1980s, or until the introduction of the one made by Fujitsu in 1981.

[8] For this reason, the telecommunications system in China was one of the poorest in the world. There were merely 3,972,000 telephone lines for a population of over 900 million, with about 4 phones per 1000 people in 1978 (Wu 1997: 7–8; Xin and Wang 2000: 7; Shen 1999: 16–17).

switches from 1991 (Shen 1999: 16–21). Fearing that the two JVs would dominate the Chinese market, other multinational suppliers started to actively pursue JV negotiations with their Chinese partners and eventually established their own ones after 1993.[9] As a result, the involvement of FDI had transformed China's switch market from one dominated by "direct imported goods" to a "JV dominated" one in the early 1990s.

Large-scale installation of imported switches in China's telecom networks and the presence of many JVs in China fostered the diffusion of technology know-how across the country. As Section 2.5 elaborates, there was a broad-ranging knowledge transfer and exchange involving R&D, production, subcontracting, marketing, after-sales services, and local human resource training (Tan 2002; Q. Zhang 2000: 148). Domestic researchers and engineers, teamed with entrepreneurs, quickly grasped the opportunity to develop competitive indigenous products. A specific project to indigenously develop digital electronic telephone switches implemented in the mid-1980s (or 1984), with the initiation of Professor Wu Jiangxing at the Center for Information Technology (CIT) under the Zhengzhou Institute of Information Engineering of the People's Liberation Army. Wu's team at the CIT was joined by the LTEF (Luoyang Telephone Equipment Factory) under the MPT, which used to produce crossbar (electro-mechanical) switches. Some of the specialists who formerly worked at Shanghai Bell also participated in this project to develop digital automatic switches (Shen 1999: 76–77).

What this team developed first in 1987 was a small capacity (1,000 lines), or branch-level, digital switch with model name HJD-03 (Shen 1999:108). Although the switch was registered officially with the MPT, it was notorious for software bugs and repeated breakdowns and was installed in small private networks but never in a public network (Pyramid 1996: 110). This small success was a stepping stone for bigger success a couple of years later. In 1987, a contract to develop a switch with 2,000 lines was signed between the CIT and the Posts and Telecommunications Industrial Corporation (PTIC) under the MPT. Since then, the PTIC has played the role of the general project manager and financial sponsor, with the CIT as the main technological force and the LTEF as the technical assistant and test workshop.

As Section 2.5 will elaborate later, it was in 1991 that this three-party consortium of the CIT, the LTEF, and the PTIC finally developed a central office digital automatic switch (HJD-04). Domestically designed and manufactured central

---

[9] Since January 1, 1993, in response to conditions imposed on China to rejoin the General Agreement on Tariffs and Trade, the tariff for direct imports of SPC switches had been reduced, and other SPC switches technologies transfer projects had been approved by the government (Shen 1999: 21). Thus, several new JVs were established: Tanjin NEC Electronic & Communications Industry, AT&T Qingdao Telecommunications Equipment and Services Co., Beijing Nokia Hangxing Telecommunications, Nanjing Ericsson Communications Co. Ltd., Jiangsu Fujitsu Telecommunication Technology Co., Ltd., and Guangdong-Nortel Telecommunication Switching Equipment. For more details, see Mu (2002) and Pyramid (1996: 104–105).

office SPC switches (a kind of digital automatic switch) started to serve rural markets in 1992. In the mid-1990s, indigenous manufacturers began to compete directly with JVs first in rural and subsequently in urban markets, with significantly improved product quality and added features. Starting from a 10.6 percent market share in 1992, the four indigenous manufactures—led by Great Dragon (Julong) and followed by Datang, ZTE, and Huawei (the so-called *Ju Da Zhong Hua* in Chinese, which means "great China")—held 43 percent of China's digital automatic switch market in 2000 (see Figure 2.1). They even began to export their switches to many developing countries in East Asia, Central Asia, Eastern Europe, and Latin America.

The preceding overview indicates that in catching-up in the telephone switch technology, China experienced a "stage-skipping catch-up," to use the term of Lee and Lim (2001). China had only some experience in developing or producing electro-mechanical switches but skipped the development and production of analog electronic switches to jump directly to digital automatic switches. According to Shen (1999), crossbar switches mainly installed in provincial capital cities were replaced by digital automatic switches (skipping analog automatic switches). In rural areas, manual switches were replaced by digital automatic switches (skipping step-by-step switches, crossbar switches, and analog automatic switches), and in some areas, the first telephone switch installed directly entered the digital age (skipping all stages).

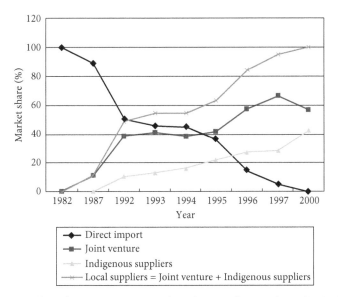

Figure 2.1 Local products versus imported products in the switch market in China, 1982–2000

Source: Mu and Lee (2005), where the original source of the data is explained.

2.3 The Model of Technological Catch-up and the Chinese Factors

This chapter utilizes the Schumpeterian model of technological leapfrogging and catch-up explained in Chapter 1 (Figure 1.4). In this model, the technological capability of a firm is determined as an outcome of the interaction between the available R&D and the amount of its R&D effort (or technological effort). The amount of a firm's R&D effort depends on the probability of success of the R&D project or product. Firms assess two kinds of probability in this regard: the probability of successful development of target products and the expected marketability (competitiveness) of to-be-developed products. Technological regimes enter the model as determinants of the expected chance for product development. We consider the predictability of the technological trajectory to be one element of the technological regime relevant for product development by a latecomer. A technological trajectory with a greater uncertainty implies a smaller chance for success, because it would be more difficult for the latecomer firms to predict the direction of the technology's future development and to fix the R&D target. The model also observes that the technological regime featured by higher cumulativeness implies a smaller likelihood of success, because more R&D effort would be necessary for the latecomer firms to catch up. Access to external knowledge base (technology transfer) is also taken as an element relevant to the success of the R&D project. This access can be arranged in diverse forms: informal learning, licensing, FDI, strategic alliance, co-development, and so on. Later in the chapter, we will emphasize the role of FDI in the case of the telecommunications industry in China.

We now provide a brief explanation of how we utilize the model to elaborate the process of technological catch-up in the Chinese telecommunications industry.

First, let us examine the technological regime of telecommunications equipment, telephone switches in particular. The nature of the technical trajectory can be addressed by examining the ages and life cycles of new technologies in switches, and the frequency of innovation, by patent counts.

Given the history of telephone switches from the manual switch (1880s–1920s) to the electro-mechanical switch (1920–1960s) and then to the electronic switch such as the SPC switch (1965–now), we can notice that the lifespan of each generation of telephone switches is relatively long. The average lifespan of electro-mechanical switches in service was roughly 35–40 years, while some individual users had adopted them for as long as 55 years (Dittberner 1977). It has been over 35 years since the inception of the digital automatic switch, but it is still in use all over the world. This shows that the telephone switch industry is characterized by a technical trajectory that is more predictable than that of other industries such as the computer industry. Whereas computer products are characterized by life cycles of about 6 years, telecommunications switch equipment traditionally had

Table 2.2 Trends of the US patents in telephone switches and DRAM

	Telephone switches patents		Dynamic RAM + DRAM patents	
	Count	3-year moving average	Count	3-year moving average
1976	13		1	
1977	13	16.67	3	2.00
1978	24	17.00	2	2.33
1979	14	16.00	2	2.67
1980	10	10.67	4	4.67
1981	8	10.67	8	9.00
1982	14	10.33	15	11.67
1983	9	11.67	12	13.00
1984	12	11.00	12	14.33
1985	12	11.00	19	18.67
1986	9	15.00	25	31.33
1987	24	16.00	50	42.00
1988	15	18.33	51	50.00
1989	16	15.33	49	59.00
1990	15	17.00	77	70.33
1991	20	14.67	85	85.67
1992	9	15.33	95	103.67
1993	17	13.33	131	130.67
1994	14	18.67	166	159.67
1995	25		182	

Average annual growth rates of the patents

	Telephone switch	Dynamic RAM+DRAM
1977–1982	−9.1%	42.3%
1982–1987	9.1%	29.2%
1987–1992	−0.8%	19.8%
1977–1992	−0.6%	30.1%

Source: Calculations using the data from the USPTO website; keyword search.

life cycles of 20 to 40 years and transmission equipment was replaced every 10 to 20 years (Duysters 1996).

Next, the patenting trend in telephone switches shows that the regime is featured by low frequency of innovation (see Table 2.2). Checking the number of patents related to telephone switches by keyword search in the United States Patent and Trademark Office (USPTO) website for the 1977–1992 period,[10] we find that the average annual growth rate is only minus 0.6 percent, while other

---

[10] We observe this period, because the Chinese project to develop indigenously digital electronic telephone switches started in the mid-1980s, to succeed in 1991.

emerging technologies such as DRAM (dynamic random access memory chips) show much higher growth rates, for example, 30 percent in the case of DRAM during the same period; the same is true of wireless communication technologies as well.[11] The frequency of innovation is also related to the age of the technology, such that old technologies tend to exhibit more stable technological trajectories.

This discussion shows that the technological regime of the telephone switches is featured by a more predictable technological trajectory and less frequent innovation, at least as of the 1980s—the time the Chinese were starting their catch-up effort. It implies that, according to the model, the telephone switch is a relatively easy target for latecomers to emulate and develop. However, there will be a higher chance for success only if there is effective access to available foreign knowledge. This is a finding that is common to the six industries analyzed in Lee and Lim (2001), although those industries resorted to different channels of access.

As the channel for access in the Chinese context, we emphasize the knowledge transfer through FDI or JVs. Given the huge market in China, access to knowledge was made possible by a purposeful strategy adopted by the Chinese authorities—the so-called trading market for technology policy in the JVs. As detailed analyses in Section 2.4 (on the transfer agreement) and Section 2.5 (on the knowledge diffusion from the JVs to other Chinese firms and workers) will show, the case of a JV, Shanghai Bell, is a remarkable example of how China took advantage of its large market size to push BTM to sign a contract for the transfer of core technology, even though it was restricted by Coordinating Committee for Multilateral Export Controls (COCOM), which is an agreement among Western countries to control exports of high-tech products to Communist countries.[12] Through the establishment and operation of Shanghai Bell, China was able to acquire related technologies of manufacturing, installing, and engineering. Shanghai Bell and other JV establishments fostered the diffusion of technological know-how across the country.

Now, we examine the chance for market success of developed products. According to the model, factors such as cost edge, product differentiation, and first-mover advantages serve as determinants of market success. In the Chinese context, we emphasize a new element, the segmented nature of the Chinese market, featured by a kind of dualism: rural–urban dualism and core–periphery dualism. As the detailed analysis in Section 2.5 will show, the non-JV, indigenous Chinese firms, although they were technologically inferior to foreign firms and JVs, took advantage of rural, peripheral, and lower end markets to sell their own digital automatic switches with a simple machine–operator interface and a

---

[11] For a comparison of the growth rates of US patents in several technology categories, see Lee and Lim (2001).

[12] In 1949, the US, Japan, and the North Atlantic Treaty Organization countries created COCOM to restrict the flow of strategic goods and know-how to Communist countries. Industrial sectors such as electronics and telecommunications were of particular concern in this context.

Chinese-based screen menu that was easy to operate. Due to its low development and production costs, this kind of switch was provided to the Chinese users at much lower prices, making them initially popular in rural areas.

Finally, regarding the remaining components of the model, namely, the strategies of the firms and the role of the government, we will investigate the role of the consortium of public (even military) research institutes (CIT) and the manufacturing companies (LTEF) in Section 2.5, as well as government policies during the initial development and promotion stages of the digital automatic switches in Section 2.6.

Chapter 1 (Section 1.2.1) identifies three patterns of catch-up. First, the path-following catch-up refers to instances in which latecomer firms follow a path that is identical to that of the forerunners. However, the latecomer firms go along the path in a shorter period of time than the forerunners. The second pattern is the stage-skipping catch-up, in which the latecomer firms follow the path to an extent but skip some stage and thus save time; an example is the development of fuel injection type engines by Hyundai Motors in Korea. The third pattern is the path-creating catch-up, which means that the latecomer firms explore their own path of technological development; an example is the development of the CDMA technology by Korean firms. This kind of catching-up may occur when latecomers, after having followed the path of the forerunners, try to create a new path. Among the three patterns, the first type is the more traditional pattern, while the latter two types contain some aspects of leapfrogging. Of course, the three patterns are not necessarily a once-and-for-all occurrence; there can be a mixed pattern.

As explained earlier, China had only some experience of developing or producing electro-mechanical switches but skipped the development and production of analog electronic switches to jump directly to digital automatic switches. Thus we propose the following hypothesis.

Hypothesis (stage-skipping catch-up and technological regime): The growth of indigenous digital switches in China can be considered as a case of "stage-skipping catch-up" according to the model; such a catch-up was possible in part by the fact that the technological regime of the telephone switch industry is featured by a high predictability of technical trajectory and a lower frequency of innovation.

This chapter measures technological catching-up by the Chinese firms in terms of whether or not and the extent to which the firms were able to develop and produce the products to catch-up "market share within China."

In sum, we emphasize the strategy of trading market for technology as a means of access to the foreign knowledge base for the JVs and the factor of market segmentation as the source of competitive advantage for the indigenous firms (see Figure 2.2). The following sections give a detailed examination of the hypotheses and explain how the "stage-skipping catch-up" was realized in the telecommunications equipment industry in China.

2.4 Trading Market for Technology and Getting Access to Knowledge

2.4.1 Bargaining Power in JVs

The bargaining power perspective suggests that the implications of resource dependence for JV control may be mediated by the bargaining powers of prospective partners (Fagre and Wells 1982; Lecraw 1984). Prospective partners negotiate for a level of JV control, given the assets that they command (Blodgett 1991: 64). Yan and Gray (1994, 2018) developed a model of international JV focusing on the bargaining power that, in effect, incorporates two dimensions, namely, the critical resource provision ("capital" and "noncapital" resource) by each partner and the substitutability of the partners.

Brouthers and Bamossy (1997) explore the role of governments in transitional economies in Central and Eastern Europe as key stakeholders and how they influence international JV negotiations. The role is described and analyzed by examining eight cases of Western and Central/Eastern European enterprises that had negotiated agreements. The findings suggest that transitional governments are key stakeholders that intervene at different stages of the negotiation process, have both direct and indirect influences on the process, and can change the balance of power in the negotiations.

The Chinese government and policy-makers seemed to have a good understanding of the market size as a source of bargaining power for China. According to Yu Weixiang, the director of the Study Center for the World Trade Organization under the Research Institute on International Trade and Cooperation which belongs to the Ministry of Foreign Economics and Trade, more than 80 percent of direct foreign investments in China since 1978 have been based on the principle of trading market for technology, especially in industries such as automobiles, chemicals, and electronics (Chen and Yue 2002). It is believed that the strategy of trading market for technology was first adopted in the automobile industry during the early 1980s.[13] The spirit of such a strategy was implicitly reflected in the first "Law of Sino-Foreign Equity Joint Ventures" adopted in July 1979; its Article 5 states that the technology and equipment contributed by a foreign JV as its investment must be advanced technology and equipment that suits China's needs.

Besides the size of the market, the state monopoly must also be mentioned as an additional source of bargaining power for China. The state was the sole provider of telecommunications service as well as the single purchaser and producer

---

[13] Cheng, Yuan, "Over Protection and Inefficient Development Whose Mistakes Brought out Backward Development in Automobile Industry?" [Baohu Guodu yu Fazhan Buzu—Qiche Luohou Shuizhiguo?], http://b-car.com/cywj/11.htm.

of telecommunications equipment and facilities. Within China, the MPT was completely responsible for both regulation and operation of networks. The MPT, together with the provincial ministries of posts and telecommunications, was the monopoly provider of international, domestic, and local telecommunications services as well as the purchaser of the related equipment throughout the country. Telecommunications equipment was subject to approval by another state agency, the MEI, until the MPT and MEI were restructured to form a single ministry called the Ministry of Information Industry (MII) in 1998. Until 1980, the MPT controlled 28 telecommunications equipment factories; in 1980 the PTIC was formed and took over the management of these 28 factories. However, the PTIC still remained under the control of the MPT.[14]

In what follows, details on how China took advantage of its bargaining power for effective technology transfer will be elaborated.

2.4.2 Technology Transfer in Shanghai Bell

While the Chinese government had allowed the import of large-scale digital switches to alleviate the immediate bottleneck in the telecommunications infrastructure following the reform, its belief was that direct imports of finished foreign digital automatic switches should be only a short-term solution for China. Being the world's most populous country with a huge potential market, transferring technologies by setting up JVs was considered necessary for China, with added benefits of increase in local valued-added and job creation. More importantly, it anticipated the effects of technological learning and the building-up of indigenous technological capabilities. The MPT approached almost every major telecommunications company around the world to explore opportunities for technology transfer through JVs. Several state councilors and premiers paid official visits to industrialized countries and explored the possibility of the ventures (Q. Zhang 2000: 228).

However, at that time, most of the telecommunications companies were only interested in exporting their finished products to China. BTM was one of the few firms who were willing to exploit the potentially huge market while at the same time allowing for some technology transfer in manufacturing components by conducting a comprehensive "turnkey" project. Obviously, the attractions of a potentially large market and the opportunity for long-term partnership with local

---

[14] The PTIC was renamed as the Pu Tian Information Industry Group of China on January 1, 1999. In 1993, a new division, the Directorate General of Telecommunications (DGT), was split off from the MPT to handle telecom network operation and maintenance. In practice, however, the DGT still depended on the MPT for funding and personnel.

manufacturers were the key elements for BTM's decision to show interest in the project (Shen 1999: 64).

As the huge size of the domestic market provided the Chinese government with strong bargaining power in dealing with MNCs, it could afford to demand that three conditions be satisfied when a foreign firm entered China to establish a JV in the telecommunications business. The first condition was that the Chinese side must hold a majority share of more than 50 percent (in the case of Shanghai Bell, the share was 60 percent), the second was that the foreign side must transfer important technology to the Chinese side, and the third was that the custom large-scale integrated (LSI) chips used in telecommunications equipment must be produced within China (Zhu 2000).

Following these conditions, BTM agreed to transfer the technologies that the Chinese requested in its JV, Shanghai Bell. The first preliminary agreement between BTM and the PTIC was signed at Luoyang in November 1980.[15] In May 1981, the MPT submitted the project to the State Planning Commission and the State Import and Export Commission and got approval. In March 1982, it sent a delegation to Belgium for an on-the-spot investigation (Q. Zhang 2000: 228).

China was convinced that the digital automatic switching system named System-12 was, at that time, the most advanced as well as the most appropriate technology for its telecommunications network. System-12 was the only switching equipment available at that time with fully distributed controls. It was designed to avoid the weakness of central control systems and to be relatively failure-safe. It was able to handle the complex user interface and large call-processing densities that were essential for operation in China. ITT's reputation was an additional attraction, as BTM was one of the son companies of ITT at that time, until Alcatel of France took over ITT in 1987 (Q. Zhang 2000: 138). In addition to these considerations, the Belgian government had agreed to lend a long-term loan at a "country to country" level, which guaranteed the continued financial support from the Chinese government. However, one of the most important factors was that BTM agreed to transfer technologies for component production, including the production technology of its custom LSI chip. At that time, no other supplier was willing to offer the transfer of such advanced technology (Shen 1999: 64).

The initiation of the System-12 technology transfer project involved the Belgian and Chinese governments, MPT, BTM, ITT, and PTIC. Since this was by far the largest high-technology transaction in the history of China (Zhou and Kerkhofs 1987), the Chinese side set up a strong negotiating team. The chief representative of the team was a deputy minister of the MPT (also a senior specialist

---

[15] In 1980, BTM was convinced that its technology could be successfully transferred to China, given China's skilled personnel, sound financial policies, and a suitable partner, the PTIC (Zhou and Kerkhofs 1987: 186).

in telecommunications technology). Many senior experts in both technologies and foreign trade from various state institutes also took part. The negotiation was an arduous marathon lasting 33 months, from November 1980 to July 1983.[16] As far as China was concerned, the major technological issue was whether or not the System-12 technology suited the conditions of its telecommunications network. Hence, the features of System-12 were checked one after another (Shen 1999: 65). The whole process was a challenge for the Chinese team. As noted above, the transfer of the production technology for the custom LSI chip was also an important factor, as it was an advanced technology within the category of COCOM's restrictions. China insisted that all technologies of component production had to be included in the transaction, lest the component provision be stopped in future as a result of a change in political relations between the two countries. On this issue alone, both sides took a year to reach an agreement (Shen 1999: 65). At last, the contract on the establishment of the JV, Shanghai Bell Telephone Equipment Manufacturing Company, was signed by Ma Shengshan, the president of the PTIC, and Mondeck, the president of BTM, on July 30, 1983 (Q. Zhang 2000: 229).

According to the contract, Shanghai Bell was registered with a capital of USD 27 million and designed to produce 300,000 lines per year of System-12 switches. BTM equity share amounted to 32 percent of the total, the Belgian government contributed 8 percent, and the PTIC of the MPT held the remaining 60 percent (Q. Zhang 2000: 228). In addition, depending on the regulation of the contract, the PTIC was primarily responsible for providing land, buildings, and necessary facilities for the plant and for selling in the domestic market for locally produced System-12 exchanges; BTM provided the technology together with various services; and the Belgian government contributed the capital (Alcatel Bell Telephone 1992). We should note that the PTIC, which was in charge of marketing, was under the control of the MPT, and the MPT was completely responsible for both regulation and operation of networks in China (Tan 1994). It was both the telecommunications equipment supplier and the purchaser. This was an additional reason for the willingness of the foreign side to transfer the technology to Shanghai Bell.

The contract for the rest of the technology, with the exception of the LSI chip, was agreed and signed on July 30, 1983. However, the production technology for the custom LSI chip was under COCOM's restriction, so BTM undertook to lobby COCOM to ease the restriction (Q. Zhang 2000: 231; Shen 1999: 65). The Belgian government, from time to time, took up the matter as its involvement became necessary. In 1983, the Belgian minister of foreign affairs sought to convince the US government to lift the restrictions against China. In June 1985, even the Belgian prime minister intervened. The Belgian Embassy in Washington

---

[16] This is a calculation using information provided by Zhang (2000: 228–229).

acted on behalf of the Belgian government in obtaining the US government approval for the LSI technology transfer. During this period, the BTM delegations had traveled frequently to Washington and Paris to pursue this goal. Even the ITT was involved in these efforts. In March 1987, approval for the transfer of the (LSI) chip production technology to Shanghai Bell was at last obtained from the US and other relevant governments (Shen 1999: 65).

The technology to be transferred between BTM and Shanghai Bell included manufacturing and installation as well as engineering technologies (Shen 1999: 66). This was to be carried out during the contractual period of 15 years with an extension option for a period of 5 years. It concerned the transfer of hardware and software technologies. The hardware technologies included custom LSI chip production of 3-micron CMOS (Complementary Metal Oxide Semiconductor) and 8-micron Bi-MOS (Bipolar MOS); thick film hybrids, double-sided and multiplayer printed circuit boards, and assembly line technology; computerized test facilities; and numerically controlled equipment for piece-part manufacturing.

BTM was committed to transfer all the technologies that the Chinese requested. However, the Chinese did not order all the technologies but only those that were considered necessary (Shen 1999: 66). For example, the Chinese did not want the fully automated production assembly that BTM used in its own factories, in order to save on capital costs. They decided instead to conduct manually many jobs that could be carried out by hand without compromising on the production quality. In other words, where possible, the Chinese preferred to use labor rather than expensive automatic machines. Some equipment that they judged could be made in China was also not ordered.

The first System-12 technology to be transferred was the "release-5.0" based on the evolution line circuit technology, which at that time was the latest version. Subsequently, Shanghai Bell selectively transferred the later innovations of System-12. In 1989, Shanghai Bell obtained the latest development of the version 5—release-5.2. In 1992, a new contract between BTM and Shanghai Bell was signed, extending the project of technology transfer for another 20 years from 1994 to 2014.

In the process of adopting, assimilating, and learning the foreign technology, Shanghai Bell encountered a range of problems. These resulted not only from the technical imperfections of System-12 per se but also from the inappropriateness of this technology to the Chinese environment. However, Chinese government policy and its direct support for Shanghai Bell helped the company out of a crisis that emerged at the beginning of the production period and provided the JV with privileges (e.g., low tax, autonomy in management, and human and material resource supply) that allowed Shanghai Bell to conduct its business free from many of the constraints faced by other local firms (Shen 1999: 67). For example, to ensure Shanghai Bell a leading position in the domestic market, the MPT even decreed in an internal circular that System-12 was one of the principal switching systems for use in the telecommunications network in China. It also helped

Shanghai Bell to obtain funds and loans from relevant government departments. Thus, with the Chinese government's help, Shanghai Bell overcame the crisis and ended up capturing 31 percent of the switches market in 1999.[17]

In sum, owing to the huge domestic market that implied strong bargaining power, the Chinese government was able to demand more technology transfer when they approved foreign firms to establish local JVs in the telecommunications equipment industry. The technology transferred to Shanghai Bell included manufacturing and installation as well as engineering technologies, including both hardware and software technologies. As Section 2.5 shows, the System-12 technology transfer by BTM to Shanghai Bell led to the dissemination of technological knowledge about the central office digital automatic switches across a network of players in the telecommunications equipment producers, users, and research institutes in China. This provided a springboard for the later development of HJD-04 by the indigenous Chinese R&D consortium.

2.5 Knowledge Diffusion and the Indigenous Development of Digital Automatic Switches

2.5.1 Interfirm Knowledge Diffusion and Innovation

Knowledge diffusion between firms plays a critical role in the development of technology. The existing literature (Rogers 1982; von Hippel 1987; Schrader 1991) suggests that knowledge diffusion through informal channels, such as informal contacts, happens in the form of information trading. Studies have shown that this type of informal exchange of knowledge between firms is a frequently observed phenomenon during the phases of product development, production, and diffusion of technological innovations (Martilla 1971; Czepiel 1974; Allen 1984). Information trading refers to the informal exchange of information between employees working for different, sometimes competing, firms (von Hippel 1987). Colleagues working in different firms provide each other with technical advice in the expectation that their favors will be returned in the future. Inter-personal communication is relatively more important for sharing knowledge with customers than with competitors (Lissoni 2001). In high-tech industries, another important method of diffusion is through employee mobility (Franco and Filson 2000).

Knowledge diffusion from multinational enterprises (MNEs) to domestically owned firms of a less developed country is often regarded as a major source of its technical progress and productivity growth. Through its past innovative activity and the professional experiences of its employees, a firm can catch up in technological knowledge. Analyzing establishment-level panel data for the Indonesian

---

[17] Company profile of Shanghai Bell, available at its old, no more existing, site of http://www. shanghaibell.com.cn.

manufacturing sector during the period 1995–1997, Todo and Miyamoto (2002) find the R&D activities and human resource development conducted by MNEs as one more important source of knowledge diffusion. They also find that domestic R&D is effective only when MNEs are present in the same industry, enabling the domestic firms to absorb knowledge from the MNEs through R&D.

2.5.2 Shanghai Bell as the Source of New Knowledge

Before Shanghai Bell's establishment in China, nobody knew how to manufacture digital automatic switches or how to develop or design them. Thus, it was strange for the Chinese to operate and maintain digital switches (Q. Zhang 2000: 232; Cheng 1999: 49). The establishment of Shanghai Bell gave them the opportunity to experience the core technological areas as well as the operating and manufacturing of the system. China had also generated a batch of trained personnel (Q. Zhang 2000: 232). In the process of adapting System-12 to the Chinese environment, Shanghai Bell cooperated with local universities and research institutes. This process brought about the diffusion of related knowledge and skills.

As the production capacity of Shanghai Bell expanded rapidly, it hired several MPT engineers to carry out installation works in neighboring areas that they were familiar with. It also used engineers who had been technically trained in Shanghai Bell to carry out a relatively difficult job in installation–software testing. To provide adequate after-sales services, Shanghai Bell had established a number of maintenance centers, and its computer centers had been providing 24-hour services for its users. Apart from this, it also established a customer association with members across the country. Every six months, it invited users to meetings to give feedback on using its products. It also arranged a "System-12 Column" of two pages in a telecommunications journal—*Telecommunications Technology*—whereby it regularly introduced the system to users and discussed troubleshooting experiences. In addition, Shanghai Bell widely circulated an occasional publication titled *Bell Dispatches*, where it ran an "information" system that included many items on the utilization of System-12. Some essays were instructions written by specialists and others were engineers' experiences; all were carefully classified to allow users to search easily online. Taking advantage of the MPT's traditional arrangement of involving the development of a couple of highly experienced engineers in each district, Shanghai Bell cooperated with them to solve technical problems on the spot.[18] These programs and publications were of substantial help to the Chinese in learning about advanced switching.

---

[18] From company profile and the Shanghai Bell newspaper. Used to be available its old site, http://www.shbell.com.cn.

Next, when taking advantage of external resources and training, Shanghai Bell fostered a great number of qualified engineers in China. The firm managed to get many highly skilled external staff members working for the company. By agreement between Shanghai Bell and its customers, after their six months' training course, these engineers would continue their practice in Shanghai Bell for 1.5 to 2 years. As a result, given their previous experience in the field and their newly acquired knowledge about System-12, they became very capable. They played an important role in helping Shanghai Bell to install and maintain System-12 in the field. At the same time, they could acquire new expertise. The Chinese general manager told jokingly that Shanghai Bell had been a "big school," fostering a great number of qualified engineers for this country (Shen 1999: 83). Every year, around 3 to 4 percent of the engineers left the company to work elsewhere, while more new ones joined.

2.5.3 The R&D Consortium by the Three

Before discussing the specific linkages between Shanghai Bell and the indigenous Chinese firms, we first provide an introduction of the three organizations constituting the R&D consortium, which were also jointly responsible for the indigenous development of digital switches (HJD-04) in China. These are the CIT, under the Zhengzhou Institute of Information Engineering of the People's Liberation Army, the LTEF, and the PTIC. The CIT was the research arm of the army and served as the initiator of the project; the PTIC was originally the procurement unit of the MPT and played the role of the general project manager and financial sponsor; and the LTEF was formerly a producer of crossbar switches and later emerged as the initial producer of HJD-04. These three organizations had different backgrounds and motivations for joining this consortium.

The CIT's involvement can be traced back to the early 1980s when this institute worked on national defense-related technology. Once economic growth became the national agenda of China, the state budget for national defense, including military R&D projects, decreased. At the same time, the Military Commission of the Central Committee of the Communist Party issued several documents encouraging the army to make a contribution to the civil sectors. Under this pressure, the military research team of the CIT began looking for R&D projects that were applicable to civil sectors. Professor Wu played a key role in this episode. Formerly a senior engineer who later became the head of the CIT, in the early 1980s Wu worked in Fuzhou (the capital of the Fujian province on the southeast coast of China) as a research fellow doing computer design. This was the time and place at which the first foreign digital automatic switches, the Japanese F-150 system, were imported and installed. China encountered many problems with this system.

From the day the contract was signed, it took two years to get the system into operation. This frustrating experience highlighted the dangers for China of lacking its own technology and deeply affected Wu. Thereafter, he established a research team in the CIT to work on telecommunications technologies (Shen 1999).

The LTEF was established in the 1970s to produce crossbar telephone exchanges. As one of the 28 MPT-controlled manufacturing firms, the LTEF was a company with relatively new equipment. However, since the open door policy went into effect and as foreign-made advanced digital automatic switches began to pour into the Chinese market, the firm encountered a serious crisis in the 1980s. Following the "foreign technology fever," the LTEF first bid, unsuccessfully, to be the Chinese side of a JV with the Belgium BTM (which eventually became Shanghai Bell) and, later, was involved in another bid organized by the MPT, for one of ten JVs to produce digital switches. Having failed twice, in 1986 the LTEF decided to cooperate with the military-based CIT's research team to seek new technological opportunities.

The PTIC was established by the MPT at the start of the economic reforms to co-ordinate the activities of the 28 firms under the MPT. It had previously undertaken the provision of equipment for the MPT's public network. Since the MPT was one of the few ministries that were historically quasi-militarized, it enjoyed a strong monopoly-like position in several areas. However, economic reforms had not left the MPT untouched. The PTIC and the MPT's R&D institutions were allowed to become increasingly independent of the MPT control. Under the MPT, there were 31 R&D institutes. In the past, any technologies developed in these institutes were freely given to manufacturing firms under the MPT. The reforms changed this relationship, because technologies were now perceived as profitable and valuable in the market. Without an R&D base of its own, the PTIC feared the loss of its technological leadership. The pressure to save its loss-making state-owned firms also concerned the PTIC. As a result, the PTIC took a risk and joined the CIT-initiated R&D projects at a later stage.

Although this tripartite R&D consortium played a key role in the development of indigenous digital electronic switches in China, diffusion of knowledge from Shanghai Bell to this consortium was critical. We illustrate this point now.

2.5.4 Specific Linkages between Shanghai Bell's System-12 and HJD-04

Regarding the linkages, we will show here that the designers of HJD-04 absorbed the knowledge of Shanghai Bell's System-12 and that the main manufacturer, the LTEF, sought technical help from Shanghai Bell. This was possible because the LTEF was the PTIC's subsidiary factory and the PTIC was Shanghai Bell's major shareholder.

First, Wu, the key designer of HJD-04 at the CIT, acquired information about System-12 and other foreign public digital switch systems through publicly available documents. Some of the other engineers who had experiences in helping the System-12 project also contributed to the development of HJD-04. For example, the control system of HJD-04 assimilated the advantages of Fujitsu's F-150 and Shanghai Bell's S1240 (Q. Zhang 2000: 148). F-150 adopted a centralized control system, and S1240 adopted a distributed control system. But HJD-04 adopted a multiprocessor distributed control system. In particular, the switching network of HJD-04 consisted of up to 32 identical, relatively independent modules, and the interconnection between modules was via cables linking the buffer memories of each module.

Second, many local Chinese were involved in the process of adapting System-12 to the Chinese environment, and they contributed their learned knowledge and skill to the development of indigenous switches. When producing, installing, and maintaining System-12, they continuously sought help from the MPT engineering teams and experienced engineers in local Posts and Telecommunications Authorities in provinces (Q. Zhang 2000: 230). The MPT brought together a group of highly skilled staff from its R&D institutes, universities, and factories across the country to Shanghai Bell. Among them were many experienced senior engineers and knowledgeable professors in the field. They played a crucial role in building up the company in the early stages. Thereafter, most of them returned to their institutes, and some subsequently used the knowledge they had obtained from System-12 to carry out various R&D projects for Shanghai Bell. Some of these specialists participated in the development of the HJD-04 technology (Shen 1999: 76–77). This process of technology diffusions gave birth to, and enabled the operation of, new types of digital automatic exchanges developed by the indigenous units (Q. Zhang 2000: 232; Wu 1997: 75–76).

Third, the LTEF sought help by sending delegations to Shanghai Bell to explore suitable solutions while developing its production facilities and management approaches (Shen 1999: 153). The LTEF was a fairly typical state-owned enterprise, in terms of the institutional structure, incentives, and operating mechanism. It would not have been able to fulfill the task of the production of HJD-04 if it had not reformed itself. Under internal and external pressures, it had to restructure its entire organization, including its management institutions and operating system. Hence, the LTEF sent delegations to Shanghai Bell to study and explore suitable solutions for its production facilities and management approaches. As a result, it was able to upgrade its technological capabilities.

Finally, as Shanghai Bell brought up the components production facilities to meet global quality standards and technologies, the manufacturers of HJD-04 were able to buy such components readily and cheaply within China.

Based on the above points, it can be said that without the diffusion of the technology related to digital automatic switches embodied in System-12 and other projects in Shanghai Bell, the indigenous technological development of HJD-04 might not have been possible. According to the president, Zhang, of Great Dragon, HJD-04's development can be regarded as an assimilation of Shanghai Bell's System-12 (Q. Zhang 2000: 232).

To summarize, the designers of the indigenous switch HJD-04 first started with conducting research on Shanghai Bell's System-12, using publicly available documents. Also, some of the engineers participating in the development of HJD-04 were recruited from those who had participated in Shanghai Bell's System-12 project. Moreover, the main manufacturer (LTEF) of HJD-04 sought direct technical help from Shanghai Bell. Therefore, with some experience of computer technology and telecommunications technology, together with an array of available foreign technologies from JVs, the institute (CIT/ZIIE) in cooperation with the LTEF and PTIC developed the first successful central office digital switches in China in 1991. It should also be noted that the project was initiated by engineers who were led by Wu, working in the CIT. The CIT first invited the LTEF and later sought help from the PTIC as a financial sponsor (Shen 1999: 174; Mu 2002: 233–234). During its early stage, the MPT did not provide much direct help to this project initiated by the CIT because it was focusing on developing digital switches on its own. This project was called the DS series and was developed in isolation by the MPT's 10th Research Institute in 1991. However, as explained in detail in Mu (2002), the project was not successful. The main cause of failure was the lack or ignorance of access to foreign knowledge and technology transfers.

As a next step, to produce HJD-04 on a large scale, the consortium cooperated with the joint initiatives by the MPT and MEI to establish a manufacturing company called Great Dragon (Julong). Great Dragon was actually a business group comprising nine affiliated companies including the LTEF (Q. Zhang 2000: 151). With the joint sale activities of the nine affiliated companies, HJD-04 has experienced rapid growth in sales since 1992. The average annual growth in sales has been over 200 percent for the past three years. In 1994, the market share of HJD-04 increased from 0 to 16 percent.[19] The annual single shift capacity for HJD-04 was 4.6 million lines in late 1995. By October 1998, cumulative sales of HJD-04 were 16 million lines, while Shanghai Bell's were 23 million lines.[20]

After the development of HJD-04 in 1991, knowledge diffusion was further amplified through the inter-flowing of engineers or related persons, which finally led to successive development of four other types of digital automatic switches (C&C08, EIM-601, ZXJ-10, and SP-30) by other indigenous firms. The later development of other types of digital switches by firms such as ZTE, Datang, and

---

[19] The Birth of the Great Dragon [Zouxiang Lianhe—JuLong Dansheng Ji], Renmin Youdian Bao [People's Post & Telecom], 1995.

[20] Woguo Juyong Jiaohuanji Chanye de Fazhan Xianzhuang yu Qianjing Zhanwang [Development and prospects of central office SPC switches in China], http://202.96.31.133//information/industryy.nsf.

finally Huawei all benefited from knowledge diffusion via interfirm mobility of skilled engineers. For example, Huawei's location at Shenzhen and its higher salary levels attracted skilled manpower from Great Dragon (original manufacturer of HJD-04). Consequently, many skilled young engineers who had mastered or at least had some knowledge of the HJD-04 system left Great Dragon for Huawei (or ZTE). They contributed to the R&D of another digital switching system, C&C08, in Huawei.

In sum, in the case of digital switches in China, knowledge diffusion from the foreign JVs and its absorption by public research institutes were critical.

2.6 Segmented Market and the Competitive Advantage of Indigenous Firms

2.6.1 Market Segmentation in China

Since the issue was first introduced by Smith (1956), market segmentation has become a central concept in both marketing theory and practice. Smith states that market segmentation involves viewing a heterogeneous market as a number of smaller homogeneous markets. A segmentation basis is defined as a set of variables or characteristics used to assign potential customers to homogeneous groups. From a market segmentation perspective, China is a typical segmented market, based not only on geography but also on socio-demographics and lifestyle—a market that therefore requires differentiated implementation campaigns (Schmitt 1997). The Chinese market should not be treated as a single market of 1.3 billion consumers. Geographically, there are at least three markets in China, a developed east coast market, a developing mid-China market, and an emerging frontier market in the far west (Kotler 2001).

In the color TV industry, major indigenous firms have secured market shares by taking advantage of the segmented market. An example is Changhong, which originated in the city of Mianyang in the Sichuan province and started to manufacture color TVs in May 1980. The company geographically expanded its market through three phases: it focused on Sichuan and then, having maintained 90 percent of the market from 1980 to the mid-1980s, expanded to southwestern China until 1989, and later entered northeast China and expanded to cover the entire market. Since 1992 Changhong has been one of the largest color TV makers; its domestic market share was 27 percent in 1996 (Kang and Ke 1999a). During this process of expansion, initial success in the geographically segmented market of the Sichuan and southwestern China regions was important for later expansion to other regions such as the developed market of Beijing and Shanghai.

With a market share of 9 percent, Konka became the second-largest color TV maker in China in 1995. A JV established by Hongkong and Guangdong firms,

Konka initially exported all of its color TVs from 1983 to 1987. In 1988 the company also began selling to the domestic market. Upon observing the saturation of the east coast market, however, it swiftly targeted inland areas by establishing JVs with "local" inland firms such as Mudanjiang Konka in Heilongjiang in 1993 for the northeastern market, Shanxin Konka in 1995 for the northwestern market, and Anhui Konka in 1996 for the eastern market. Konka also developed differentiated color TVs for consumers in rural areas in 1995 (Kang and Ke 1999b: 40–47). Differentiated product development for rural markets and a regionally segmented market-oriented expansion strategy enabled Konka to capture a larger market share.

The telecommunications equipment market in China was not only huge but also segmented. One of the most important characteristics of this market was a kind of dualism: rural–urban dualism and core–periphery dualism. In other words, there existed two different markets in China: one similar to developed countries and the other more often found in underdeveloped countries. In terms of the level of general economic development as well as the existing telecommunications network conditions, different areas of China varied to a considerable extent. Many inland districts and rural areas lagged far behind the coastal urban areas and large cities. Thus demands for telecommunications services from inland districts or rural areas were different from those of large cities. They were often not able to afford expensive foreign digital automatic switches. Given their knowledge about the Chinese market, the Chinese firms first targeted the rural or lower end market in China's public telecommunications network, while all the foreign companies were aiming at large cities.

Apart from the three international gateways, there were five levels in the public network: levels one to four (known as C1, C2, C3, C4) were transit switches, and level five (known as C5) was comprised of terminal switches. There were 8 level-one (C1) transit switching centers; 22 level-two (C2) transit switching centers were located in the capital cities of provinces or autonomous regions; level-three (C3) transit switching centers were located in each district and level-four switches (C4) at the county level; and level-five (C5) terminal switches were located in every major city and town. The HJD-04 system could be used at the C4 or lower level (although technologically it was designed also to meet the requirements at the C3 level). It had a capacity of approximately 30,000 (later 60,000) subscriber lines and could be used as local or tandem switches. Until 1993, the C3 and higher levels were dominated by foreign systems. However, there was a large market for HJD-04 at the lower levels (about four times bigger than the C3 and higher markets), which foreign systems either had not yet focused on or had difficulties entering.

HJD-04 had a simple machine–operator interface with a Chinese-language screen menu. Owing to its low development and production costs, this kind of switch was provided at much lower prices, which made it popular in rural areas in the initial stage. According to *Shenzhen Special Zone Daily*, in the mid-1990s, 90 percent of Huawei's products were installed in C4 or C5, and 100 percent of ZTE's products were applied to C4 or C5. In 1997, ZTE's products began to enter C3; in contrast, 90 percent of Shanghai Bell's products were installed in C3 or upward.[21]

Given the ex post importance of the rural market, one might ask why the MNCs or JVs did not pay attention to this market. Our first answer is that the urban markets were large enough for the MNCs to indulge themselves in when they entered China during mid-1980s to the early 1990s. A more important answer is the fact that even if they wanted to go for the rural market, their products were not suitable for it. Transmission quality and transmission lines varied greatly in different areas of China. Under the low network level and poor network conditions, the foreign systems were rarely able to work. In addition, many foreign systems were designed around presumptions of lower usage of lines; however, the rural market was featured by a combination of low telephone penetration rate and intensive use for each telephone set. Thus the foreign systems ran into problems, sometimes even leading to breakdowns in the local network. Furthermore, the screen menu of all the foreign systems was in English. Outside the big cities, it was difficult to find operators who could understand English. Moreover, the products of the MNCs and JVs were more expensive than their local counterparts.

In sum, in terms of the source for competitive advantage, the likelihood of market success was high for indigenous Chinese firms. On the one hand, in its competition with foreign or local JV firms within China, indigenous firms took advantage of the segmented nature of the Chinese market. On the other hand, in their later competition in the international export market, the indigenous firms took advantage of relatively cheap labor costs and numerous other resources. The cost of labor in China was no more than one-tenth of that in advanced countries. Other costs were also much lower than those in other countries. For example, LSI chips for digital automatic switches can be manufactured in China at half the international price. With the volume of production expanded, the price can decrease greatly (Xin and Wang 2000). Thus the digital automatic switches manufactured by indigenous firms enjoyed several sources of competitive advantage. After having significantly improved product quality and added new features, indigenous manufacturers began to compete directly with local JVs in both the rural and urban Chinese markets after the mid-1990s. They eventually entered world markets.

---

[21] Guanyu Woshi Chengkong Jiaohuanji Chanye de Sikao [Thinking about SPC switching industry in Zhenshen city], *Shenzhen Special Zone Daily*, May 13, 1997.

2.6.2 Role of the Government and Catch-up by Indigenous Firms

The role of the government also became decisive when indigenous Chinese firms started to compete directly with the JVs in both rural and urban areas. The basic role of the Chinese government was to provide market protection and to give incentives for the adoption and use of domestic products. In 1996, the government stopped arranging foreign government loans to import digital automatic switch equipment. Instead it imposed tariffs on imported communication equipment, to promote the purchase of locally made equipment. The sum of the market share of local firms (including Sino-foreign JVs) was 63.1 percent in 1995 (see Figure 2.1). One year after tariffs on imported communication equipment went into effect, the figure reached 84.8 percent in 1996, and in 1997, it reached 94.9 percent (Figure 2.1).

Since 1997, the MPT had organized coordinating conferences every year with the Administrative Bureau of Posts and Telecommunications. Through these conferences, the MPT encouraged the Administrative Bureau of Posts and Telecommunications to purchase indigenous equipment if the equipment was suitable in character and proper in price. During the first conference, contracts for more than 5 million lines were signed, and finally more than 7 million lines of digital automatic switches were sold. In the second coordinating conference, contracts for 17 million lines of digital automatic switches were agreed on and 18 million lines were sold eventually. These two coordinating conferences were a turning point for the growth of the communication manufacturing industry in China (Xin and Wang 2000). For example, in the second coordination conference, Huawei gained orders for 6.505 million lines, which was 40 percent of the total orders of 1997 and 1998 (Xu and Fu 1997). Under the encouragement of the People's Bank of China, the China Construction Bank supplied Huawei buyer's credit of RMB 3.85 billion, which was 45 percent of the bank's total buyer's credit in 1998.[22]

Affected by the coordinating conferences and financial support, since 1998 the market share of the indigenous firms had increased rapidly, and they became the main suppliers in the domestic market. In the urban market, indigenous firms claimed 21 percent of the market; but in the rural market, they dominated with a market share of 80 percent.[23] The four indigenous manufacturers—Great Dragon, Datang, ZTE, and Huawei—held more than 60 percent of China's digital automatic switch market in 1998 (see Table 2.3).

In Table 2.4, we can observe the growth of sales of the indigenous firms and JVs. Huawei started to produce large-scale central office digital automatic

---

[22] Including Zhongxing and other telecommunications manufacturing firms, the volume of buyer's credit supplied by the China Construction Bank was RMB 8 billion in that year. From *Shenzhen Special Zone Daily* [Sehnzhen Tequ Bao], July 30, 1998.

[23] Source: China telecommunication, U.S. Department of Commerce—National Trade Data Bank, November 3, 2000 (http://www.tradeport.org/ts/countries/china/isa/isar0024.html).

Table 2.3 Market shares of the four indigenous firms in 1998

Company	Capacity (lines)	Market share
Huawei	7,000,000	24%
ZTE	5,100,000	20%
Great Dragon	3,000,000–3,500,000	13.45%–15.6%
Datang	1,560,000	7%
Total	16,660,000–17,160,000	64.45%–66.6%

Source: Woguo Juyongjiaohuanji De Fazhan Xianzhuang Yu Qianjing
Zhanwang [The Development and Prospects on Central Office Exchange
Industry in China], http://sd-ep.cei.gov.cn/fanzhan/shehui/eea5-sd.htm,
1999, and Xin and Wang (2000).

switches only in 1995, but it has been the biggest manufacturer since 1998. Also, its sales are much bigger than that of the other companies. The sales of ZTE in 1995 and 1996 were clearly less than those of Tianjin NEC and Jiangsu Fujitsu. However, since 1997, the situation has been reversed: ZTE became one of the top five makers, next to Huawei, Shanghai Bell, and BISC. Datang's progress was also substantial. In the domestic central office switching market, Shanghai Bell remained the leader until 1998, but in 1998, Huawei surpassed it to become the largest digital automatic switch manufacturer in China. The market shares of Huawei and Shanghai Bell can be compared in Table 2.5 and Table 2.6. Among the four indigenous firms, only Huawei is a private company while the other three are state-owned. It is interesting that Huawei eventually emerged as the leading company. The reasons for its success may be numerous, including ownership and governance, corporate culture and strategy, and human capital development.[24]

In sum, due to the segmented nature of the Chinese market, the indigenous firms were able to utilize the rural or lower end market as their nurturing bases. They were also given active government support, until they were developed enough to compete directly with foreign JVs in urban or coastal regions.

2.7 Summary and Concluding Remarks

This chapter examines the growth of technological capabilities in the telecommunications industry in China. It is based on a technological learning and catching-up model for China that focuses on the neo-Schumpeterian concept of technological regimes. This study first investigates the technological regime of telephone switches and the evolution of the telecommunications industry in China. Then, with case studies of Shanghai Bell, the CIT-led R&D consortium (and later Great Dragon), and Huawei, it analyzes how catching-up in the

---

[24] For more details, see Mu (2002).

Table 2.4 Sales volumes of the central office digital (SPC) switches by firms, 1995–2000 (unit: lines)

	1995	1996	1997	1998	1999	2000 (Jan.–June)
Shanghai Bell	---	---	5,880,000	4,460,000 (Jan.–Aug.)	4,600,000 (Jan.–Jul.)	3,260,000
Beijing Int'l Switching Co (BISC)	1,472,754	2,450,978	3,406,708	6,356,042	6,943,610	4,042,613
Qingdao Haixin Group Co	691,000	992,760	1,628,136	2,394,394	3,381,108	1,879,400
Tianjin NEC	955,600	1,053,300	764,000	834,600	1,367,947	---
Jiangsu Fujitsu	---	1,252,000	1,434,000	1,601,000	1,151,000	---
Shenzhen Huawei#	---	---	3,934,678	9,332,734	13,750,445	9,582,290
Shenzhen ZTE#	425,000	767,000	1,880,000	5,103,600	5,980,000	---
XiAn Datang#	---	58	845,000	1,393,000	1,527,400	---
Great Dragon#	1,508,518*	1,235,072*	1,605,136*	2,024,493*	994,958*	675,321

Source: Production Ranking of Central Office SPC Switch Maker (1995–1999) (Chengkong Juyong Jiaohuanji Chanliang an Qiye Paiming) and Sales of Switch Maker in Top 100 IT in China (Jan.–Aug. 1998; Jan.–Jul. 1999; Jan.–June 2000), CCID database.

Note: # refers to indigenous firms;

* refers to the figure that comes from the total capacity produced by the four major factories.

Table 2.5 Huawei's market share in switches in China

1997		1998		1999		2000	
Sales (1,000 lines)	Market share	Sales (1,000 lines)	Market share	Sales (1,000 lines)	Market share	Sales (1,000 lines)	Market share
4,115	20%	7,000	24%	7,500	32%	16,500	35%

Source: Xin and Wang (2000: 41) and Huawei (2001: 15).

telecommunications industry was realized. Figure 2.2 summarizes the whole process. The first digital switches to be made locally were in 1984 by the JV Shanghai Bell. They were indigenously developed seven years later in 1991 by the R&D consortium of the CIT–PTIC–LTEF and mass-produced by a state-owned business group, Great Dragon (Julong). Other state-owned companies also developed and produced diverse variants of HJD-04. The final winner, however, was a private firm, Huawei, which outpaced its state-owned rivals with its unique corporate culture and strategy.

The major findings of this study may be summarized as follows.

First, regarding the technological regime, we find that the technological trajectory of the switching system is more predictable and less cumulative and that it is one of the factors that facilitated the technological catch-up of the telephone switch makers in China. It is a case of stage-skipping catch-up in terms of the model mentioned in Chapter 1 (Figure 1.3). That is, the development of the switching system in China underwent the stages of manual switching, step-by-step switching, and crossbar switching, and then skipped the stage of analog electronic switches to jump to digital electronic (SPC) switches. One may think that it is inevitable for latecomers to skip some stages or outdated models and that all kinds of catch-up should contain some element of skipping. But not all cases of catch-up by latecomers include such aspects of skipping; skipping is not always inevitable. The stories of Hyundai Motors and Samsung Electronics validate this point.[25] The point is that whether or not, or the extent to which, catch-up involves stage skipping or even path creating depends on the initial level of technological

---

[25] When Hyundai started to develop engines in the early 1980s, the carburetor-based engine was the standard type and the R&D team considered developing and going along this proven technology. But, knowing that the trend of engine technology was moving toward a new electronic injection-based engine, the founding chairman J.Y. Chung, after long consultation and debate, firmly decided to target this emerging technology. It was not an inevitable but a deliberate choice. The same was true of Samsung's production of DRAM memory chips. Samsung's DRAM business started with producing 64-Kbit DRAM chips in the early 1980s. At that time, the government's position (Ministry of Industrial and Trade) was that the Korean firms had better start with 1-Kbit DRAM, but it was the

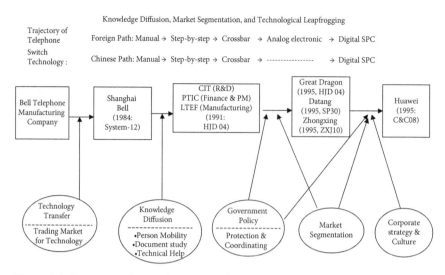

Figure 2.2 Summary of stage-skipping catch-up in telephone switches in China
Source: Author; author's article of Mu and Lee (2005).

Table 2.6 Huawei and Shanghai Bell's rank in top 100 IT firms in China, 1996–2002

Year	Huawei		Shanghai Bell	
	Rank	Total sales (million RMB)	Rank	Total sales (million RMB)
1996	21	2,215.9	8	4,574.8
1997	18	4,189.3	12	5,005.7
1998	10	7,180.4	12	6,046.1
1999	10	10,214.7	11	8,646.9
2000	8	15,200.0	12	10,820.5
2001	7	16,229.0	9	15,101.1
2002	7	17,214.2	12	11,138.4

Source: Top 100 electronics and information enterprises in China, http://www.ittop100.gov.cn.

capability (or so-called absorptive capacity) and the nature of arranged access to knowledge and terms of transfer.

Second, given the huge market in China, access to knowledge was made possible by the strategy of trading market for technology, while the public research institute initially played an important role in the development of the indigenous switching system. The case of the JV Shanghai Bell shows that China took advantage of its large market size to push Alcatel's BTM into a contract enabling

---

purposeful decision of the private firm to skip 1- to 16-Kbit DRAM to enter directly into 64-Kbit DRAM. See Lee and Lim (2001) for details.

technology transfer. Through the establishment and operation of Shanghai Bell, China was able to acquire technology related to manufacturing, installing, and engineering. In return, the JV gained a large share of the new market and kept a dominant position in the Chinese market. Shanghai Bell and other JV establishments fostered the diffusion of technological know-how across the country. Having benefited from such technology diffusion, the public research institutes led by the CIT developed the first indigenous digital automatic switch, HJD-04, in 1991. Following continuous knowledge diffusion, other switching systems were later developed by other firms.

Third, indigenous Chinese firms were able to secure their competitive advantage owing to the segmented nature of markets. The telecommunications equipment market in China is a segmented one; indigenous firms differentiated their products to meet different demands in the segmented markets. The HJD-04 system was developed to cater to the less developed market, with characteristics of high processing capacity, simple and open structure, and simple interface. The rural market made it possible for indigenous firms to realize their first-stage growth.

Fourth, initial protection and promotion by the government provided additional competitive advantage for indigenous firms. For example, the new policy of levying high tariffs on imported communication equipment helped local firms to secure their market share. The two coordinating conferences organized by the MPT in 1996 and 1997 and the state-owned banks' financial support encouraged telephone service operators to buy the products of indigenous firms.

In sum, the key success factors include the coordinated acquisition of foreign technology by taking advantage of the bargaining power associated with the market size, the regulation of the JVs to allow knowledge diffusion, and the existence of a plan for domestic capability building given the initial condition of segmented markets. The contribution of this chapter is that it has elaborated the process of technological catch-up in China, thereby identifying new and important factors that are different from other countries like Korea. The new factors are the trading market for technology strategy, the role of the JVs in diffusing knowledge to other firms, and the role of segmented markets as the source of competitive advantage for indigenous firms. This study deviates from other studies on similar subjects by providing a comprehensive elaboration of the long and complex process in a consistent theoretical framework.

3

Origins and Growth of Big Businesses in China[1]

3.1 Introduction

The importance of large businesses in the process of economic development has long been recognized in the literature, since Schumpeter (1934: 71–72) discussed the contribution of large businesses in stimulating innovation by large R&D investment. Moreover, having a certain number of large businesses has recently been recognized as one of the important factors for an economy to grow beyond the middle-income stage (Lee et al. 2013). There is no doubt that China has already generated a large number of Fortune Global 500-class firms, or a similar number to that in the US; the number of Chinese firms in the list increased from 3 in 1994 to 20 in 2005, to 61 in 2010, and to 119 in 2018 (see Table 9.2 in Chapter 9). These firms are the leading engines of China's technological and economic catch-up. This chapter discusses the origins of large businesses in China, going back to the 1990s and 2000s. The focus is particularly on business groups, which are the main form of large businesses in China.

China has its own specific definition of business groups, used in official statistics and government policies. The National Bureau of Statistics of China (NBS) defines a business group as a collection of legally independent entities that are partly or wholly owned by a parent firm and registered as affiliated firms of that parent firm. Apart from some incidence in the early twentieth century, modern-style business groups emerged in China in the mid-1980s as a consequence of the reform and restructuring of state-owned enterprises (SOEs), which aimed at increasing economies of scale and specialization (Lee and Jin 2009; Keister 2000). As of the late 2000s, several Chinese business groups succeeded in becoming major players in the world economy, and the Chinese government, both at the central level and at the local level, played an important role in the formation and development of business groups (Lee and Jin 2009; Hahn and Lee 2006).

In terms of ownership, the state still holds the dominant position as the controller of business groups in China. However, non-government ownership has

[1] This chapter is a re-writing of an article, Keun Lee and Young Sam Kang (2010), "Business Groups in China," in: A. Colpan, T. Hikino, and J. Lincoln (Eds.), *Oxford Handbook of Business Groups* (Oxford: Oxford Univ. Press, pp. 210–36).

been growing at a fast pace. Business groups with private and other ownership accounted for about 45 percent of a total of 2,856 business groups in 2007, although their share in terms of sales was still less than 20 percent. In terms of the socio-economic context, business groups in China have their own unique characteristics, while sharing some features with those in other countries. They are also diversified but comparatively less so than their counterparts in other countries, and even a refocusing tendency was reported in the 2000s in some studies (Seo, Lee, and Wang 2006).

This chapter provides a descriptive analysis of business groups in China, extending and updating the literature, such as Hahn and Lee (2006). Section 3.2 discusses a basic profile of business groups in China. Section 3.3 outlines their history, and Section 3.4 focuses on the role of the state in the emergence of the business groups. Section 3.5 discusses the problems of ownership structure and agency costs in these business groups, Section 3.6 explains their business structure and diversification, and Section 3.7 examines the competitiveness of business groups in China.

3.2 Basic Profile of the Business Groups in China

Business groups in China are registered with the State Administration for Industry and Commerce. Only large business groups, *qiye jituan*, and not the small and private business groups, can be registered. According to the State Administration for Industry and Commerce, the core company of a business group in China should have a registered capital of over 50 million RMB (*yuan*) plus at least five affiliated companies, and the business group should have a total registered capital (including the core and other affiliated companies) of over 100 million yuan. One of the most important differences between large business groups in China and their counterparts in Korea and Japan is that the former are mostly multi-industry entities owned by the state and not by particular families, while small business groups are family-owned.

The importance of business groups in the Chinese economy can be seen in Part A of Table 3.1. First, the number of business groups registered increased from 2,472 to 2,926 during the period 1998–2007, about 20 percent increase. In terms of the number of total workers employed in the groups, its growth was much faster, namely, about 60 percent, with an increase from 20.9 million to 32.4 million over the same period. The sales revenue of all the registered business groups, calculated as a ratio to GDP, was already substantial, or about 90 percent, which is comparable to other countries. The ratio had grown rapidly by about 150 percent (from 41.6 percent in 1998 to 93.2 percent in 2007) during the 10-year period, indicating the fast growth of business groups in the economy.

Table 3.1 Basic statistics of business groups in China, 1998–2007

Part A: Share in the economy

Variable	1998	1999	2000	2001	2002	2003	2004	2005	2006	2007
Number	2,472	2,757	2,655	2,710	2,627	2,692	2,764	2,845	2,856	2,926
Total assets (billion yuan)	6,699	8,732	10,698	12,805	14,254	17,017	19,472	23,076	27,121	34,355
Percentage of GDP	79.4	97.4	107.8	116.8	118.5	125.3	121.8	126.0	128.0	137.7
Total revenue (billion yuan)	3,508	4,377	5,326	6,562	7,712	10,010	12,639	15,551	18,964	23,257
Percentage of GDP	41.6	48.8	53.7	59.8	64.1	73.7	79.1	84.9	89.5	93.2
No. employees (thousand)	20,900	23,420	22,820	25,240	25,180	25,850	26,712	28,359	30,104	32,393
Percentage of urban workers	9.67	10.45	9.86	10.54	10.16	10.08	10.09	10.38	10.63	11.04

Source: Calculated from the data in National Bureau of Statistics, China (2008a, 2008b).

Part B: Sales revenue by ownership type of business groups

Ownership type	2000	2001	2002	2003	2004	2005	2006	2007
State ownership (billion yuan)	4,749	5,806	6,709	8,485	10,365	12,396	14,965	18,127
(%)	89.2	88.5	87.0	84.8	82.0	79.6	78.9	77.9
Collective ownership (billion yuan)	316	344	409.3	463.5	570.7	616	1128.3	1,331
(%)	5.9	5.2	5.3	4.6	4.5	4.0	5.9	5.7
Private ownership and others (billion yuan)	261	413	594	1,061	1,703	2,559	2,870	3,799
(%)	4.9	6.3	7.7	10.6	13.5	16.4	15.1	16.3
Total (billion yuan)	5,326	6,562	7,712	10,010	12,639	15,571	18,964	23,257

Source: Calculated from the data in National Bureau of Statistics, China (2008a, 2008b).

Notes:

1. Enterprises owned by town and village, so-called township and village enterprises (TVEs), are classified into collective ownership.

2. "Others" includes foreign firms and Sino-foreign joint ventures.

Part B of Table 3.1 compares the share of total revenues by ownership type of business groups. It shows the share of state ownership was almost 90 percent in 2000 but decreased to less than 80 percent by 2007. In contrast, the share of private ownership and others increased, from 4.9 percent in 2000 to 16.3 percent in 2007. The share of total revenues of the collectively owned business groups was around 4 to 6 percent. Although these figures show the dominance of state ownership in the size of revenues, the shares in terms of the number of companies are quite different. Figure 3.1 shows that the share of business groups with private and other ownership was substantial, at 44 percent, in 2007, a rapid increase from 19 percent in 2000. In other words, in 2007 almost half of the business groups in China were private. In contrast, the share of business groups owned by the state decreased rapidly, from 65 percent in 2000 to 45 percent in 2007, when it accounted for less than half. The share of business groups under collective ownership hovered around 10 percent, not showing a big change.

The number of Chinese firms included in the Fortune Global 500 list also reflects the growth of big business groups in China. As shown in Table 3.2 the number of Chinese firms on the list was 24 in 2006, including two Hong Kong firms. Among these, Sinopec, the largest firm in China, was ranked 17th, with

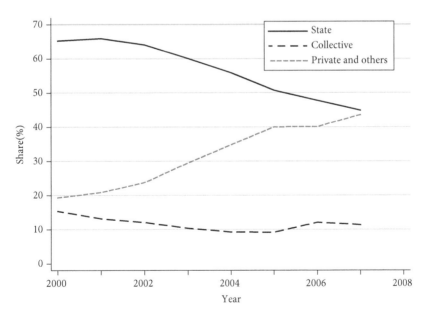

Figure 3.1 Trend in the number of Chinese business groups by ownership type (% in total)

Source: Calculated from the data in National Bureau of Statistics, China (2006c, 2008b).

Note: State, Collective, and Private and others denote state ownership, collective ownership, and private ownership and others, respectively.

an asset of USD 131.6 billion. China National Petroleum and China Grid Corporation were ranked 24th and 29th, respectively.

Table 3.3 lists the top 30 business groups in China, selected in terms of the size of sales in 2006. They were enormous in size and had a selected strategic sector. One can easily notice that in terms of the listed strategic sectors, manufacturing was not dominant, different from the groups in Korea and Japan, with more incidence of firms in energy, utilities, and trading. Moreover, they were mostly SOEs, with 27 out of the 30 being state-owned.

If we look at the top 500 Chinese business groups, instead of the top 30, the industrial distribution changes, with manufacturing being more dominant. Using the data of the top 500 business groups, Table 3.4 shows that the manufacturing sector had the biggest share of around 70 percent in all criteria, including the number of firms, shareholders' equity, sales revenue, profit and tax, and the number of employees. The service sector had the second-largest share of the indicators, accounting for 20 to 35 percent depending upon the indicator.

3.3 History of Business Groups in China

Most of the large business groups in China emerged around the mid-1980s, more specifically as a result of the reform measures by the government 1985 and 1986 (Keister 2000). The concept of a "business group" appeared in the State Council's official documents for the first time in 1986. However, even before the SOE reform and experiment, there had been various attempts by enterprises to expand their scope of integration since economic reform began in the late 1970s. For instance, firms in the same business sector formed a horizontal association to share brands, marketing channels, and production facilities to fill the gaps in underdeveloped markets (Hahn and Lee 2006). These attempts eventually led to the recognition of several limitations of a loose horizontal association without centralized ownership and control. An attempt to solve these problems led to the transition of horizontal associations into business groups that had a clear power structure (Hahn and Lee 2006).

From 1987, when the regulation "Several Suggestions on Forming and Developing Business Groups" was enacted, business groups were formed at a quite rapid rate, both voluntarily and with the state's assistance, predominantly in the state-owned sector (Keister 2000). The Chinese government encouraged the restructuring of the SOEs into business groups in order to provide them with economies of scale and increasing specialization. It also thought that it could implement industrial policies more effectively with business groups. Learning from the experience of Korea and Japan, the government believed that it would be would be less costly and more efficient to implement industrial polices in an economy led by a few big business groups.

Table 3.2 Chinese firms in Fortune Global 500, 2006

Ranking	Name	Headquarters	Revenue (million USD)	Profit (million USD)
17	Sinopec	Beijing	131,636	3,703
24	China National Petroleum	Beijing	110,520	13,265
29	State Grid Corporation	Beijing	107,186	2,238
170	Industrial & Commercial Bank of China	Beijing	36,833	6,179
180	China Mobile Limited	Beijing	35,914	6,260
192	China Life Insurance	Beijing	33,712	174
215	Bank of China	Beijing	30,751	5,372
230	China Construction Bank	Beijing	28,532	5,810
237	China Southern Power Grid	Guangzhou	27,966	1,074
275	China Telecom	Beijing	24,791	2,280
277	Agricultural Bank of China	Beijing	24,476	728
290	Hutchison Whampoa	Hong Kong	23,661	2,578
299	Sinochem Corporation	Beijing	23,109	345
307	Baosteel	Shanghai	22,663	1,622
342	China Railway Engineering	Beijing	20,520	143
384	China Railway Construction	Beijing	18,736	70
385	First Automotive Works	Changchun	18,711	70
396	China State Construction	Beijing	18,163	281
402	Shanghai Automotive	Shanghai	18,010	90
405	COFCO Limited	Beijing	17,953	281
435	China Minmetals	Beijing	16,902	154
457	Jardine Matheson	Hong Kong/ Hamilton	16,281	1,348
469	China National Offshore Oil	Beijing	16,039	3,007
488	China Ocean Shipping	Beijing	15,414	1,093

Source: http://money.cnn.com/magazines/fortune/.

The government articulated the concept of business groups and accordingly encouraged the state-owned firms to form business groups by providing them with incentives. It granted preferential policies for business groups, such as the right to set up finance companies that can play the role of intragroup banks. The State Council also selected the first batch of 57 large business groups as the national trial group in 1991.[2] The national trial group was extended to comprise 120 business groups after the second batch was chosen in 1997. The business groups in the national trial group were granted various privileges, including

---

[2] According to Ma and Lu (2005), there were two reasons why the government chose the national trial groups: to make groups in a particular sector to become international players and to solve the matter of poorly performing SOEs by incorporating them into business groups led by well-performing SOEs.

Table 3.3 Top 30 business groups in China, 2006

Name of the group	Revenue (billion yuan)	Employee (thousand)	Ownership	Major business lines
China Petrochemical Co.	1,097.5	649.7	State	Oil refining and petrochemicals
China National Petroleum Co.	923.2	1,012.8	State	Oil (fuels, lubricants), natural gas, petrochemicals, oil exploration services, oil exploration equipment
State Grid Co. of China	855.3	794.5	State	Build and operate power grids and provide power supply
China Mobile Communications Co.	286.3	371.0	State	Telecommunications, mobile communications
China Southern Power Grid	223.5	173.2	State	Power generation
China Telecom	198.7	400.3	State	Fixed service telecommunications provider
Sinochem Group	184.5	17.8	State	Chemical fertilizer
Baosteel Group Co.	183.4	91.3	State	Steel, finance, coal processing, engineering
China Railway Engineering Co.	163.8	268.0	State	Railways
China FAW Group Co.	158.6	117.6	State	Automobiles
China Railway Construction Co.	150.7	218.3	State	Railways
Dongfeng Motor Co.	147.2	134.2	State	Automobiles
China State Construction Engineering Co.	144.8	404.1	State	Property and real estate construction
Shanghai Automotive Industry Co.	144.1	82.0	State	Passenger cars, commercial vehicles, and components
Legend Holdings	138.9	30.3	Privately owned company	IT, equity investment and real estate development
China Minmetals Co.	135.0	36.3	State	Production and trading of metals and minerals; finance, real estate, and logistics

Company				
China National Offshore Oil Co.	132.4	48.0	State	Oil and gas
China Ocean Shipping (Group) Company	127.6	64.0	State	Freight forwarding, shipbuilding, ship-repairing, terminal operations
China Communications Construction Company	115.1	77.0	State	Construction and design of transportation infrastructure, dredging and port machinery manufacturing
Haier Group	108.0	54.0	Collective, TVEs	Electronics, white goods, financial services
Aluminum Corporation of China	106.1	188.2	State	Aluminum products
China Resources (Holding) Company Limited	100.4	171.5	State	Retail, power, breweries, real estate, food, medicine, textiles, chemical products, gas, compressor
China Netcom Group	97.0	248.7	State	Fixed-line telephone services, telecommunications and data services
China Metallurgical Group Co.	90.7	113.3	State	EPC business (engineering, procurement, and construction), natural resources exploitation, papermaking business, equipment fabrication
China Unicom Group	87.9	145.9	State	Mobile communication service，Unicom Horizon CDMA Service，mobile value-added service
China Huaneng Group	84.2	66.7	State	Power generation, IT, transportation, renewable energy, environment protection
Shenhua Group Co. Limited	83.6	141.2	State	Coal production, transportation, electricity generation
Ping An Insurance (Group)	81.7	48.8	Privately held	Insurance and financial services
China International Trust and Investment Company (CITIC Group)	81.3	77.6	State	Financial services: banking, securities business, insurance, trusts business, funds, futures
COFCO Group	75.4	82.5	State	Producer and supplier of processed agricultural products (including oilseed, wheat, and rice)

Source: The list of business groups and data of employees and revenue come from Enterprise Research Institute in Development Research Center of the State Council (2007). Other information is collected from related websites.

Table 3.4 China's top 500 business groups by sector, 2006

Sector	Number of groups	Total assets (billion yuan)	Total share holders' equity (billion yuan)	Revenue (billion yuan)	Employees (million)	Profit and tax (billion yuan)
Total	500	20,432	7,837	14,724	19.01	1,789
Primary sector	5	228.3	46.6	145	1.41	5.9
Manufacturing sector	363	12,917	5,435	10,942	13.81	1,411
Service sector	132	7,287	2,355	3,637	3.78	372.7
Share (%)						
Primary sector	1.00	1.12	0.59	0.98	7.42	0.33
Manufacturing sector	72.6	63.2	69.4	74.3	72.7	78.9
Service sector	26.4	35.7	30.1	24.7	19.9	20.8

Source: Enterprise Research Institute in Development Research Center of the State Council (2007: 7). Notes: Yuan is units of the Chinese currency (RMB).

investment decision-making, financing, foreign trade, debt–equity swap, and capital injection (Hahn and Lee 2006).

Business groups in China were formed and evolved through three paths (Hahn and Lee 2006; Lee and Hahn 2007). The most common way of setting up a business group was establishing subsidiaries through spin-offs. Firms separated core parts of their production, established subsidiaries that would be profitable businesses, and transformed themselves into holding companies.[3] Spin-offs sometimes involved the establishment of new firms with investment from parent firms and other firms, which is the second path—joint ventures with other companies. In this case, the joint venture could often take advantage of the pooling capital, equity, or brand names. The last path through which business groups were formed was mergers and acquisitions (M&As). Intense market competition led firms to be involved in M&As through which firms hoped to increase market share, achieve economies of scale, enhance brand names, and capitalize on the superior managerial talent (Lee and Hahn 2007). Hair Groups, the biggest in the household electric appliances industry, and China International Marine Container Group, a globally dominating producer of marine shipping containers, are good examples of groups whose growth has been propelled by M&As.

Lee and Jin (2009) discuss three alternative theories to explain the emergence of the business groups in China, namely, the market-based view, the state-activism view, and the resource-based view. Using firm-level data and variables representing different theories, they verify that the joint venture path should be the most dynamic and privately motivated way toward forming a business group and is consistent with market-based and resource-based views; that the M&A path seems to be consistent with the state-activism view, implying top-down manner of restructuring; and that the spin-off path seems to be close to the resource-based view. They also find that the greater autonomy given together with or after changing into a shareholding corporation is one of the most consistent and significant factors leading to a business group, regardless of whether it is through an M&A, a spin-off, or a joint venture path. This implies that the SOEs have gone through the path from being traditional SOEs to shareholding corporations and then finally to business groups.

With the decision of the Communist Party to establish a socialist market economy in 1993, private ownership began to be recognized officially in China. As a result, many non-state firms emerged and many of them built their own business groups to show up their sizes and reputation (Ma and Lu 2005). From 1998, the state made efforts to create "highly competitive large business groups" in the key pillar industries in the national economy. In 1998, the 15 industrial ministries

---

[3] Establishing business groups through spin-offs often involved irregular diversion of the parent firms' resources for the benefit of subsidiaries. Expropriation of state property in the form of asset stripping, tax evasion, debt reduction, and dividend manipulation has been reported.

were closed and the State Council began to directly control state-owned groups at the central level. In 2003, the Chinese government established the State-Owned Assets Supervision and Administration Commission of the State Council (SASAC), which played a crucial role in the reform of state-owned business groups. Charged with exercising the rights and authority of ownership on behalf of the government, SASAC took over the supervisory role that all the former industrial ministries previously had and clearly demarcated authority among different levels of the government.

SASAC owned several hundred firms that were controlled at many layers, with the individual enterprise at the bottom level, an investment or holding company in the middle, and the SASAC at the top. In 2006, SASAC was the controlling shareholder of the 168 largest companies listed on the Chinese stock exchanges in Shanghai and Shenzhen, accounting for 33.8 percent of the domestic market value (Naughton 2008).

3.4 Role of the State in the Growth of Business Groups

The role of the state in the emergence and development of business groups have been more important in China than its neighbors in East Asia such as Japan and Korea, because the Chinese groups emerged through a gradual transition, guided and controlled by the Communist Party, from a planed to a market economy. In fact, the government was actively involved in the establishment and development of Chinese business groups, at the central and provincial levels.

The central government as a developmental state promoted big business groups because it considered them a useful "device for economic catch-up" (Lee 2006a), as was the case for Korea and Japan. The State Council designated and made relevant benefits and privileges available to certain business groups. Moreover, the local governments and their ministries tried to promote their own business groups through various schemes, which included the transformation of former government units in charge of state-owned companies into holding companies.

Table 3.5 shows the importance of the 131 business groups directly controlled by the central government or the State Council in 2007. These 131 (4.5 percent) out of a total of 2,926 business groups accounted for 48.3 percent of the total assets and 41.8 percent of the total revenue of all business groups in China in 2007. The state gave them a variety of grants and favorable treatments to help them grow. Relevant ministries of the State Council also played a similar role in boosting big business groups; 141 business groups (4.8 percent) registered with relevant ministries of the State Council represented 10.9 and 9.9 percent, respectively, of the total assets and total sales revenue of all the registered business groups in China.

Table 3.5 Distribution by the level of state units in charge, 2007

Level of state units	Number of groups		Assets			Revenue		
	Number	Share (%)	Amount (billion yuan)	Share (%)	Average (billion yuan)	Amount (billion yuan)	Share (%)	Average (billion yuan)
State Council	131	4.5	16,607	48.3	126.77	9,718	41.8	74.18
Relevant ministries of the State Council	141	4.8	3,738	10.9	26.51	2,296	9.9	16.28
Provincial governments	777	26.6	6,585	19.2	8.48	5,321	22.9	6.85
Bureau of provincial governments	670	22.9	3,106	9.0	4.64	2,136	9.2	3.19
Others	1,207	41.3	4,319	12.6	3.58	3,787	16.3	3.14
Total	2,926	100.0	34,355	100.0	11.74	23,257	100.0	7.95

Source: Calculated from the data in National Bureau of Statistics, China (2008b).

Table 3.6 Distribution by ownership type of parent companies, 2007

Ownership type of parent companies	Business groups		Assets			Revenue		
	Number	Share (%)	Amount (billion yuan)	Share (%)	Average (billion yuan)	Amount (billion yuan)	Share (%)	Average (billion yuan)
SOEs	300	10.3	15,840	46.1	52.80	9,522	40.9	31.74
WSOEs	662	22.6	10,284	29.9	15.53	6,339	27.3	9.57
SOEs + WSOEs	962	32.9	26,124	76.0	27.16	15,861	68.2	16.49
Limited liability companies	1,331	45.5	4,882	14.2	3.67	4,746	20.4	3.57
Limited companies	397	13.6	2,533	7.4	6.38	1,743	7.5	4.39
Sino-foreign joint ventures	38	1.3	170	0.5	4.47	189	0.8	4.98
Joint ventures with Hong Kong, Macao, and Taiwan	33	1.1	70	0.2	2.12	60	0.3	1.82
Others	165	5.6	575	1.7	3.49	658	2.8	3.99
Total	2,926	100	34,354	100	11.74	23,257	100	7.95

Source: Calculated from the data in National Bureau of Statistics, China (2008b).

Many strategic considerations were also involved in building business groups. Starting in the early 1990s, the Chinese government began to encourage the creation of big business groups with the intention of strengthening the international competitiveness of Chinese firms. To aid the formation of big business groups, the government promoted M&As among big firms with a policy initiative called a "strong-strong combination" (*qiangqiang lianhe* in Chinese). Administrative means were often used in this process. For example, Shanghai Baosteel Group, the biggest business group in the Chinese iron and steel industry, was founded in 1998 through mergers and restructuring of Shanghai Metallurgical Holding Group and Shanghai Meishan Group with the former Shanghai Baoshan Iron and Steel Corporation, which became the core company of this new group. The biggest difficulty in building this group was the different affiliations of the firms involved. The Shanghai city government controlled some companies, whereas the central government controlled others. Extensive negotiations took place before the Shanghai city government finally agreed on the merger of the firms (Hahn and Lee 2006: 215).

In the provinces the formation of some business groups was initiated by the local governments with the aim of improving enterprise performance by sharing existing managerial resources across a wider array of businesses in order to respond to the increasing market competition. The supply of skillful managerial talent was very limited in many localities in China. Some local governments restructured all SOEs under their supervision into several business groups. In 1993, Siping county in Liaocheng city of the Shandong province restructured 29 SOEs under its supervision into 5 business groups, based on these groups' industrial categories, in order to share both established brands and managerial talent (Lee and Hahn 2007).

In some cases, business groups were formed under public policy considerations. Regarding the SOEs under their control, local governments had conflicting objectives: the promotion of profitable enterprises and social stability. As market competition increased, the profitability of many SOEs decreased. The local governments were often more concerned about the social tension that might be caused by massive layoffs. Accordingly, they tended to emphasize their responsibility to maintain social stability. In dealing with unprofitable enterprises, they often merged these enterprises with better-performing enterprises, "forced marriages" (*lalangpei* in Chinese), rather than having them go bankrupt, leading to the emergence of new business groups or the expansion of existing business groups.

3.5 Corporate Ownership, Governance, and Agency Costs

In China, there are several types of enterprises by firm type: state-owned enterprises (SOEs), wholly state-owned enterprises (WSOEs), limited liability companies, and limited companies. SOEs are firms owned by the central or a provincial government. Both SOEs and WSOEs are owned by the state; however, the latter group firms, which are100 percent owned by the government, are granted special autonomy and privileges. A limited liability company (*youxian zeren gongsi* in Chinese) is a legal form of business company offering limited liability to its owners. A limited company (*gufen youxian gongsi* in Chinese) is a corporation whose liability is limited by shares.

Depending on whether an enterprise is wholly owned by foreigners or jointly by foreigners and Chinese, or more specifically whether owned by non-mainland Chinese or both non-mainland and mainland Chinese, enterprises are classified into foreign-invested limited companies, Sino-foreign joint ventures, Hong Kong, Macao, and Taiwan-invested limited companies, and joint ventures with Hong Kong, Macao, and Taiwan[4]. Table 3.6 shows that the state-owned economy (including SOEs and WSOEs) maintained the leading position among the ownership types of parent companies in China in 2007. Although the proportion of both SOEs and WSOEs in terms of number was relatively small at 32.9 percent, they accounted for 76.0 percent of the total assets and 68.2 percent of the total sales revenue. However, it is interesting to see that limited liability companies, accounting for only 20.4 percent of the total sales revenue, had the leading position in terms of the number of business groups. SOEs and WSOEs were also dominant in terms of the average size of assets of the parent company of a business group. In particular, the average size of the parent companies of SOEs was about 4.5 times the average size of parent companies of all other business groups in terms of assets.

The dominance of state ownership is more pronounced when we focus on the top 500 business groups. Table 3.7 shows several basic statistics of the top 500 business groups by ownership type in 2005. In terms of numbers, 101 SOEs were ranked in the top 500 groups, accounting for 20.2 percent, and 177 WSOEs, accounting for 35.4 percent; thus, the number of corporations in the state-owned economy (both SOEs and WSOEs) comprised 55.6 percent of the 500 business groups. Comparison with statistics in Table 3.6 indicates that a larger number of state-owned business groups were included in the top 500 business groups, indicating that the state owned bigger business groups.

Among the top 500 business groups, SOEs and WSOEs constituted 51.6 percent and 31.0 percent in terms of assets, 58.8 percent and 27.1 percent in terms of shareholders' equity, 49.9 percent and 26.6 percent in terms of revenue, 27.7 percent and 37.9 percent in terms of exports, 61.0 percent and 24.9 percent in terms of profit and tax, and 44.3 percent and 32.1 percent in terms of the number of employees, respectively. Totaling the two groups, the state-owned economy represented 82.6 percent, 85.8 percent, 76.5 percent, 65.6 percent, 86.0 percent, and

---

[4] In Table 3.7, the data of two types of business groups, namely, foreign-invested limited companies and Hong Kong, Macao, and Taiwan-invested limited companies, are included in Others.

76.4 percent in terms of total assets, shareholders' equity, revenue, exports, profit and tax, and the number of employees, respectively. When compared with statistics in Table 3.6, it is evident that bigger business groups were owned by the state although time difference between the data in the two tables should be considered.

For the rest of the groups, in terms of the number of units, limited liability companies accounted for 28.6 percent while limited companies accounted for 9.0 percent.[5] The share of the other remaining groups was negligible. In terms of total assets, limited liability companies comprised 9.9 percent and limited companies 5.7 percent. In terms of revenue, limited liability companies accounted for 14.6 percent and limited companies 5.6 percent, and so on.

Table 3.8 shows the average size of the top 500 business groups by firm type in 2006. It is seen that the state-owned ones were quite bigger than the others. In terms of assets, SOEs were the biggest among the top 500. In 2006, SOEs had average assets of 104.5 billion yuan, which means that their asset size was 2.56 times the average asset size of the top 500 groups, while that of the business groups with other ownership types was below the average of the top 500. The others can be ranked as follows in terms of the average asset size: WSOEs (35.8 billion yuan), limited companies (25.7 billion yuan), limited liability companies (14.1 billion yuan), and joint ventures with Hong Kong, Macao, and Taiwan (13.6 billion yuan).

In terms of average revenue, SOEs were again bigger, with an average revenue of 72.8 billion yuan, 2.47 times the top 500 average. It was followed by WSOEs (22.1 billion yuan), limited companies (18.3 billion yuan), limited liability companies (15.0 billion yuan), joint ventures with Hong Kong, Macao, and Taiwan (9.9 billion yuan), and the Sino-foreign joint ventures (9.8 billion yuan). Similar results are drawn from the analysis of the average number of employees.

As seen in the previous discussion, the dominance of the state in ownership was an important characteristic of the business groups in China. Such ownership structure should have some implications for corporate governance and agency costs. In the listed business groups in China, a large portion of shares were non-tradable shares owned by state-related agencies, and the minority shareholders, including holders of tradable shares, played a negligible role (Tenev, Zhang, and Brefort 2002). Such weak legal and market mechanisms for exercising control over the managers provided a good ground for managerial entrenchment and often led to severe agency problems (La Porta, Lopez-De-Silanes, and Shleifer 1999).

Given this situation, the formation of business groups may lead to more private benefits for managers and controlling shareholders because the potential agency costs are aggravated in group-type firms with more serious asymmetric

---

[5] Limited companies consist of two types of firms, the private company limited by shares and the public limited company. In limited liability companies, a member's liability to repay the companies' obligations is limited to his or her capital contribution.

Table 3.7 Main economic indicators of the top 500 business groups by ownership type of parent companies, 2005

Ownership type of parent companies	Number of units	Assets (billion yuan)	Shareholders' equity (billion yuan)	Revenue (billion yuan)	Exports (billion yuan)	Profit and tax (billion yuan)	Employees (thousand)
SOEs	101	10,550.25	4,605.04	7,348.19	276.77	1,091.72	8,423.8
WSOEs	177	6,329.58	2,119.62	3,911.32	379.39	446.20	6,103.4
Limited liability companies	143	2,020.15	724.46	2,147.64	226.74	163.75	3,067.8
Limited companies	45	1,156.02	235.06	821.28	66.35	54.56	1,010.5
Sino-foreign joint ventures	10	67.09	30.19	98.20	9.87	8.80	127.3
Joint ventures with Hong Kong, Macao, and Taiwan	3	40.69	21.47	29.78	1.93	4.31	43.4
Others	21	268.41	101.20	367.06	40.09	19.61	228.7
Total	500	20,432.19	7,837.03	14,723.48	1,001.15	1,788.95	19,005
Share (%)							
Ownership type of parent companies	Number of units	Assets	Shareholders' equity	Revenue	Exports	Profit and tax	Employees
SOEs	20.2	51.6	58.8	49.9	27.7	61.0	44.3
WSOEs	35.4	31.0	27.1	26.6	37.9	24.9	32.1
SOEs + WSOEs	55.6	82.6	85.8	76.5	65.6	86.0	76.4
Limited liability companies	28.6	9.9	9.2	14.6	22.7	9.2	16.1
Limited companies	9.0	5.7	3.0	5.6	6.6	3.1	5.3
Sino-foreign joint ventures	2.0	0.3	0.4	0.7	1.0	0.5	0.7
Joint ventures with Hong Kong, Macao, and Taiwan	0.6	0.2	0.3	0.2	0.2	0.2	0.2
Others	4.2	1.3	1.3	2.5	4.0	1.1	1.2

Source: Enterprise Research Institute in Development Research Center of the State Council (2007: 18).

information. Under the pyramid structure of business groups, controlling shareholders easily transfer profits across firms, often from firms that have low cash flow rights to ones that have high cash flow rights, so-called tunneling.

In China, irregular diversion of parent companies' resources to subsidiaries was often reported (Fan 1996). Such a diversion took various forms of expropriation of state property, such as tax evasion, debt reduction, and dividend manipulation. Lee and Hahn (2004) investigated these phenomena in the context of the history of economic reform and explained how the control power over firms had changed over time since economic reform took place in China. According to them, the outsiders—the supervisory state and party organs—had strong power in controlling firms until the 1980s. However, from the end of the 1990s managers started to have de facto and de jure control over firms.

A series of empirical studies reported agency problems related to state-dominant ownership as well as weak legal and market mechanisms for exercising control over managers. Xu and Wang (1999) reported a positive correlation between ownership concentration and profitability using the data of Chinese listed companies during the period 1993–1995. They found that a firm's profitability was positively correlated with the fraction of shares held by legal persons, whereas it was either negatively correlated or uncorrelated with the fraction of shares held by the state. Their findings indicate that ownership concentration, especially by legal persons, alleviates the agency problem by strengthening shareholders' control over managers.

Tian (2001) uses data of listed firms in China during the period 1994–1998 and finds that firms having a non-government majority shareholder outperform those having the government as a majority shareholder. Moreover, he observes a U-shaped relationship between the size of government equity holding and corporate value. According to him, the U-shaped relationship indicates the interest-maximization behavior of the state. The grabbing hand by the state tend to reduce corporate value under a certain threshold, but the government may also increase corporate value by providing a helping hand when its financial interests become sufficiently large.

Using public company data for the period 1994–2000, Wang et al. (2004) show that the degree of ownership concentration is positively correlated with operating performance. They also report that legal person ownership shows no difference from state ownership in terms of its impact on performance.

3.6 Business Structure and Diversification

Typical business groups in China have a core company at the first tier, closely related companies at the second tier, semi-closely related companies at the third tier, and loosely related companies at the bottom. Core firms are also called the

Table 3.8 Average size of the top 500 business groups by ownership type, 2006

Ownership type	Assets (billion yuan)	Revenue (billion yuan)	Employees (thousand)
SOEs	104.5	72.8	83.4
WSOEs	35.8	22.1	34.5
Limited liability companies	14.1	15.0	21.5
Limited companies	25.7	18.3	22.5
Sino-foreign joint ventures	6.7	9.8	12.7
Joint ventures with Hong Kong, Macao, and Taiwan	13.6	9.9	14.5
Others	12.8	17.5	10.9
Total average	40.9	29.4	38.0

Source: Enterprise Research Institute in Development Research Center of the State Council (2007: 13).

parent company or group company because they have majority rights to the assets of their subsidiaries and unite the business group into a single controlled structure. They are generally a large industrial or commercial enterprise, with their business defining the primary business area of the group. They have their business and thus they can survive independently of their member firms. It is possible for core companies to exist as a pure holding company, but this is not the common case (Keister 2000; Lee and Hahn 2007).

Core firms also directly control and manage several specialized affiliate companies such as finance companies (*caiwugongsi* in Chinese) and R&D companies. A finance company is an independent non-bank financial firm responsible for a business group's financing activity. The main role of a finance company in a business group is to raise funds from banks as well as from member firms and to lend them to member firms in need of financing. In the early stage of economic reforms, the capital market in China was underdeveloped, and thus firms had difficulties in accessing the required capital. Finance companies emerged to overcome this situation. The government gave business groups the rights to set up finance companies. The first finance company in China was established in 1987. In 2007, there were 81 finance companies that were registered with China National Association of Finance Companies.

Many business groups also have R&D companies to fulfill the demand for R&D. Table 3.9 shows the aggregate amount of R&D investments by Chinese business groups, which was hovering around 1 percent of sales revenue during the period 2001–2005.

In addition to the relation between a core firm and its member firms in a business group, member firms have diverse types of interfirm relations. It is typical for firms in a business group to be connected to each other through cross-shareholdings, interlocking directorates, loan dependence, transaction of intermediate goods, and joint subsidiaries (Goto 1982). Cross-shareholding developed in China to help member firms share their interests with other firms in the same group, without which they would be competitors. It enables member firms to be involved in joint projects and to increase overall investment in R&D, which would be too risky otherwise (Keister 2000). Interlocking directorates take place when several firms in a business group share a manager on their boards of directors. According to Li (1995), interlocking directorates are the consequences of the practice of the state appointing key positions in the SOEs. However, it should not be overlooked that they emerged in order to fully utilize insufficient managerial resources in a business group. Firms in Chinese business groups are also linked among themselves through cross-lending as well as cross debt guarantee toward the commercial banks. Production relations often can be seen among member firms because many firms in a business group do business in the same industry. Joint venture-based subsidiaries with foreign firms in other Asian countries or in Western countries (*zhongwai hezi gonsi* in Chinese) are often built to access high technology as well as foreign markets. However, empirical evidence shows that they have a limited impact on technology transfer (Kang and Lee 2008).

Regarding diversification, it seems certain that business groups in China have also pursued diversification. Part A of Table 3.10 shows that during 2000–2007 the business groups had on average more than 10 subsidiaries, which cannot be taken as small. While Part A, based on the whole sample, cannot show the exact number of segments the Chinese business groups were doing business in, part B, based on the listed business groups for the period 1994–2003, shows that they had on average 7.62 subsidiaries and were doing business in 2.2 out of a total of 19 business segments. In Part C, when we divide the sample (about 220 business groups as of 2000) into those that have 2 or less segments of business and those that are diversified and thus have more than 2 segments of business, we can see that roughly half of the listed sample can be classified as diversified. As shown in Part C, some of them (more than 70) were doing business in more than 4 business segments as of 1999. However, this number drops rapidly toward 2003, which indicates some refocusing in the 2000s (Seo, Lee, and Wang 2006).

Nevertheless, this refocusing tendency cannot be verified by the data of the whole sample shown in Part A of Table 3.10. It is shown that the average number of subsidiaries was still increasing in the 2000s, from 8.3 in 2000 to 9.7 in 2003 and to 9.9 in 2007. This might indicate that the listed business groups were more exposed to market competition and sensitive to profitability and thus had conducted some refocusing. The theory is that business groups in China pursued diversification in the early 1990s, but fierce market competition forced them to withdraw to their traditional core line of business, as argued by Lee and Woo (2002). However, Chinese business groups that have diversified business tend to diversify into related rather than unrelated fields. Huang (2000) also reports that a great majority of M&As in China involve horizontal, vertical, and related diversification. In general, listed business group are relatively less diversified than Korean *chaebols* (Lee and Woo 2002).

Table 3.9 R&D expenditure of business groups

Year	Sales revenue (billion yuan)	R&D expenditure (billion yuan)	R&D ratio (%)
2001	6,562	66.9	1.02
2002	7,712	80.7	1.05
2003	10,009	90.5	0.9
2004	12,639	120.1	0.95
2005	15,551	150.7	0.97

Source: Calculated from the data in National Bureau of Statistics, China (2006b).

Less diversification of the Chinese business groups implies that they cannot expect the diverse benefits enjoyed by the Korean *chaebols*, such as the diversification of risks and the related cross-subsidization of temporary loss-making but potentially promising business (Lee and Woo 2002). Most of new businesses of Korean *chaebols*, including the memory business of Samsung, incurred heavy losses during their early days, which were subsidized by sister companies in the same business group. Affiliate companies in Chinese business groups would have more difficulties in finding such help from other member companies. In this respect, they would be more vulnerable to firm-specific or sector-specific risks than Korean *chaebol* firms, unless supported by the government.

3.7 Efficiency and Competitiveness

Now let us turn to the issue of competitiveness. Statistics of the top 500 business groups provide some evidence of the competitiveness of big business groups in China. Table 3.11 indicates the strong growth orientation of big business groups during 2002–2006. According to the table, aggregate total assets of the top 500 business groups annually grew by between 9.32 percent and 20.29 percent, profit and tax grew by between 18.47 percent and 38.70 percent, and revenue grew by between 18.59 percent and 29.98 percent during the period.

Table 3.12 confirms the overall tendency of China's top 500 business groups to improve efficiency for the period 2002–2006. The total factor productivity increased over the period, from 4.49 percent in 2002 to 7.30 percent in 2006, while the output per worker increased from 357.6 thousand yuan to 756.7 thousand yuan. Moreover, the profit and tax ratio increased from 8.00 percent to 11.59 percent, the ratio of profit to stockholders' equity increased from 7.59 percent to 13.83 percent, and the profit and tax per worker increased from 41.0 thousand yuan to 94.1 thousand yuan. However, the R&D to sales ratio shows some stagnating tendency.

To further examine the competitiveness of business groups in China, in comparison with stand-alone firms, we conducted some econometric analysis with the data of the firms listed on the Shanghai or Shenzhen Stock Exchange during the period 1995–2006. We classified the listed firms into business group firms and

Table 3.10 Trends and degree of diversification
Part A. Number of subsidiaries by firm type

Ownership type	2000			2005			2007		
	No. of parent companies	No. of subsidiaries	Average number of subsidiaries	No. of parent companies	No. of subsidiaries	Average number of subsidiaries	No. of parent companies	No. of subsidiaries	Average number of subsidiaries
SOEs	538	6,805	12.6	349	5,603	16.1	301	5,002	16.6
WSOEs	696	2,067	3.0	676	2,446	3.6	661	2,576	3.9
Limited liability companies	665	6,392	9.6	1,202	13,033	10.8	1331	15,509	11.7
Limited companies	438	1,562	3.6	390	1,805	4.6	397	1,793	4.5
Sino-foreign joint ventures	43	1,747	40.6	29	1,663	57.3	38	1,615	42.5
Joint ventures with Hong Kong, Macao, and Taiwan	28	597	21.3	33	794	24.1	33	831	25.2
Others	247	2,778	11.2	166	2,135	12.9	165	1,775	10.8
Total	2,655	21,948	8.3	2,845	27,479	9.7	2,926	29,101	9.9

Source: Calculated from the data in National Bureau of Statistics, China (2002, 2006c, 2008b).

Part B. Average number of subsidiaries and segments of listed groups

Year	Observation	No. of business groups	Average number of subsidiaries	Average number of segments	No. of segments per subsidiary
1994	270	162	6.29	2.22	0.35
1995	270	162	6.29	2.24	0.36
1996	270	162	6.29	2.25	0.36
1997	270	164	6.78	2.30	0.34
1998	270	165	7.28	2.36	0.32
1999	270	170	7.77	2.47	0.32
2000	270	184	8.26	2.50	0.30
2001	270	191	8.76	2.31	0.26
2002	270	189	9.27	2.09	0.23
2003	270	189	9.27	2.09	0.23
Average		173.8	7.62	2.28	0.30

Source: Manually collected from annual reports of public companies listed on the Shanghai Stock Exchange or the Shenzhen Stock Exchange.

Notes:

1. A firm is defined as a business group when the firm has at least four subsidiaries.

2. One of 22 industries (segments), which comprise 12 industries based on one-digit standard industry classification (SIC) system plus 10 manufacturing industries based on two-digit, is assigned to each firm.

Part C. Distribution of business groups by the number of business segments, 1994–2003

	1994	1995	1996	1997	1998	1999	2000	2001	2002	2003
SEGMENT	2.6	2.63	2.6	2.61	2.7	2.7	2.8	2.5	2.3	2.3
1	38	38	38	47	46	44	44	60	59	56
2	63	61	60	67	63	74	73	74	88	88
DIVER 0	101	99	98	114	109	118	117	134	147	144
3	62	63	63	55	59	58	60	51	65	66
4	38	38	38	42	33	30	24	31	19	18
5	8	9	10	11	20	20	21	16	4	4
6	1	1	1	3	4	9	11	4	1	1
7	0	0	0	0	0	0	2	1	0	0
DIVER 1	109	111	112	111	116	117	118	103	89	89

Source: Seo, Lee, and Wang (2006).

Note: DIVER 0 counts the number of business groups with one or two segments, and DIVER 1 counts those with three or more. This table shows distribution of listed firms with more than two subsidiaries.

Table 3.11 Growth performance of the top 500 business groups (yearly growth in %)

Variable	2002	2003	2004	2005	2006
Total assets	11.32	20.29	9.32	18.74	17.55
Number of employees	−0.17	1.14	−4.74	6.45	5.67
Export sales	18.57	16.93	29.31	13.74	25.37
Profit and tax	33.70	18.47	38.70	22.41	23.72
Net profit	29.90	32.79	49.75	23.90	22.58
Revenue	18.59	29.98	21.79	22.03	21.50
Total stockholders' equity	11.27	13.00	8.99	16.60	15.43

Source: Enterprise Research Institute in Development Research Center of the State Council (2007: 2).

stand-alone firms, and we also divided the period into two subperiods (1995–2000 and 2001–2006). For the first period, 1995–2000, we defined a firm as a business group if it had at least four subsidiaries in 1998. For the second period, 2001–2006, we defined a firm as a business group if it had at least four subsidiaries in 2002. Table 3.13 summarizes the results of comparing the size, accounting performance, and growth propensity of these two types of firms during the period 1995–2006.

First, Part A of Table 3.13 shows that business groups were definitely larger than non-business group firms in terms of both assets and sales. Accounting performance and growth of business groups compared to non-business group firms can be seen in Part B of Table 3.13. Business groups were apparently outperformed by non-business groups in terms of return on assets in both periods. However, they were not much different from non-business groups when return on sales is used as a comparison. Given that return on assets is composed of two components, sales to assets and return to sales, we can conclude that the poor performance of business groups mainly stemmed from poor turnover rate (sales to assets), not from profit margin.[6]

In terms of firm growth, business groups appear to have grown slightly slower than non-business group firms during the period 1995–2000. In the period 2001–2006, the growth of business groups was not different from that of non-business group firms. Overall, business groups grew almost at the same rate as non-business groups.

3.8 Summary and Concluding Remarks

The Chinese government has an explicit definition for business groups, which have to be registered with the State Administration for Industry and Commerce.

---

[6] Return/Assets = Return/Sales * Sales/Assets

Table 3.12 Economic efficiency of China's top 500 business groups

Variable	2002	2003	2004	2005	2006
Total factor productivity (%)	4.49	5.29	6.31	6.85	7.30
Output ratio per worker (thousand yuan/worker)	357.6	459.6	587.6	673.6	756.7
Profit and tax ratio (%)	8.00	8.26	10.44	11.28	11.59
Profit ratio of stockholders' equity (%)	7.59	8.92	12.26	13.02	13.83
Profit and tax per worker (thousand yuan/worker)	41.0	48.0	69.9	80.4	94.1
R&D ratio (%)	1.05	0.91	0.79	0.78	0.89

Source: Enterprise Research Institute in Development Research Center of the State Council (2007: 3).

Table 3.13 Comparison of business groups with non-business groups

Part A: Size

Dependent variable	Control variable	1995–2000	2001–2006
Log (asset)	Sector dummies	Larger than non-BG	Larger than non-BG
Log (revenue)	Sector dummies	Larger than non-BG	Larger than non-BG

Part B: Performance

Dependent variable	Control variable	1995–2000	2001–2006
ROA	Size, sector dummies	Lower than non-BGs	Lower than non-BGs
ROIC	Size, sector dummies	Lower than non-BGs	Lower than non-BGs
NI/Sales	Size, sector dummies	Slightly lower than non-BGs	Indifferent
EBIT/Sales	Size, sector dummies	Lower than non-BGs	Indifferent
$(Sales_t - Sales_{t-1}) /$ $Sales_{t-1}$	Size, sector dummies	Slightly lower than non-BGs	Indifferent

Notes:

1. Non-BGs stands for non-business group firms. A firm is defined as a business group when it has at least four subsidiaries. So one is assigned as group dummy for firms with at least four subsidiaries, zero otherwise. Size is measured by sales.

2. ROA (return on assets) = Net income/Total assets; ROIC (return on invested capital) = EBIT/ Total assets; EBIT = earnings before interest and tax; NI: net income; $Sales_t$: sales at time t; $Sales_{t-1}$: sales at time $t-1$.

The business group should have at least five affiliated companies and as a total should have a registered capital of over 100 million RMB (*yuan*). The number of registered business groups increased from 2,472 in 1998 to 2,926 in 2007, about 20 percent increase. The chief differences between large business groups in China and those in Korea and Japan are that the former are less diversified and owned by the state, not by particular families or commercial banks. The government had controlling power over 45 percent of business groups in 2007. The dominance of the state is more evident in terms of the total revenue, with the state-controlled ones accounting for 78 percent. However, non-government ownership was growing fast, with business groups with private and other ownership accounting for about 45 percent of a total of 2,856 business groups in 2007 although their share in terms of sales was still less than 20 percent. In terms of sectors, firms in the top 30 were mostly in energy, utilities, and services, whereas the share of manufacturing was dominant in the top 500 business groups.

Chinese business groups typically maintain a vertical structure, with the core company at the first tier, closely related companies at the second tier, semi-closely related companies at the third tier, and loosely related companies at the bottom. Core firms are also called the parent company or group company because they have majority rights to the assets of their subsidiaries and unite the business group into a single controlled structure. They are generally a large industrial or commercial enterprise, with their business defining the primary business area of the group. Some large business groups have finance companies and R&D companies as their affiliates.

While the performance of business groups seems to have improved over time, they are showing some inferior or comparable performance relative to stand-alone firms. It is observed that Chinese business groups also have both strengths (high growth) and weaknesses (lower profitability) similar to those in other countries.[7] This is understandable, as business groups in China are also known to have a multitier structure, leading to asset-stripping and agency costs, as in their counterparts in other countries. Our regression results confirming low asset turnover seem to be compatible with this argument. It remains to be seen what the long-term growth path of the Chinese groups will be.

---

[7] Korean *chaebols* in the 1990s also have both strengths and weaknesses. As analyzed well by Choo et al. (2009), those business groups that promoted strengths (investment in R&D) while minimizing weaknesses survived the financial crisis and have shown long-term viability.

4

Role of Science and Technology Institutions in Limited Catch-up: Semiconductor Industry[1]

4.1 Introduction

China's economic success owing to the reform and open door policy since 1978 is an interesting case, and thus diverse views have been suggested from different angles. The traditional view attributes the success of China's reform—another East Asian miracle—to policy changes that maximized its comparative advantage in labor-intensive goods (Lin et al. 1996; Lin 2003). While some studies noted the similarity between China and neighboring South Korea and Taiwan (Li and Lian 1999; Li, Li, and Zhang 2000), others tended to pay more attention to the disparities (Nolan 2002; Lee, Hahn, and Lin 2002). Specific factors for China's economic growth have also been considered, such as the influx of private or foreign capital, education, and openness (Chen and Feng 2000; Lee 1996), financial liberalization (Liu and Li 2001), new development policies to prioritize its coastal region (Berthélemy and Démurger 2000; Tian et al. 2004), and various structural changes (Phillips and Shen 2005; Kawakami 2004).

Since the mid-2000s, studies on China's growth with focus on innovation and knowledge have also gained some attention. The Chinese government has emphasized "indigenous innovation" since the 2000s and has supported technology innovation led by Chinese firms as well as emphasized firm-level R&D investment, accumulation of knowledge, and organizational learning. Jin, Lee, and Kim (2008) verified that the engine of growth has changed from privatization, exports, and foreign direct investment (FDI) to innovation and exports. Gu and Lundvall (2006a) explained the trends of China's innovation capacity from the perspective of the national innovation system.[2]

This chapter follows this trend of paying more attention to the microfoundation of the overall economic growth of China. It especially investigates

[1] This chapter is a re-writing of an article, Sungho Rho, Keun Lee, and Seong Hee Kim (2015), "Limited Catch-up in China's Semiconductor Industry," *Millennial Asia*, 6(2), 147–75.
[2] There are many cases and industry studies on technology capability building and catch-up in China, such as Mu and Lee (2005), Zhu et al. (2006), and Li and Pu (2009).

China's Technological Leapfrogging and Economic Catch-up: A Schumpeterian Perspective. Keun Lee, Oxford University Press. © Keun Lee 2021. DOI: 10.1093/oso/9780192847560.003.0004

industrial catch-up in China's semiconductor sector. Though the industry has accomplished some catch-up, it is still limited. The chapter also discusses the sources for the limitations of China's semiconductor industry.

In general, the semiconductor industry is the industry that manufactures semiconductors such as discrete devices, memory chips, and microprocessors, with integrated circuits (ICs hereafter) being the most important product type. The production of ICs is preceded by the processes of layout design and mask production and followed by lithography—including the stages of exposure, etching, and development—that transfers mask patterns to silicon wafers as well as hundreds of repeated fabrication processes. After being wired, the wafer undergoes assembly and testing before being made into the final product. In this chapter, our analysis focuses on the IC manufacturing industry. IC manufacturing is an important part of the value chain of the semiconductor industry and plays a key role in the catch-up of the industry as a whole. Hence developed countries did not want it to be transferred to China and tried to restrict technology transfer.

Our analysis will adopt the theoretical framework proposed in Chapter 1, focusing on the sectoral systems of innovation (SSI hereafter), a framework that originates from the concept of the national systems of innovation (Freeman 1987; Lundvall 1992). SSI scholars observe that innovation systems differ from industry to industry and depend largely not only on the individual agent's innovation efforts but also on the interactions between the actors and social and economic conditions. Malerba (2004) advanced the discussions on SSI and conducted analyses of the industries of various countries according to this framework. Since then, many papers, including Chapters 2, 6, and 7 in this book, have sprung up, applying the framework to industry analyses of China, Korea, and India. Industry-by-industry comparative studies can be conducted more conveniently using the SSI framework.

The structure of this chapter is as follows. Section 4.2 reviews the situation of China's IC manufacturing industry and its catching-up performance. Section 4.3 presents a SSI of the semiconductor industry. Using specific cases and data, Sections 4.4 and 4.5 analyze the impact of technological regimes and actors' behavior on the evolution of innovation systems in China's IC industry. Section 4.6 provides the conclusion.

4.2 Limited Catch-up in China's IC Manufacturing

The Chinese government had attempted supportive industry policies to promote its manufacturing sector since the early stage of its reform period. However, indigenous companies did not achieve a big market share and had limited abilities to catch up in the technological aspect, even until the 2010s.

Table 4.1 Top 10 semiconductor suppliers in the Chinese market, 2012–2013

Rank		Company	Revenue in USD million			Market share
2012	2013		2012	2013	% Change	
1	1	Intel	25,076	24,941	−0.5	13.8
2	2	Samsung	11,450	13,723	19.9	7.8
5	3	SK Hynix	5,108	7,230	41.5	4.0
4	4	Toshiba	5,152	5,886	14.2	3.3
3	5	TI	5,398	5,650	3.8	3.1
10	6	Qualcomm	3,171	4,658	46.9	2.6
6	7	ST	4,359	4,546	4.3	2.5
7	8	AMD	4,219	4,050	−4.0	2.2
8	9	Freescale	3,561	3,958	11.1	2.2
9	10	Renesas	3,260	3,008	−7.7	1.7

Source: PWC (2014).

First of all, in terms of market shares, China's domestic companies lagged behind in the standard IC market. Since the standard IC market has a large market size and huge potential, competition among the firms is fierce. Product innovation speed is also very high. Central process unit (CPU) and dynamic random access memory (DRAM) chips are two of the main products of this market. However, the share of China's domestic companies in the standard IC market was rather stagnant if not decreasing. Notably, the profit margin of Semiconductor Manufacturing International Corporation's (SMIC) DRAM products considerably decreased due to Korean, Taiwanese, and Japanese firms. Huahong-NEC, a JV firm, failed to enter the DRAM market in its early stage and was focusing on the application-specific integrated circuit (ASIC) chip market. In addition, in the foundry market, that is, the ASIC chip market, the market share growth of domestic companies also remained stagnated due to the Taiwanese companies. As seen in Table 4.1, all of the top 10 companies that dominated China's semiconductor industry in 2012–2013 were from abroad. They were all from the standard IC segment. China's semiconductor market accounted for half of the world's market and these companies accounted for 42.9 percent of the Chinese IC market as of 2013 (PWC 2014).

This situation can also be inferred from China's degree of dependence on IC imports. China imported more than 29 percent of the semiconductors consumed within the country in 2011. It is known that it imports mainly from Korea, Taiwan, and the US. This is due to the developed countries' strategic decision of not transferring IC manufacturing value chains to China. Additionally, IC designing and fabrication counted very little in China's entire semiconductor industry,

Table 4.2 China's wafer fab capacity by design rule and wafer size, 2012

	China			Worldwide	
	Capacity	%	Ratio of China to World in capacity (%)	Capacity	%
Design rule					
> 0.7 μm	621.4	27	20	3,089.2	14
< 0.7 to > 0.4 μm	159.6	7	14	1,175.0	5
< 0.4 to > 0.2 μm	202.9	9	10	2,073.6	10
< 0.2 to > 0.12 μm	315.0	14	14	2,269.2	11
< 0.12 to > 0.06 μm	467.3	20	18	2,888.6	13
< 0.06 to > 0.028 μm	562.5	24	11	5,333.7	25
< 0.028 μm	0	0	0	4,088.8	19
n/a	0	0	0	611.0	3
Total	2,328.7	100	11	17,932.7	100
Wafer size					
> 4-inch	345.7	15	34	1,019.8	5
5-inch	186.9	8	28	724.6	3
6-inch	396.3	17	13	3,093.9	14
8-inch	619.0	27	11	5,814.1	27
12-inch	780.8	34	7	10,874.8	51
Total	2,328.7	100	11	21,527.2	100

Source: PWC (2013).

Notes: Capacity = 1000s 8-inch equivalent wafer starts per month.

Current capacity = World Fab Watch probability > 1.0.

compared to assembling and testing value chains. Given that designing and fabrication require the most advanced technology and thereby correspond to higher value added within the value chain, it can be said that the catch-up of China's IC manufacturing industry has a long way to go.

The main reason behind this standstill in market catch-up is that catch-up is limited in terms of fabrication technology. Table 4.2 demonstrates the 2012 trends in technology catch-up of China's IC manufacturing industry. We can see that none of the products were made from less than 0.028 μm as of December 2012. On the other hand, the share of worldwide products from less than 0.028 μm accounted for 19 percent. Moreover, the Chinese had only four—not many—12-inch fabs, which does not show a very high yield rate, indicating a big gap in productivity.

Given the limited catch-up in China's IC sector, our goal in this chapter is to find out what the reasons are and whether this phenomenon will persist in the future. We answer this question by comparing the IC sector with other more successful sectors in China, as well as with the success of other economies (Korean and Taiwan) in this sector.

4.3 Innovation Systems of Semiconductor Industry

4.3.1 SSI Framework and Catch-up Literature

The building blocks of SSI consist of (1) knowledge and technological regimes, (2) demand conditions (or market regimes), (3) actors and networks and the coordination among them, and (4) surrounding institutions, including intellectual property rights (IPRs), laws, and culture. These elements are supposed to interact to generate a variety of outcomes in terms of selection of agents and co-evolution of sectors. Many studies have used the SSI framework to perform research on industrial catch-up in developing countries. Among the studies emphasizing industry-specific technology and knowledge systems, the research of Lee and Lim (2001) is a representative example using the Korean case. Lee, Mani, and Mu (2012), Mu and Lee (2005), and Lee, Cho, and Jin (2009) implemented the case study approach to explain catch-up phenomena in China. Lee, Mani, and Mu (2012) also tried to explain both initial commonalities and later divergence among the four countries of China, Korea, India, and Brazil in telecommunications equipment sector. They concluded that paradigm shifts (short cycle) can act either as a window of opportunity (as for China and Korea) or as further entry barriers (as in India and Brazil) for latecomers' successful endeavor. Lee, Cho, and Jin (2009) adopted the concept of modularity into the pre-existing framework concept and analyzed technology catch-up trends of China's mobile phone and automobile industries.

According to the analysis, indigenous automakers in China were making a quick catch-up upon entry because the auto sectors tended to be featured by a higher degree of embodied technical changes and increasing modularity in many components. Similarly, in the mobile phone industry, early stage catch-up was relatively easy owing to the high modularity of production and the availability of knowledge pool around the nation. Mu and Lee (2005) paid special attention to developing countries' special market structure. Their study examined China's telecommunications industry and explains that its local follower firms dominated the rural or lower end market because China had segmented markets that had different market structures between the urban and rural areas, which served as the groundwork for technology catch-up.

4.3.2 Technology/Knowledge Regime of Semiconductor Industry

The semiconductor industry is a high-technology industry that is related to various academic fields such as electromagnetism, solid state physics, material science, chemistry, optics, and architecture. Even seismology can be counted as a related academic field, as semiconductor equipment is sensitive to oscillations and can cause tremendous losses to the company using it in case of earthquakes.

Moreover, exploratory studies on alternative materials are being conducted in many academic fields to overcome the physical limits of materials. That is, the semiconductor industry's knowledge domains vary and are constantly expanding. Academic research findings of related fields are rapidly reflected in this industry's development so that innovations are frequent and fast. In other words, there exist plenty of technological opportunities.

In terms of technology appropriability, as product life cycles are short, a company may secure appropriability by being the market leader. This is why it is important to have the ability to rapidly produce next-generation products. In the semiconductor industry, facilities of different generations are needed in order to fabricate wafers of longer diameters, which exponentially increase productivity (refer to Table 4.3). We can argue that the degree of embodied technical change is high for high-technology fabrication facilities. Furthermore, high-technology facilities are needed in order to realize more stable fabrication process for the testing and production of next-generation products from newly built facility lines. Additionally, tacit knowledge is very important in order to efficiently manage these facilities and raise operating ratios from the facilities.

In many countries, the semiconductor industry is protected as the nation's strategic industry, and thus, it is not easy to acquire fabrication technology. Moreover, as semiconductor manufacturers fiercely compete with each other, means such as patent lawsuits restrict imitation. In other words, there is very low accessibility in terms of the industry's high technology. In order to overcome the situation, semiconductor manufacturers strengthen their R&D capacity, accumulate IPRs, and defend themselves from patent lawsuits through cross-licensing agreements. In the semiconductor industry, patents are important because they are strategically useful. A leading company dominates the patents used in the fabrication process and thereby restricts follower companies. A follower company, on the other hand, owns patents that can be used to respond to leader firms that use their patented technologies in lawsuits.

The next important point in terms of the semiconductor industry's technology/knowledge regime is that the degree of technology cumulativeness in incumbent dominant firms has become higher, and it has become a typical Schumpeter Mark II industry. The fundamental reason for this change is that as technology

Table 4.3 Productivity by production line

Wafer	8-inch	12-inch
Products per wafer (64 MB, 0.18 μm)	700	1,600
Investment (USD billion)	1.8	2.5
Productivity (products/investment)	1	1.7

Source: Korea Industrial Technology Foundation (2003).

develops and becomes complicated, the price of the equipment for next-generation innovations and the complexities of production processes increase. For instance, compared to USD 1.5 billion spent towards reaching the production capacity of 30,000 per month for 8-inch wafers in the 1990s, USD 2.5 billion were consumed in the 2000s to achieve the production capacity of 20,000 per month for 12-inch wafers (Joo 2004). In order to increase the density of semiconductors, production technologies of smaller line widths are needed, which calls for costlier devices. In addition, devices for clean room technology and automation, planning, and measuring equipment for the development of high-performance circuits become more expensive after innovation.

As investment increases, a firm bears higher risks, which enables incumbent firms to compete in a more advantageous position than follower companies. Also, in terms of cognitive capability for next-generation technology and organizational capability for production and planning, incumbent big corporations have an edge over follower firms. Moreover, as catch-up proceeds toward later stages, tacitness of involved knowledge tends to increase and access to next-generation technology becomes more important and probably difficult, which place the followers in a difficult position to catch up. This situation can be verified by industry concentration ratio. The leading semiconductor manufacturers, Intel and Samsung, dominate the semiconductor industry's main sectors, microprocessor and DRAM, respectively, with power. This trend is also affirmed in the research of Kim and Lee (2003), which proved using a history-friendly model that bigger corporations are in a more favorable position than small-scaled competitors in the DRAM industry. If we relate this to China's semiconductor industry, we conjecture that China's small-scaled follower companies will face difficulties in catch-up due to its technological regimes.

4.3.3 Demand Condition/Market Regime of Semiconductor Industry

An important trait of the demand conditions of the semiconductor industry is that next-generation products can completely replace existing products. Hence, after a launch of next-generation IC products, prices of the previous IC products sharply fall. Furthermore, as next-generation products become cheap due to the increase in the number of companies producing them, the previous products disappear from the market. In general, electronic products have short product life cycles compared to automobiles, machines, or ships, and IC products have an even shorter product life cycle as they undergo frequent product innovations. Of late, product life cycles are becoming shorter and shorter. Additionally, as IC products are small in size and light in weight and therefore easy to transport, as long as the tariff wall does not interfere with trades, the degree of world market integration is high. Judging from the fact that many of the electronic devices produced in China are being exported again, China market and the world market are not divided into two separate classes.

These demand conditions affect innovations of the semiconductor industry in many ways. First, it is important for a firm to implement rapid marketing strategies so that it maximizes profits when prices are high immediately after the launch of its product. Furthermore, as a result of production experiences in this stage, it has to increase the yield rate and rapidly flatten the learning curve in order to save costs and secure profits amid price competitions with the competitors. Therefore, a firm that possesses leading R&D capacity and develops up-to-date fabrication technology that rapidly increases its yield rates can maintain its competitiveness and survive. Therefore, technologically regressive innovations (e.g., thin slab mold technology) are nearly impossible except in several ASIC areas.

As a result of the semiconductor industry's demand conditions, follower firms and follower countries face several difficulties in catching up. Although the market is increasing in size, because the period of maintaining products in the market without being thrown out by the next-generation products is shortening, firms bear high risks. Moreover, if follower firms cannot constantly achieve this kind of innovations, it is impossible to catch up. That is, with mere temporary introduction of facilities and technology transfers, catching up in the market cannot be realized.

The demand conditions of the semiconductor market mentioned above have a market structure that is quite different from that in telephone switches, analyzed in Chapter 2 of this book, where markets are clearly segmented into high- and low-end markets. Thus, we can conjecture that China's domestic firms will have difficulties in catching up in the semiconductor market, where markets are unified than segmented. In other words, there is no low-end market that plays a protected or niche market for indigenous products.

4.3.4 Actors in China's Semiconductor Industry

Regarding the actors in China's semiconductor industry, our focus is on indigenous players, such as domestic firms, the Chinese government, universities and research institutions, and industry associations. Surely, we cannot ignore the influence of foreign companies established within China on Chinese semiconductor industry's innovation system. As of the early 2010s, SK Hynix, a Korean company, ranked the first in terms of sales among China's semiconductor manufacturers because it had a joint venture inside China (Wuxi city), and Samsung was also coming up as a main actor in China's semiconductor industry since it had built a local production facility in Xian in 2013. However, foreign firms function with respect to their mother nations' innovation systems, and for strategic reasons, technology transfer effects into China is very limited. Therefore, in order to analyze the evolution of China's industry innovation system, we allocate more space in discussing indigenous firms. Moreover, we have to be careful in discussing the Chinese government, as the central government and the local governments are different entities that function within the innovation system. The central government and the local governments have different motivation systems and frequent conflicting interests, which rationally calls for the necessity to separate these as two different factors that affect innovation systems.

4.4 Failure to Catch-up during the 1950s to the Early 1990s

4.4.1 The Period from the 1950s to the 1970s

China began to show interest in semiconductor technology as early as in 1956. At the time, the government selected computer, semiconductor, automation, and wireless electric technologies as the four national emergency technologies. With respect to semiconductor technology, China established plans for technology procurement of material and related facilities and for upbringing human resources, which became its first science and technology policy. Institute of Applied Physics in Chinese Academy of Sciences, being the center of raising human capital by inviting returned scientists from abroad and of conducting research and development, manufactured its first transistor in 1956, with the semiconductor-related technology it acquired from the Soviet Union. However, as diplomatic relations with the Soviet Union ceased, China faced technological isolation, and it became impossible to adopt external semiconductor manufacturing technology in the economic management system of autarky. In the 1960s, producing mainly transistors used in radios was the main role of the semiconductor industry. Later, 878Fab, established in 1968, and Shanhai19Fab, established in 1970, were important hubs for semiconductor research and development (Zhu 2006).

Soon after, during the Chinese Cultural Revolution, strange policies regarding the semiconductor industry were implemented. "All people must make semiconductors" was the campaign during the 1970s, when around 40 semiconductor factories sprouted. Because of this, 878Fab, which had relatively good technology, plunged in productivity with decreased yield rates. This Cultural Revolution period hindered the development of China's semiconductor industry later when the government-funded research institute's technology accumulation stopped, limiting the government's further efforts for industry development. Table 4.4 demonstrates the years when China and the US succeeded in developing primal ICs. The table shows that the gap started to widen in the early 1970s. Although in 1972 the diplomatic relations between China and Japan began to recover, which led to Chinese firms observing Japanese firms and adopting three 3-inch production facilities in Beijing's 878Fab, Shaanxi's 771Fab, and 4433Fab, fundamentally

Table 4.4 US–China IC development in years

	SSI	MSI	LSI	VLSI	ULSI
US	1958	1964	1966	1976	1986
China	1965	1972	1972	1986	1999
Lagged year	7	8	6	10	13

Source: Zhu (2006).

catching up in the IC industry under the closed system was a very difficult job. For instance, in 1977 and 1978, the Chinese government attempted, but failed, to establish three fake companies with government money in order to procure IC manufacturing technology (Zhu 2006).

4.4.2 The Government as the Unique Actor: From the Early 1980s to the Early 1990s

During the initial stage of the reform, the government had to be the main actor in transforming the industry innovation system. In the early 1980s, there was a rush into semiconductor facilities by the local governments. There were 24 lines of IC production facilities in 33 units nationally, which were mainly old facilities from the developed countries. Most of the facilities that were brought in did not function well, and the number of their monthly wafer output was merely in the range of several hundreds to 2,000. This was because the local governments did not have any technology or human capital for facility management and lacked the capital to purchase manufacturing equipment in shortage. The reason for this is explained by the "sponsored partisanship" of Naughton and Qi (2000). According to them, the central government delegated the rights for facility importation to the local governments. The local governments, without any accumulation of related technology, competitively decided to bring in facilities for technology that was out of their reach. Their failure in this endeavor was predicted as there were many restrictions, including budget limits for the facilities (Naughton and Qi 2000). However, there was one case with minor success—742Fab of Jiangsu Wuxi. This factory introduced a 3-inch line to produce ICs to be used in TVs and manufactured over 10,000 wafers a month, which was possible due to the successful transfer of Toshiba's technology necessary for facility management (Zhu 2006).

In 1986, the central government developed a strategy to overcome this situation. This resulted in the 531 Plan, which was a representative plan formed during the seventh five-year plan. According to the plan, China was to discontinue 5-mm technology, acquire 3-mm manufacturing technology for main players, and start R&D for 1-mm technology. In 1985–1986, the central government's Ministry of Electronics Industry made an effort toward structural reform and decentralization, such as delegating ownerships of parts manufacturers—except 742Fab of Wuxi and 4400Fab of Shaanxi—to cities, provinces, and local governments and undergoing organization restructuring. Along with this, in 1986, it supported the IC firms through policies such as eliminating production tax, cutting income tax, supporting 10 percent of R&D costs, and giving tax breaks in facility import taxes for important projects. Moreover, in 1989, Wuxi Huajing, Shaoxing Huayue, Shanghai Beiling, Shanghai Philips, and Beijing Shougang-NEC were selected as main players. Among these, Shanghai Beiling, Shanghai Philips, and Beijing Shougang-NEC were Sino-foreign joint ventures. Establishing a Sino-foreign joint firm was one of the means to obtain technology, which reflected the Chinese government's passion for acquiring IC technology. The central government, which solely owned the bargaining rights, demanded technology transfers from its foreign negotiating partners in return for the rights to access the Chinese market and offered joint ventures in the IC industry, a high-technology area. This strategy is widely known as "trading market for technology," as noted in Chapter 2 and also by Mu and Lee (2005).

In this matter, the Chinese government functioned as the sole actor in transforming the IC industry's innovation in a situation where domestic firms could not establish themselves and research institutes and universities did not have R&D capacity. However, in the circumstances where organizations constantly changed due to the public sector reform, it was difficult to maintain steady industry development policies.

A case illustrating this point is the "908 Project," formed during the eighth five-year plan period. It consisted of building 6-inch production lines and obtaining 0.8–1-mm manufacturing technology with RMB 2.5 billion funding. Although the project was a reflection of some political ambition, it took eight years to get the central government's permission for capital investment. In August 1990, it was finally authorized and named 908. Although it was the outcome of a difficult decision, there were constant disputes over which products to produce as processes of allocating capital were not facile. Finally in 1995, the project team started to build production lines and, in January 1998, began to produce pilot products. This project is considered a failure because, at the time, it was impossible to maintain competition with 6-inch production lines (Chen 2005).

4.4.3 Causes of Policy Failures: Immature Innovation System and Institutional Factors

In the initial stage of the reform, government-led industry policies failed due to the absence of an innovation system and related institutional factors.

First, there were no reliable firms and R&D organizations. In the early days of the reform, China was in such a state that firms had to be created as part of its transition from planned economy to market economy. Its universities and public research organizations had low competitiveness due to lack of learning and exchange opportunities with the external world. Moreover, a legacy of its Cultural Revolution was that many R&D centers, where resources were concentrated, were disrupted. In this calamitous scenario, industry catch-up was not to be accomplished with the sole effort of the government.

On the contrary, in Korea, big corporations (e.g., Samsung, Hyundai, and LG) pioneered technological advancements and industry innovations such that they accumulated technology in the DRAM industry, while in Taiwan, government research institutions (e.g., ITRI) developed basic IC manufacturing technology and provided it freely to private firms, accomplishing industry catch-up (Choi 1996; Cho, Kim, and Rhee 1998; Cho and Mathew 2000). However, China could not pursue any of these models.

Second, we can point out the government's limitations as the leader of industry innovations. Chen (2005) demonstrates this by interviewing several policymakers who participated in policy decisions related to the IC industry at the time. According to Chen (2005), during the process of implementing the 908 Project, 28 government departments disputed over a dredging approval. Local governments first disputed over the locations of production line facilities and, later on, over the countries and companies to import the technology from. Finally, choosing between ASIC and DRAM was a challenge as some voiced concerns that DRAM products were not competitive. After a series of fierce debates, the conclusion was not choosing one strategy over another but an inefficient decision to produce DRAM and ASIC products with equal emphasis on both. This example illustrates the government's limitations in functioning as an innovation actor in terms of capacity and decision-making efficiency at the time.

Third, we highlight external institutional factors surrounding innovation systems with respect to accessibility of external knowledge. In regard to the policy environment of China's semiconductor industry, the most conspicuous fact was that adopting technology from foreign sources was restricted. This type of restriction originated from the Coordinating Committee for Multilateral Export Controls (COCOM), which was formed in 1949. At the time, the committee banned the export of member countries' material and technology to around 30 Communist East European countries, which could possibly use them for strategic purpose. After the Korean War in 1950, China was included in the list. This agreement restricted exporting wafers bigger than 5 inches and production facilities of design rule smaller than 2 μm to the sanctioned countries, which was one of the reasons for China's mass import of old facilities during the initial stage of reform. After 1994, when this agreement was dismissed, it was succeeded by the Wassennar Arrangement in 1996 under the leadership of the US. This arrangement also restricted the member countries exporting materials and technologies that could be of strategic use to the Communist countries. Because of this agreement, we conclude, China's adoption of the IC manufacturing technology was constrained at a certain level. Thus, this external institutional barrier was a hindrance to China's access to foreign technology (Lin 2009).

Along with the Western countries' restrictions on technology transfers, another important institutional barrier was Taiwan's ban on IC manufacturing investment. Taiwan, competing with mainland China, did not permit transfer of facilities—except the ones at least two generations behind—to China in order to protect its industries. This measure was an obstacle for Taiwanese IC firms advancing to China's markets. As for China, the restriction on the entry of Taiwanese firms meant the easiest way to obtain IC technology and access external knowledge was blocked. In the situation where China lacked the systematic capacity to catch up internally with the existing trends in technology innovation of the semiconductor industry, the government's effort for industry catch-up was even more bound to fail because of such restricted access to external technology.

4.5 Limited Success from Late 1990s to Early 2000s

4.5.1 Emergence of Innovation System and Limited Success

As discussed above, China faced difficulties in industry catch-up in the early days of the reform, but several new innovative actors started to evolve and made an effort to develop industry innovation systems. The "909 Project," formed during the ninth five-year plan period, was the beginning of such development. The project planned to build an 8-inch production line that mainly produced DRAMs. Learning from the failure of 908 that resulted from the absence of political authority, the Chinese government's political figures actively led the construction of IC manufacturing firms this time. The 909 Project was initiated in 1996 and included the negotiation and cooperation with NEC as a partner for technological learning. It started producing wafers in 1999. While negotiating the joint venture agreement, the government clearly stipulated conditions for technology transfers, which resulted in detailed technology transfers on production line operations from NEC. Thanks to these efforts, the product yield rates soared within a short period. Huahong-NEC, built during the project, ranked second in terms of sales among China's IC manufacturers for some years in the 2000s (Hu 2006).

In 2000, SMIC was established by a CEO who moved to China from Taiwan. With the support of the Chinese government, it grew rapidly and was listed on the Hong Kong Stock Exchange and on Nasdaq later on. By successfully accumulating funds, SMIC obtained a 12-inch fab for the first time in China. In 2005, it completed building a factory for 12-inch wafers in Beijing, and in 2007, it started operating a 12-inch production line in Shanghai. Additionally, SMIC is a

Table 4.5 SMIC's fab capacity, 2013

City	Wafer size	City	Design rule	Capacity
Beijing	12	Wuxi	90 nm–65 nm	36,000
Shanghai	12	Beijing	45 nm–28 nm	14,000
Shanghai	8	Beijing	$0.11\,\mu$m–$0.35\,\mu$m	96,000
Tianjin	8	Shanghai	$0.18\,\mu$m–$0.35\,\mu$m	39,000

Source: http://smics.com/download/factsheet_1Q13.pdf.

Note: Capacity =Wafer starts per month.

consigned manager of a 12-inch line, built in Wuhan after investment decision rights in high technology were transferred to local governments. Among the firms in China, it has the most up-to-date wafer process technologies, including 90-nm technology from Quimonda and 45-nm from IBM (Wang 2009).

The establishment and fast growth of SMIC in the 2000s have important implications for the development of China's innovation systems in several aspects. First, China acquired the 12-inch wafer production capacity. As seen in Table 4.5, SMIC owned three 12-inch production lines in 2013. Excluding foreign firms, it had the best facilities in China. In other words, it led the technology catch-up of China's entire IC industry. Second, SMIC demonstrated the development path that well suited the government's industry catch-up strategies—promoting indigenous firms. Naughton and Qi (2000) classified the Chinese government's means to acquire technology and develop innovation systems: establishing joint venture firms, attracting foreign capital, and promoting domestic firms. All these are found in the semiconductor industry. However, in the IC manufacturing industry, foreign Western companies had not been making direct investments because they strategically chose not to transfer important value chains to China. Since the owner and the initial capital were both from abroad (Taiwan), SMIC was initially regarded as a foreign holding company. The key human resources, too, were the engineers from Taiwan. However, as its headquarters were in China, and the company was listed on the Hong Kong Stock Exchange, it was often regarded as a domestic company. In addition, when SMIC faced difficulties, China's Datang purchased 16.55 percent of the company's stocks to become its biggest shareholder. After the Taiwanese CEO resigned, the situation resulted in the firm's clear position as a domestic company (Wang 2009). In this limited sense, it can be said that the establishment and the development of SMIC were a successful case of the government's efforts to foster entry of domestic firms for later catch-up.

Since the 2000s, leading firms such as SK Hynix, Intel, and Samsung have decided to invest in China's production lines, which can be considered as another innovation actor that affects China's sectoral innovation systems. As its market gains importance and the infrastructure for companies improves, China is considered a viable production location. Foreign companies have immensely contributed in the semiconductor industry's fixed asset investment since the 2000s. The Chinese government also wants to attract FDI in the IC manufacturing industry; it has the goal of completing the value chains within China even if foreign companies become main players. In fact, it places emphasis on the development of the IC design industry. In terms of wafer production, it prefers competitive domestic firms to be established, which, however, has a low probability in reality. Therefore, China demands an active role of foreign companies. This trend, along with the local governments' efforts to promote the high-technology industry, welcomed foreign companies' investment in China.

As companies invest actively and evolve as an important innovation actor, universities, related research institutes, and industry associations play a greater role. Additionally, companies in the value chains of semiconductor designing and assembling, testing, and system operators are rising as a key innovation actor by strengthening their relationship with IC manufacturers.

4.5.2 Reasons for Limited Success 1: Technological Regimes

Indigenous firms in China had shown limited performance in catch-up in the 2000s. As seen in Table 4.6, SMIC, a representative firm, experienced a decline in sales in 2008 and, thus, realized constant deficits. In its financially difficult situation due to the investment in 12-inch production lines, it is experiencing further troubles because of low yield rates in high-technology products. It does not have room for cost cuts as it cannot invent and control the production processes by itself but depends on technology transfers of micro-processing technology. Huahong is also experiencing difficulties in its initial public offering stage as it could not satisfy the conditions to be listed on the Shanghai Exchange Market, where companies have to show positive profits for three years in a row. Moreover, it has constantly tried to introduce 12-inch production lines but has experienced delays in investments because of its limitation as a state-owned enterprise. Huahong contends that it has the capacity for its own process development, which, however, shows a wide gap with the international level.

Furthermore, as fierce competitions in the industry lead to an increase in patent lawsuits and low accessibility to recent high technologies, Chinese domestic firms are experiencing difficulties in catch-up. For instance, SMIC had fallen into hard times after losing the patent lawsuit that began in 2003 with Taiwan Semiconductor Manufacturing Company (TSMC). In California, after TSMC filed a suit against SMIC for manufacturing products by using the company's confidential information, it was awarded a compensation of USD 175 million in 2005, which seemed to be the end of the dispute. However, it filed another suit in August 2006 with an accusation that SMIC violated conditions in their agreement

Table 4.6 Wafer capacity of China's top five IC manufacturers, 2005–2008

	2005 sales	2006 sales	2007 sales	2008 sales	Ownership	Wafer capacity ratio (China)
1 SK Hynix (IDM)	n/a	n/a	93.59	122.07	Foreign	13%
2 SMIC (foundry)	94.88	113.50	111.43	93.03		13%
3 Huahong Grace (foundry)	24.12(8.53)	28.48(13.52)	35.09(15.34)	46.79(14.56)		6%
4 TSMC (foundry)	n/a	12.86	13.40	11.00	Foreign	5%
5 Intel (IDM)	n/a	n/a	n/a	n/a	Foreign	5%

Source: CCID (2006–2009), PWC (2014).

Notes: Capacity measured in terms of 8-inch equivalent WSpM (wafer starts per month).

Ranks are in terms of sales revenue (RMB 100 million).

and tried to block manufacturing products of 0.13 µm or less. SMIC lost this suit as well and was placed in the situation of making reparations of USD 1 billion and of losing the US market. In the suit filed by SMIC at a high court in Beijing, the court took sides with TSMC, and SMIC's accusation was dismissed in the first trial in June 2009. Because of this crisis, SMIC's founder, who had a grudge against TSMC, had to step down, and the new CEO agreed to implement the following conditions in order to reach an agreement. First, SMIC would pay USD 0.2 billion compensation until 2013. Second, it would give up 1.79 billion shares of SMIC along with 695 shares of call options with HKD 1.3 strike price (Wang 2009). Thus, Chinese follower companies should avoid this kind of situation by composing IPR portfolios with their own technologies made by their R&D resources and by organizing partnership networks through license and using them strategically in the case of lawsuits with leader firms.

In a situation where access to external knowledge is restricted, universities and research organizations have to play an important role. However, they are not competent enough to function as an innovation actor. In the US, Japan, Korea, and Taiwan, universities and research institutions were pioneers in the development of the semiconductor industry. But, in China, because of their peculiar history, universities and research centers do not command reliable R&D capacity than firms yet. The instance that reflects this reality is the "Hanxin Event." It refers to the incident wherein Chen Jin, after just changing the package, presented Motorola's Moto-Freescale 56,800 chip as his own DSP chip developed in China. He eventually was discovered as a fraud in 2006. Chen Jin, in the meantime, gained a chair position in the School of Micro Electronics of Shanghai Jiaotong University and enjoyed millions of yuan of R&D funding by the government. This incident reveals that Chinese universities and research institutes lack professional human resources that can lead the semiconductor industry and that human resources and systems that can professionally execute the R&D budget are absent within the government.

In sum, China's semiconductor industry showed limited catch-up because of the industry-specific technology and knowledge regimes. This is quite a contrast to the fast catch-up in its automobile and electronics industries. In the automobile industry, domestic firms in China are rapidly catching up, as the probability of modularity increased due to parts suppliers' growth and as the next-generation electronic cars emerged—a paradigm shift (Lee, Cho and Jin 2009). In the case of the semiconductor industry, the situation is the opposite.

4.5.3 Reasons for Limited Success 2: Institutional Barriers

Other than the technology and knowledge regimes mentioned above, institutional barriers also serve as a cause for the limited catch-up in the semiconductor industry. Specifically, the Chinese government tried to initiate industry innovations through aggressive policy supports but ended up with mixed results or failures. The most important instance is the failure of the "18th Provision" after China's entry into the World Trade Organization (WTO). The 18th Provision is the most important government policy with respect to the development of the IC industry during the tenth five-year plan period. This policy was strengthened by the 51st Provision (Chen 2005).

The problem began when China joined the WTO in 2001. As the US raised issues about China's tax break policy from the perspective of fair trade rules, this policy could not be executed. In April 2005, some parts of the tax break policy were annulled although some element of the policy was reborn in the form of the New 18th Provision. Moreover, the development of Chinese domestic IC manufacturers was hindered to a certain degree due to zero tariff regulations with respect to semiconductor imports that started in 2002.

Meanwhile, the Taiwanese government continued to regulate investments in China. The representative case is Hejian, a company founded by a retiree of Taiwan's United Microelectronics Company (UMC) in 2002. This firm had high technology capacity owing to the efforts of the engineers transferred from UMC and was able to make profits starting from the second year. Later on, UMC implemented initial technology support in the form of strategic alliance and filed for a merger and acquisition (M&A) with the Taiwanese government. However, at the time, the Democratic Progressive Party (i.e., Min Jin Tang) was the major party and brought an indictment against UMC for an act of treachery, which, of course, led to the stop of the M&A deal. Because of this, Hejian's development was stalled. In the 2000s, international policy mechanisms that restrict technology transfers to China became much lenient but their influence cannot not yet be dismissed (Lin 2009).

In addition to foreign restrictions, policy limits exist within China as well. An example is that China maintained export-oriented tax rebate policy and maintained a strict foreign exchange control. China's tax breaks on exports countered the government's tax incentives policy toward semiconductor companies. Rebating 17 percent of value added tax on exports countereffected the tax break policy for semiconductor companies. However, since the conditions to benefit from tax rebates were not easy for most of the semiconductor manufacturers, they first exported manufactured chips and then imported them back as raw materials for assembling and testing. Additionally, since semiconductor firms had big blind spots of not benefiting from tariff exemption, there were cases in which Chinese products lost price competitiveness compared to imported ICs with zero tariffs. Moreover, even though companies frequently faced situations in which they have to use foreign exchange for facility and raw material imports, many of the policy restrictions were not resolved due to the institutional systems that fundamentally repressed foreign exchange outflows.

Such restrictions of China can be compared with situations in Korea and Taiwan, which are politically and geographically close to Japan. With this background, these countries could rapidly access various new semiconductor facilities made by the US and Japan, the leaders of the world's semiconductor industry, and up-to-date manufacturing technologies that enhance the performance of semiconductor production. Through the efforts of their students who returned after studying in the US and Japan, Korea and Taiwan were able to build fairly early the human capital systems necessary for the development of the semiconductor industry.

4.6 Changing Situations since the mid-2000s

4.6.1 Prospect of Catching up 1: Improvement in the Innovation Systems

Though the development of innovation systems in China's semiconductor industry was in the stage of limited success until the early 2000s, the potential for the development of industry innovation systems remained high. First, some actors in the innovation systems started evolving; for example, research institutions specializing in semiconductors were being formed, and universities and industry associations were exceling in development. A case illustrating such systematic evolution was the establishment of the Shanghai Integrated Circuit Research and Development Center (SICRD). Three exchange researchers, sent to Europe's Interuniversity Microelectronics Centre (IMEC) from the Chinese Academy of Sciences in 1999, led a project while working with Huahong NEC in 2002 upon their return, which became the organization's matrix. With these members in the center, SICRD was formed on December 29, 2002, jointly financed by Shanghai's Huahong Group, Fudan University, Shanghai Jiaotong University, Huadong Normal University, and Shanghai Beiling. Their research centers were to work with the first production factory of Huahong NEC, which would facilitate the application of their technologies to the mass production in the factory. As of 2007, 50 researchers, composed of a third with bachelor's degree, another third with master's, and the final third with PhDs, strove for R&D of initial process technologies, and they planned to increase their researcher capacity to 150 by the end of 2009. Many of these researchers were dispatched to IMEC where they continued the R&D activities. Later on, the organization expanded as Shanghai's local government increased its shareholdings.

Through these efforts, Huahong's patents increased in number, and it strategically formed technology partnerships with companies such as Jazz Technologies, Silicon Storage Technology, Inc., and Cypress Semiconductor through joint licenses (Rho 2008). Likewise, as a firm's R&D capacity improves, its own process development capacity increases, forming a basis for technology catch-up. R&D organizations strengthen their capacity for absorbing and digesting introduced technologies and remarkably improve the accessibility to systems' external technologies. This R&D organization of Huahong independently develops processors, although not in the high-technology area. Innovation systems evolve as these kinds of independent experiences accumulate. Given the increasing trend of patenting by China's IC manufacturing firms, it can be said that China's capacity of innovation actors such as firms' internal R&D organizations, universities, and research institutions is constantly augmenting. This may serve as the basis of an "early indigenous innovation system" that enables China to get out of the level of simple facility and technology imports, to develop its own processes, and to bring them to the mass production stage.

4.6.2 Prospects of Catching up 2: Institutional Dimension

As China's market expands and gains importance in the world market (for instance, as much as more than 55 percent share in the global demand in the mid-2010s), the institutional factors that used to restrict transfers of IC production value chains to China were becoming less prominent in the 2000s. As China's demand increase was strong in the electronics industry, the forward-linkage semiconductor industry gained more importance; moreover, as its semiconductor sector managed to maintain the demand level even after the world's financial crisis, foreign firms could not ignore China's market, and restrictions of facility and export ban agreements lost their meaning. Following this trend, political restrictions that hindered the development of China's semiconductor industry gradually loosened their importance at least before Trump came to power in 2017. Moreover, many Chinese students studied abroad in the countries that are leaders in semiconductor technology, such as the US, Japan, and Korea, and acquired technology capacity by working with multinational companies. If China's human resource pool forms and industry innovation systems became organized, its industry catch-up would become a possibility.

In addition, Taiwan became more lax with regard to institutional restrictions as it could not give up China's market. In fact, along with the change in the political leadership in Taiwan, the relationship between the two economies was improving, resulting in a more favorable investment environment, such as less regulations in investing in China for semiconductor manufacturers. If more exchanges between the two economies, including technology partnerships, had happened, it would have positively influenced the evolution of China's semiconductor industry innovation systems. However, the situation changed again with another change in the political leadership in Taiwan in the late 2010s. Most importantly, a significant and negative change happened for China since the Trump administration in the US. Further updated analysis of semiconductor sector will be presented in Chapter 6 in comparison with Korea and in Chapter 10 involving the recent actions by the US.

4.7 Summary and Concluding Remarks

This chapter analyzed China's semiconductor industry from the sectoral innovation systems perspective. The innovation systems of China's semiconductors have long been evolving, with the government playing a crucial role as a policy actor. However, in terms of catch-up in market shares and in technology, the industry still remains limited. The chapter explained the reasons for the limited catch-up in terms of the characteristics of the technology and knowledge regimes of the industry. In the semiconductor industry, innovations are frequent and technologies are highly cumulative, which put the latecomers in a disadvantageous position. Furthermore, the market for IC chips is not segmented but highly integrated, which implies no (low-end market) room for the latecomers. Therefore, it is very difficult for latecomer firms to seize the market opportunity through marketing. The situation is getting worse with the continued increase of the required investment and the shortening of product life cycles. Furthermore, the existing practice of Western countries restricting transfer of core technologies to Communist countries like China has been aggravating the Chinese difficulties, which is gaining more momentum since the US–China trade or hegemony conflict since 2018.

An interesting point in this regard is the double-edged nature of the technological regime featured by rapid technical changes or short technological cycles. As discussed in Chapter 1, whereas short cycles give a latecomer some chance for catch-up, that observation is true only when the latecomers have already accumulated certain absorption capabilities. Otherwise, frequent changes in technologies may serve as an additional barrier against catch-up. Such double nature of technological changes has also been analyzed in the comparative cases of telecom industries in Brazil, China, India, and Korea by Lee, Mani, and Mu (2012). It is also consistent with the so-called truncation of FDI-based learning process noted in Lall (1992 2000) that frequent technological change interferes with the learning and accumulation by the latecomers. Moreover, Lee's (2013: 86–9) extension of Park and Lee's (2006) idea to the case of eight second-tier catching-up countries, including India, China, Brazil, and Mexico, show that short cycles give them additional hardship.

Although China's semiconductor industry faced many obstacles in its search for catch-up, some promising signs were emerging since the late 2000s or before the 2018 US–China trade war. First, the continuing explosion of the Chinese market and its increasing importance after the global crisis was acting as a factor to push for the loosening of restrictions of technology transfer to China. Second,

China would expect an increasing flow of human capital equipped with up-to-date technology in this field as a result of the increasing numbers of Chinese working in foreign firms and getting education and training in foreign countries. When these factors are combined with the consolidation of the domestic innovation system, such as R&D capabilities of domestic firms, research organization, and universities, China's position was expected to improve, and technology catch-up might be a possibility. In other words, as the general absorptive capacity of actors in China increases, changes and the rise of new generations of technologies could serve as a window of opportunity for leapfrogging (Perez and Soete 1988; Lee and Lim 2001), rather than as a barrier as in the past. However, some of the factors have changed again and become more complicated after the US–China trade and hegemony conflicts since 2018. We will get back to this issue in the last chapter of this book, as well as in Chapter 6.

PART II

ASSESSING THE CATCH-UP IN A COMPARATIVE PERSPECTIVE

5

Assessing China's Economic Catch-up in a Comparative Perspective

Beijing Consensus, Washington Consensus, East Asian Consensus[1]

5.1 Introduction

The "Beijing Consensus" (*Beijing Gongshi*) is a very popular phrase in China, as popular as the word "catch-up" (*zhuigan*). Both terms reflect the Chinese desire for their country to progress economically. Economic catch-up by a latecomer country is about narrowing the gap in production and income vis-à-vis a leader country. In this sense, China is definitely and significantly catching up in terms of not only per capita income but also the size of the economy. In 1978, China's per capita income was less than 10 percent of the world average, while by the early 2010s, it had reached over half of the world average. Hu (2009) computed China's share in the world's total GDP using the 2000 constant dollar price. China's share was only 1.04 percent in 1980, ranking tenth in the world, but it rose to 1.86 percent in 1990 and then to 3.78 percent in 2000, ranking sixth in the world. It was 5.02 percent in 2005, ranking fourth. Since 2010, it has been ranked second.

Many latecomer economies have achieved a certain level of catch-up, but the question of why others have not has become a significant concern. Despite the sizable amounts of development aid, the gap between rich and poor countries persists. Rodrik (1996) extended this comparison in terms of the Washington Consensus and explained the reasons for the difference in performance between East Asia and Latin America. China is an example of an East Asian country that is successfully catching up yet deviates from the full package of the Washington Consensus. This chapter examines China with a focus on the country's economic catch-up strategy from a comparative perspective.

This chapter employs the Schumpeterian economics of catch-up as its theoretical framework, which considers innovation as the fundamental force of economic change. A typical sequence of catch-up by latecomers starts with learning from

---

[1] This chapter is a rewriting of an article, Keun Lee, Mansoo Jee, and Jong-hak Eun (2011), "Assessing China's Economic Catch-up at the Firm-Level and Beyond," *Industry and Innovation*, 18(5), 487–507.

forerunning countries before moving into the innovation phase (Nelson 2008a, 2008b). Thus, our primary objective in this chapter is to provide a comparative analysis of China and other catch-up countries in terms of the modes of learning and access. Specifically, we aim to assess the process through which China acquires indigenous innovation capabilities, as declared by the Chinese government as its goal. Our unit of analysis starts at the firm level and reaches further toward the national and policy dimensions.

The following section (5.2) will first put China in comparison with the Washington Consensus. Then, section 5.3 presents an analysis of China in comparison with Asian neighbors. Several unique elements of learning and access strategies of the Chinese catch-up model (i.e., the "Beijing Consensus") not found in the models of Taiwan or Korea are identified. These unique features include: parallel (indirect) learning from foreign direct investment (FDI) firms; forward engineering (the role of university spin-off firms) in contrast to reverse engineering adopted in Korea and Taiwan; and acquisition of technology and brands through international mergers and acquisitions (M&As). Section 5.4 presents the limitations of the current strategies and other challenges facing China and provides an assessment of the prospect of China's upgrading to higher end and branded producers.

5.2 China and the Washington Consensus

When China opened its door and reformed its policies in the latter part of 1978, its per capita income was less than 10 percent of the world average in terms of the purchasing power parity adjusted dollars in 2000 prices. In the 2010s, China's per capita income has reached about half of the world average (Lee 2011). This is a truly remarkable achievement. Naughton (2007: 5–6) argued that China's economic institutions are closely resembling those of other developing countries, and the challenges that China faces are shifting and increasingly resembling those faced by other middle-income developing economies (Naughton 2007: 5). Thus, it makes more sense to compare China with other developing countries than with other transition economies.

The works of Qian and Weingast (1996) and Lee, Hahn, and Lin (2002) are among the several studies that have compared China with its neighbors or with Western economies. As a study on macro policy-oriented characterization of China, Lee's (2006) work is useful in comparing the Washington Consensus with East Asian sequencing, emphasizing the three missing elements from the Washington Consensus. The idea of sequencing originated from Rodrik (1996), who first explored the puzzle of the slow growth of Latin America, the economies of which have more closely followed the Consensus compared with East Asian economies. According to Rodrik's (1996) main observation, although Latin

America endorsed and tried simultaneously all 10 elements of the Consensus, Korea and Taiwan adopted only the first half (i.e., macroeconomic stabilization, 1–5) but maintained microeconomic intervention by not committing to the second half (privatization, liberalization, deregulation, etc.) until the latter stages. A summary of this study is provided in Table 5.1.

Reviewing the experiences of several countries in Asia, Lee (2006) argued that the mixed results of the Consensus have something to do not only with policy sequencing but also with missing or neglected policies, such as technology

Table 5.1 Washington Consensus versus East Asian Consensus

A. Elements of the Washington Consensus	South Korea	Taiwan	China
A1. Macroeconomic stabilization			
1. Fiscal discipline	Yes, generally	Yes	Yes, generally
2. Redirection of public expenditure to health, education, and infrastructure	Yes	Yes	Yes, generally
3. Tax reform, broadening the tax base, and cutting marginal tax rates	Yes, generally	Yes	Yes, since 1994
4. Unified and competitive exchange rates	Yes, except for limited periods	Yes	Yes, since 1994
5. Secure property rights	Yes, except early periods	Yes, generally	Mixed
A2. Privatization, deregulation, and liberalization			
6. Deregulation	Limited	Limited	Limited
7. Trade liberalization	Limited until the 1980s	Limited until the 1980s	Limited until 2002
8. Privatization	No; many SOEs in the 1950s and 1960s	No; many SOEs in the 1950s and 1960s	Partly no; SOEs still important
9. Elimination of barriers to direct foreign investment (DFI)	DFI heavily restricted	DFI subject to state control	DFI regulated in some sectors
10. Financial liberalization	Limited until the 1980s	Limited until the 1980s	Limited until the 1980s
B. Elements missing from the Washington Consensus			
11. Export promotion + Import tariffs	Yes, very strong	Yes	Yes, very strong
12. Technology policy for upgrading (in-house R&D; public–private R&D)	Yes, since 1970	Yes, since the 1980s	Given priority since the mid-1990s
13. Higher education revolution (doubling of the number of college students)	Yes, since the 1980s	Yes, generally	Yes, since the mid-1990s

Source: Lee (2006); Part A for Korea and Taiwan is from Rodrik (1996, Table 3); China and Part B are by the author.

policies and higher education revolution. As shown in Part B of Table 5.1, we believe that these policy elements are absent from the Washington Consensus and can be considered as the core distinctive elements of the East Asian Consensus.

The shift of emphasis from the sequencing of traditional macro policies to the missing elements of technology and higher education is important in understanding the long-term growth prospects of a nation. As Ocampo (2005) emphasized, macroeconomic stability is not a sufficient condition for growth; it is more closely tied to the dynamics of the production structure. A concrete example is Korea. Like other developing countries, Korea used to be always confronted with external imbalances and persistent trade deficits during the first two decades of its industrialization in the 1960s and 1970s. However, in the 1980s, the country realized that it could not compete with other emerging economies offering cheaper wages, and thus switched to higher-value-added goods. Korea promoted private R&D through tax incentives and even initiated public–private joint R&D for larger—albeit riskier—projects. This intensification of R&D expenditure and higher education in Korea laid the basis for its knowledge-driven growth.

In these aspects, China seems to have been closely following the East Asian Consensus. First, China has followed the example of Korea and Taiwan in emphasizing export orientation, with some protection for local producers (Lee, Lin, and Chang 2005). Second, the similarity is clear not only in terms of the micro interventions listed in Part A but also in the emphasis on the elements missing from the Washington Consensus, such as a technology policy and a higher education revolution. China has been strongly pushing for more R&D expenditure, finally reaching the 1 percent ratio in 2000. By the late 2010s, R&D expenditure has reached more than 2.0 percent, much earlier than other middle-income countries. In terms of the tertiary education enrollment ratio, China began in 1990 at a much lower level of 3.4 percent compared with the 20 percent average of nine middle-income countries. However, by 2003, the figure reached 17 percent, a value closer to or higher than that of Brazil, Costa Rica, and Mexico (Table 6 in Lee 2006b). This rapid progress is related to the higher education revolution and the 20 percent increase in the number of college students every year since 1998.

With its R&D-to-GDP ratio reaching above 2 percent, China is fast advancing in innovation and knowledge, which have become the key engines of its growth, replacing the FDI of earlier periods. This is verified by an econometric study using provincial data by Jin, Lee, and Kim (2008). Although innovation has been the main source of economic progress in the West, learning is also considered important for catch-up in the rest of the non-West latecomers (Amsden 1989). In this light, the institution for local learning and access to foreign knowledge base have been recognized as the critical factors for catch-up. In addition, access and learning modes are becoming more important due to the tendency of developed economies to enforce their intellectual property rights on developing countries.

Therefore, our approach is different from the view of national competitive advantages by Porter (1990), which places less emphasis on learning and access to foreign knowledge and on the latecomer economies. In contrast, our approach shares a common insight with the concept of "leverage" used in Zeng and Williamson (2007) and Mathews and Cho (2000) and acknowledged in World Bank studies, particularly that of Chandra (2006). This is our point of departure for the analysis of China: we focus on the unique and innovative aspects of China's modes of learning and access to foreign knowledge base.

5.3 Beijing Consensus versus East Asian Model

5.3.1 Comparison with Korea and Taiwan

Korea and Taiwan are the two most successful catch-up economies in the world. These two countries share commonalities, but a number of important distinctions still exist. The difference in the role of big versus small firms in each economy is often cited. Korea is dominated by several giant firms and Taiwan by a large number of smaller firms (Saxenian and Hsu 2001). The difference in firm-size structure of the two economies is replicated in their catch-up strategies and learning modes (Park and Lee 2006). Seemingly, there are two catch-up pathways: the one taken by Taiwan and that taken by Korea. Variations are possible—such as the pathway taken by Southeast Asia, the Singapore pathway characterized by more roles played by FDI (Hobday 2000), and combinations of these variations.

The Korean pathway is led by several large firms that are nationally owned and independent from multinational companies (MNCs). During the 1970s, which is the early stage of the Korean pathway, private firms relied on licensing and received assistance from government research institutes, obtained R&D results freely or at a low cost, and learned by working in FDI or original equipment manufacturer (OEM) firms (Lee 2005). Eventually, they consolidated their in-house R&D capacities and emerged as technology leaders.

The Taiwanese pathway was initially led by a large number of SMEs that were more or less integrated with MNCs. During the early stage of this pathway, private firms started out as OEM contractors for MNCs and eventually integrated with the global value chains (GVCs). This helped them access new knowledge and upgrade to a higher tier in the GVCs (Ernst and Kim 2002). Several became successful and ultimately became large-scale, own-brand manufacturing (OBM) firms via own design manufacturing (ODM). However, these big firms, such as Acer, still maintain a great deal of subcontracting with MNCs. Sectors that require greater capital and risk receive assistance from government research institutes or create new spin-off firms from them to obtain sources of new knowledge.

Given the previous discussion, it would be interesting to see which pattern will prevail in other rapidly catching up countries such as China. Generally, China seems to be following a third model that includes the elements of the Korean and Taiwanese models and even the Southeast Asian model, which has demonstrated more reliance on FDI. It boasts of a relatively large number of big firms, such as Lenovo (which acquired the personal computer (PC) business of IBM), Haier (the largest refrigerator maker in the world), Changhong, TCL, Konka, and Huawei. These are brand leaders in the Chinese markets that have successfully competed against MNCs, although they are not yet powerful enough to command a strong design capability. These firms mostly undertake the final assembly and may go along the path of Korean *chaebols*. In reality, many of these big firms are similarly leapfrogging straight into OBM without engaging in ODM. In contrast, SMEs in China have been developing a close integration with smaller or larger MNCs from neighboring economies in Asia and the West. Thus, Chinese SMEs seem to be following the Taiwanese or Southeast Asian path of gradual catch-up with the intermediate stages of OEM, ODM, and OBM.

The size and complexity of China necessitates that its economy adhere to two or more model types as a combination of large companies, smaller companies, and FDI firms. However, being aware of the other aspects of China's development that can be considered as more than just a combination of existing models or companies is also important. In what follows, we explore further the different access strategies China is experimenting on in its quest for economic catch-up.

5.3.2 Parallel Learning by Trading Market for Technology

Realizing the attractiveness of its market size and the bargaining power associated with this, the Chinese government actively approached multinational suppliers to engage in technology transfer and joint venture (JV) negotiations, adopting a purposeful strategy of "trading the market for technology." According to Yu Weixiang, a director in the Ministry of Foreign Economics and Trade, more than 80 percent of FDI in China since 1978 has been based on the principle of "trading the market for technology," especially in the automobile, chemical, and electronics industries (Chen and Yue 2002). This strategy made its first appearance in the automobile industry during the early 1980s.[2]

Although it has not been entirely successful, there are cases in which this strategy worked and contributed to technological catch-up. Chapter 2 of this book and Mu and Lee (2005) explain that the telecommunications equipment industry

---

[2] Cheng, Yuan, "Over Protection and Inefficient Development Whose Mistakes Brought out Backward Development in Automobile Industry?" [Baohu Guodu yu Fazhan Buzu—Qiche Luohou Shuizhiguo?], http://b-car.com/cywj/11.htm.

is an excellent example, such as the case of Shanghai Bell, a JV established in 1984 with the Bell Telephone Manufacturing Company. They observed that China took advantage of its large market size to pressure the foreign partner to transfer core technology to the local partner. Shanghai Bell and other JV establishments fostered the diffusion of technological know-how on digital telephone switches across the country. Thus, indigenous manufacturers emerged and began to compete directly with JVs in the mid-1990s, initially in rural markets and subsequently in urban markets. Starting from a 10.6 percent market share in 1992, the four indigenous manufacturers—led by Great Dragon and followed by Datang, Zhongxing, and Huawei—held 43 percent of the digital switch market by 2000 (Mu and Lee 2005, Figure 1).

In this catch-up process, FDI firms contribute by diffusing knowledge and personnel to Chinese firms while the Chinese learn from them. This process is called "parallel learning" (Eun et al. 2006). A similar diffusion of knowledge also occurred in Southeast Asian countries, but China was more successful in turning diffusion into the promotion of indigenous companies.

The preceding overview indicates that in terms of catch-up in telephone switch technology, China skipped a stage or leapfrogged. It had limited experience in developing and producing electro-mechanical switches, but it skipped the development and production of analog electronic switches to jump directly to digital automatic switch production (Shen 1999). Similar phenomena are taking place in other sectors. Chinese authorities regard a JV as a channel through which learning about technology can take place. Thus, even after its entry into the World Trade Organization, the Chinese government has made no commitment to lift the cap on foreign shares in JVs in key industries, including automobile, telecommunications, and banking sectors. This continuing restriction on foreign shares is in sharp contrast to the market opening exemplified by the lowering of tariffs, now at about 10 percent (or less) on average, which is lower than the average in most developing countries.

5.3.3 Strategy of Forward Engineering

China has successfully reared some national champion firms in high-technology sectors by exploiting its own scientific knowledge base. This is exemplified by Lenovo, Founder, Tsinghua Tongfang, and Dongruan. Lenovo, Founder, and Tsinghua Tongfang have occupied the top three spots as the leading PC makers in China, at least since the early 2000s. Dongruan is the first Chinese software company to be listed on the stock exchange. These firms have all been established by and affiliated with academic institutions. Eun et al. (2006) designated them as academy-run enterprises (AREs). AREs are widespread in China. More than 4,800 firms are affiliated with Chinese universities (MOE 2004). Furthermore,

Table 5.2 Relative importance of UREs in China

	URE		URE/Total industry (%)		URE/FIEs (%)		URE/Domestic private (%)	
	Revenue (RMB 100 million)	Employees	Revenue	Employees	Revenues	Employee	Revenues	Employees
Beijing	517.46	61,772	7.2	5.3	16.8	19.9	156.3	42.0
Shanghai	87.95	23,926	0.5	0.9	0.9	1.7	6.2	4.6
Zhejiang	62.19	11,033	0.3	0.2	1.1	0.7	0.8	0.4
Jiangsu	56.96	27,095	0.2	0.4	0.4	1.1	0.7	1.1
Liaoning	48.8	20,664	0.5	0.8	2.1	3.9	2.9	3.5
Hubei	46.71	14,882	0.8	0.8	3.4	6.4	5.2	3.5
Shandong	45.01	11,191	0.2	0.2	0.8	0.8	0.7	0.6
Shaanxi	28.1	16,434	0.9	1.4	12.4	33.5	13.3	16.8
Guangdong	27.08	9,864	0.1	0.1	0.1	0.1	0.6	0.5
Heilongjiang	25.39	8,094	0.5	0.6	7.0	7.7	7.7	6.0
:	:	:	:	:	:	:	:	:
National Total	1071.229	289,429	0.4	0.4	1.3	1.5	2.2	1.7

Source: Ministry of Education (2006: 34–35, 37–38); National Bureau of Statistics (2006a:142); National Bureau of Statistics webpage. (http://www.stats.gov.cn/tjsj/ndsj/2006/indexch.htm)

about 40 AREs are listed on the stock exchanges in mainland China and Hong Kong. Table 5.2 shows a more systemic assessment of the importance of AREs in the Chinese economy. Although their share in the national economy is still minimal, their importance in key high-tech regions, such as Beijing and Shanghai, is substantial. In Beijing, the size of AREs in terms of sales revenues is already larger than that of the private enterprise sector and is about 17 percent of the foreign-invested enterprise sector.

The direct involvement of academic institutions in industrial business is called "forward engineering" (Lu 2000; Eun et al. 2006). In the "reverse engineering" strategy, latecomer firms acquire technological principles by conducting autopsies on final (typically imported) products. Reverse engineering is a *bottom-up* mode, whereas forward engineering is a *top-down* mode of technological development, in which the creators (academic institutions) who already possess scientific knowledge further process nascent knowledge until it can be applied to commercial use. Lu (2000) and Eun et al. (2006) pointed out that forward engineering is an inherently Chinese characteristic that differentiates China from other East Asian countries. Taiwan and Korea have rarely exploited their academic institutions for technological development until recently; the main role of the academia had been to supply engineers to local firms. In contrast, Chinese universities and research institutes, such as those under the banner of the Chinese Academy of Sciences, have played an active role in commercializing new technologies using the results of their research projects.

The Chinese central government initiated several ambitious projects to strengthen the country's knowledge base. The "211 Project," proposed in the mid-1990s, focuses on strengthening the research and teaching capabilities of 100 key universities nationwide. "Invigorating the Country through Science and Education Strategy" (*KejiaoXingguo*) is an initiative introduced by ex-president Jiang Zemin and continued by his successor President Hu Jintao. The project aimed to increase the spending on education from 2.79 percent to 4.0 percent of the GDP during the period 2006–2010. Actually, this ratio has reached 4% since 2012 and remain at the level.[3]

Partially due to the efforts of the government, China's scientific capability has enhanced significantly since the early twenty-first century. This can be verified by looking into the major countries (identified by the address of author's affiliation) that participated in the production of research papers published in top journals (i.e., top 10 journals in terms of "impact factor" in each field) in three fields, namely, information technology (IT), biomedical technology, and nano technology. By the end of the 2000s, China had steadily caught up with advanced countries to be among the top five in all three high-tech fields. By the late 2010s, it had

[3] The source: http://www.gov.cn/shuju/2020-10/20/content_5552753.htm

Table 5.3 Top 25 countries in academic publication in three technological fields

Information technology	2008		2013		2018	
Total no.	37,791	100%	47,779	100%	69,547	100%
Rank	Country	Share (%)	Country	Share (%)	Country	Share (%)
1	US	23.9	china	22.4	china	38.5
2	China	12.0	US	20.8	US	16.1
3	Japan	8.0	S. Korea	6.7	India	7.8
4	S. Korea	7.1	Japan	6.2	S. Korea	5.9
5	Taiwan	6.8	Taiwan	5.1	England	4.7
6	Canada	5.3	France	4.8	Japan	4.2
7	France	5.1	Canada	4.7	Canada	4.1
8	Italy	4.5	India	4.2	Iran	4.0
9	England	4.5	Italy	4.1	France	3.6
10	Germany	4.2	England	4.1	Italy	3.3
11	Spain	3.2	Spain	4.0	Germany	3.1
12	India	2.7	Germany	3.8	Australia	3.0
13	Singapore	2.5	Iran	3.0	Spain	2.7
14	Poland	2.5	Australia	2.5	Taiwan	2.7
15	Australia	1.9	Singapore	2.3	Singapore	1.8
16	Belgium	1.5	Brazil	1.5	Brazil	1.8
17	Netherlands	1.5	Turkey	1.5	Turkey	1.7
18	Switzerland	1.5	Sweden	1.4	Russia	1.5
19	Russia	1.4	Russia	1.4	Saudi Arabia	1.4
20	Turkey	1.4	Belgium	1.3	Pakistan	1.2
21	Greece	1.3	Switzerland	1.3	Sweden	1.1
22	Sweden	1.2	Netherlands	1.3	Switzerland	1.1

Information technology	2008		2013		2018	
Total no.	37,791	100%	47,779	100%	69,547	100%
Rank	Country	Share (%)	Country	Share (%)	Country	Share (%)
23	Iran	1.2	Malaysia	1.1	Malaysia	1.1
24	Brazil	1.1	Greece	0.9	Egypt	1.0
25	Finland	0.9	Finland	0.9	Netherlands	1.0

Note: Total number refers to the number of articles published in the top 10 journals.

Biotechnology and applied microbiology	2008		2013		2018	
Total no.	20,553	100%	25,872	100%	24,965	100%
Rank	Country	Share (%)	Country	Share (%)	Country	Share (%)
1	US	24.2	US	21.4	China	31.2
2	China	11.2	China	21.0	US	19.2
3	Japan	9.4	Japan	7.4	India	5.9
4	Germany	6.2	India	6.3	Japan	5.8
5	India	5.8	Germany	6.1	Germany	5.4
6	England	5.0	S. Korea	5.5	S. Korea	5.4
7	S. Korea	5.0	England	4.0	England	4.1
8	France	4.5	Spain	3.8	Brazil	3.6
9	Spain	3.9	Italy	3.8	Italy	3.6

(Continued)

Table 5.3 (*Continued*)

Biotechnology and applied microbiology	2008		2013		2018	
Total no.	20,553	100%	25,872	100%	24,965	100%
Rank	Country	Share (%)	Country	Share (%)	Country	Share (%)
10	Canada	3.7	France	3.6	France	3.2
11	Italy	3.5	Canada	3.4	Spain	3.2
12	Brazil	2.5	Brazil	2.8	Canada	3.0
13	Netherlands	2.3	Australia	2.5	Australia	2.7
14	Australia	2.2	Taiwan	2.0	Iran	2.5
15	Turkey	1.9	Netherlands	1.9	Netherlands	1.9
16	Taiwan	1.9	Iran	1.6	Poland	1.7
17	Sweden	1.6	Belgium	1.6	Turkey	1.5
18	Belgium	1.5	Turkey	1.5	Sweden	1.4
19	Switzerland	1.4	Sweden	1.3	Switzerland	1.4
20	Nigeria	1.3	Switzerland	1.3	Taiwan	1.3
21	Denmark	1.2	Poland	1.2	Denmark	1.3
22	Portugal	1.1	Malaysia	1.2	Mexico	1.3
23	Mexico	1.1	Mexico	1.2	Belgium	1.3
24	Thailand	1.0	Portugal	1.2	Russia	1.2
25	Scotland	1.0	Denmark	1.2	Malaysia	1.1

Source: Calculations using the data from the ISI Web of Science, provided by Dr. Jong-hak Eun.

Nanoscience and nanotechnology	2008		2013		2018	
Total no.	16,925	100%	27,441	100%		100%
Rank	Country	Share (%)	Country	Share (%)	Country	Share (%)
1	US	26.5	China	27.7	China	42.3
2	China	19.1	US	24.3	US	22.0
3	Japan	8.0	S. Korea	9.7	S. Korea	8.7
4	Germany	8.0	Germany	6.7	Germany	6.8
5	S. Korea	7.7	Japan	6.1	Japan	5.4
6	France	5.4	India	5.6	India	4.9
7	England	4.5	France	4.5	England	4.0
8	India	4.4	Taiwan	3.9	France	3.6
9	Taiwan	3.9	England	3.6	Australia	3.0
10	Canada	3.2	Italy	3.4	Spain	2.9
11	Italy	3.2	Spain	3.0	Italy	2.8
12	Spain	3.2	Singapore	2.5	Taiwan	2.6
13	Singapore	2.2	Canada	2.5	Singapore	2.4
14	Australia	2.2	Australia	2.5	Canada	2.4
15	Netherlands	1.7	Iran	2.0	Iran	1.9
16	Russia	1.7	Switzerland	1.6	Russia	1.8
17	Switzerland	1.7	Netherlands	1.4	Switzerland	1.8
18	Sweden	1.3	Sweden	1.3	Sweden	1.5
19	Belgium	1.3	Russia	1.2	Saudi Arabia	1.4
20	Brazil	1.2	Belgium	1.2	Netherlands	1.4
21	Mexico	1.2	Saudi Arabia	1.2	Poland	1.1
22	Iran	1.1	Brazil	1.0	Belgium	1.0
23	Poland	1.0	Malaysia	0.9	Brazil	1.0
24	Israel	1.0	Poland	0.9	Israel	1.0
25	Turkey	0.8	Israel	0.8	Denmark	0.8

taken the top position in all the three fields, as shown by Table 5.3, overtaking the US. Further, the gap between China and the US was quite large as of 2018, with the Chinese share often being two times bigger than that of the US—for instance, 38.5 percent versus 16.1 percent in IT, 42.3 percent versus 22.0 percent in nano technology, and 31.2 percent versus 19.2 percent in biotechnology.

5.3.4 Strategy of International M&As and Going Global

Until the 1990s, the Chinese outward direct foreign investments (hereafter called ODI) were highly regulated compared with the major source countries for FDI. In fact, ODI was generally discouraged by the central authorities. However, a significant shift in policy was made at the Chinese Communist Party's 16th Congress in 2002 when the Premier announced a new strategy for encouraging Chinese companies to "Go Global" (*zouchuqu*: Go Outside) by investing overseas. Several important measures were introduced by the government in 2004 and 2005.[4] The introduction of these new measures contributed to a rapid increase in Chinese ODI. The annual flow of Chinese ODI, excluding the financial sector, surged to USD 43.3 billion in 2009 (which was as large as half of the inward FDI) from a mere USD 2.7 billion in 2002. By the end of 2005, more than 6,000 Chinese enterprises had invested abroad. Additionally, the announced M&As of Chinese companies abroad also increased; the volume of transactions involving Chinese buyers and international targets jumped from USD 2 billion to USD 3 billion (offer value) in 2003 and 2004 to almost USD 23 billion in 2005.[5]

What are the motivations behind the dramatic change in government policy toward ODI? In the macroeconomic dimension, it can be explained as a consequence of high domestic saving rates, global financial imbalance, and efforts to cool investment demand at home (Hess 2006). China had accumulated USD 870 billion of foreign reserves by March 2006. China has thus the largest foreign reserves in the world, even surpassing Japan depending upon years. Thus, it was time for China to loosen its tight controls over foreign exchange and the outflow of capital. However, Woo and Zhang (2006) observed that the policy change may also reflect a desire on the part of the Chinese government to create world-class companies and brands.

The literature in this field offers several standard explanations about the driving forces of ODI among developing countries. Dunning et al. (1996) identified two waves of ODI of developing countries at different stages of the investment development path. The United Nations Conference on Trade and Development

---

[4] The measures decentralized the approval of ODI projects to local authorities.

[5] "Chinese Companies Abroad: The Dragon Tucks in," *The Economist*, June 30, 2005.

(2005) lists six driving forces of outward FDI of firms in developing countries. In summary, these theories suggest the presence of three major motivations for engaging in ODI: resource seeking, market seeking, and capability (asset) seeking. Hess (2006) also grouped China's ODI into three similar categories: to procure natural resources, to secure market access, and to acquire brands and distribution networks.

Among the three categories, China had focused on the former two until the new "going global" strategy was launched in 2004. Several M&As targeting foreign companies in the manufacturing sector have been launched by large companies that seek managerial know-how, technology, brands, and market access in China (Zhang 2005). Particularly, the acquisition of globally recognized brands has been a crucial factor in many deals. China is beginning to recognize the importance of brand names but is also cognizant of the fact that it will take a long time and great effort to build brands of its own. One quick way of achieving this is the acquisition of foreign brands. Moreover, with the recognition of the limited success of the "trading market for technology," international M&A is being considered as an alternative.

A well-known case is Lenovo's purchase of the PC division of IBM in 2004. Lenovo was China's largest PC maker, and through the deal, Lenovo suddenly became the world's third largest PC manufacturer after Dell and HP. Similarly, TCL acquired a German company (Schneider) and established a JV with a French company (Thomson) to obtain brands and ready-made distribution channels. Haier tried unsuccessfully to buy the Maytag and Hoover brands because its own brand was not successful in the US market.

The move by BOE, a Chinese cathode ray tube (CRT) maker, to acquire the Korean company Hynix's TFT-LCD division, HYDIS, for USD 380 million had more to do with the technology than the brand. As a CRT maker, BOE had been attempting for a long time to acquire the TFT-LCD technology by inviting foreign partners to enter into ventures with the company. However, after unsuccessful deals with a Japanese company, it turned to M&A and finally bought HYDIS in 2003. After the acquisition of HYDIS, BOE has already built a fifth-generation TFT-LCD panel line in Beijing. Then it planned to build sixth- and seventh-generation lines within the next five years, which was realized by the late 2010s. Now or as of 2021, BOE is the number one in terms of global market shares in LCD panels; BOE's acquisition of LCD panel technology has served as basis for developing OLED technology, and is as of 2021 running two OLED production facilities equipped with the sixth generation technology, with APPLE as one of its client firms. HYDIS's technology and know-how played a significant role in this development process. For instance, in 2006, more than 120 former HYDIS Korean engineers worked at BOE sites in Beijing (Jee et al. 2005: 221–222). Similar cases of targeting foreign technologies can also be cited: Geely's acquisition of Volvo, D'rong's acquisition of a German passenger airplane maker, Fairchild Dornier, and Shanghai Automobile's acquisition of a Korean automaker, SsangYong.

5.4 Challenges and the Evolution of the Chinese Innovation System

The previous section elaborated on several firm-level strategies unique to China in comparison with Korea or Taiwan. The question of whether or not these broader sets of technological learning strategies pursued by China will be able to reduce the likelihood of falling into the "OEM trap" and be able to speed up the progress toward the OBM stage remains. The answer to this question is connected to the issue of the role of national economic policies and their interactions with firm-level strategies. This section deals with these issues first through an in-depth discussion of the nature of the challenges faced by Chinese firms. We then suggest several reasons for the possibility of taking cautious optimism for the future of China.

5.4.1 Nature of the Challenges in a Comparative Perspective

China's experimentation with several unique catch-up strategies aims to create national champions with their own brands in the local markets and to move away from the traditional "OEM trap" (Lee 2005). OEM is a specific form of subcontracting wherein finished products are made to the precise specification of a particular buyer, who then markets the products under its own brand name through its own distribution channels (Hobday 2000). In Taiwan and Korea, OEM accounted for a significant share of electronic exports during the 1970s, 1980s, and even 1990s (Hobday 2000: 133). Several studies, such as Hobday (2000), Cyhn (2002), and Lee and Kim (2002), identified OEM as one of the chief institutional mechanisms used to overcome the barriers to enter into and facilitate technological learning. The OEM trap implies that latecomer firms find OEM to be an easy way of catching up at the early stage of economic growth but they will soon face difficulties when the forerunning firms move their production to other lower wage production sites (Lee 2005). Therefore, unless these companies could eventually produce and sell their own designs and brands, they would remain in the low-value-added segments. Thus, these companies and their countries would not move on to the status of rich countries. Rasiah (2006) also noted the limitations exhibited by Malaysia's rapid export expansion of low-value-added goods.

The eventual transition to OBM requires a strong design capability or an interim ODM stage, as the Taiwanese experience suggests. However, acquiring the design capability is not easy because it is not available on the market. Therefore, design capability remains an important challenge for Chinese companies. Nevertheless, large Chinese companies seem to move along the Korean pathway in jumping from the OEM stage directly to the OBM stage. Unless they succeed, these companies may experience a fate similar to the Korean companies that went ahead with their own brands without sound design capabilities. For instance, after their initial success in the 1980s, Korean car producers, such as Hyundai Motors, ran into serious difficulties during their export campaigns to the US market (Guillén 2001) largely because of their lack of design capability. It was only in the late 1990s onward did these Korean car producers regain meaningful momentum in the US market after they developed its own engines which they used to import from Japan. This example demonstrates the risk of exporting one's own brand without solid design capability. However, sticking to OEM alone is not a long-term solution either (Guillén 2001).

The Chinese strategy of resorting to international M&As to acquire brand and technology (patents) may be costly, as demonstrated by the case of LG's acquisition of Zenith. Many of the key employees of Zenith quit after the takeover by LG. Moreover, the tacitness of knowledge tends to limit the degree of effective learning after M&A. The strategy is also costly because China's aggressive ODI seems to be backed by strong government incentives, such as cheap loans from state banks.

Another bottleneck for China could be the process of localizing key capital goods (i.e., core parts and components) industries, which is necessary if these industries would like to move beyond the simple assembly of final goods with imported parts and supplies. In this regard, the Korean experience indicates the difficulty of promoting and localizing capital goods industries (Kim and Lee 2008). Korean exports in the last four decades have continued to rely on the importation of core capital goods from Japan.

Another interesting case suggesting the limitations of technological capabilities of local Chinese companies is the dynamic story of catch-up and retreat in the mobile phone market in China, as analyzed by Lee, Cho, and Jin (2009). In the 1990s, foreign phones had taken almost 100 percent of the market, with Motorola, Ericsson, and Nokia taking up almost 80 percent of the market with their advanced technology and brand names. It was only in the late 1990s that local brands of mobile phones emerged in the market, such as Kejian, Konka, Bird, and TCL. Since then, the market shares of these indigenous makers had been increasing, claiming more than half of the market in 2003 and demonstrating a huge catch-up by the Chinese firms. However, after peaking in 2003, the shares of indigenous makers began to decline again, slipping to 34 percent in 2007. This pattern of catch-up and retreat by Chinese manufacturers is in contrast to the catch-up of Korean manufacturers, who did not experience such a setback during the course of their catch-up (Lee, Cho, and Jin 2009).

However, as will be discussed in Chapter 6, it is also noteworthy that the Chinese firms have enhanced their technological capabilities to emerge as the final winner in mobile phone market in the 2010s, with the share of foreign firms (like Samsung) dropped to one digit level. China market is more dynamic and turbulent than Korea market.

5.4.2 The Chinese Responses

Although the abovementioned challenges are formidable, we also note several promising signs associated with responses from the Chinese side. First is the increasing number of patent applications, which seems to reflect the enhanced innovation capability of Chinese firms. In this situation, one important comparative criterion is whether or not China is achieving the three important "catch-ups" that have also been observed to be present in Japan, Korea, and Taiwan in the past. The "three technological catch-ups" discussed in Lee and Kim (2010) are whether or not (1) residents' patenting is catching up with the non-residents' patenting in a host country, (2) invention patents are catching up with utility model patents, and (3) corporate patenting is catching up with individual inventors' patenting. In Korea, corporate patents first caught up with individual patents as early as 1986, and the number of invention patents caught up with that of utility model patents in 1989. Ultimately, the number of domestic patents overtook that of foreign patents in 1993. This pattern in Korea indicates strong R&D capabilities led by its large indigenous corporations. These three patterns are important checkpoints as no other latecomer economies other than Japan, Korea, and Taiwan have achieved such catch-up. In typical latecomer economies, the majority of the patents are filed by non-residents or foreigners (Lee and Kim 2010).

These three kinds of catch-up all occurred in China in the 2000s (Lee 2011). In terms of the number of patent applications, the share of domestic inventors became larger than that of foreigners in 2003, with the former filing over 50,000 applications (Figure 2 of Lee 2011). In 2004, the number of regular invention patents overtook that of utility model patents. In 2007, the number of patent applications by corporations overtook that of individual inventors, signifying the importance of corporate innovation activities.

Although these are promising signs at the aggregate levels, there are other supporting evidence for the rapid rise of big businesses and their capabilities in China.

First, there are many cases of Chinese indigenous firms upgrading to the status of OBM and globally competitive companies. In consumer electronics goods, the case of Konka as analyzed in Xie and Wu (2003) and Mathews (2008a) can be cited. Konka started as an OEM contractor and began to produce its own branded products for the domestic market in 1987, competing against imported brands.

By 2007, it boasted of a 24 percent market share of color TVs in China and became a major player in diverse consumer electronics goods (Xie and Wu 2003; Mathews 2008a). The case of Konka presents several of the features observed in Korea and Taiwan, particularly upgrading the capabilities from OEM to ODM and then to OBM.

At present, China boasts of several such cases in many sectors. According to a Chinese source book, Chinese companies are successfully competing against MNCs, at least in the domestic market. For example, in the computer sectors (i.e., notebook, server, and PC), Lenovo, Dongfang, and Founder are among the top 10 brands. In the soft drinks sector, Wahaha, Xurisheng, and Wanglaoji are the Chinese companies among the top 10. In the home audio-visual sector, Haixin, Changhong, Konka, and Chuangwei-RGB are the top four in the market.[6]

Furthermore, an important study by Zeng and Williamson (2007) showed that some Chinese companies are not just leaders in the domestic market but also global players across a wide spectrum of industries. The China International Marine Container Group dominates the global shipping container industry with more than 55 percent market share. This company is far from being low-end and has gradually penetrated every segment of the container market. This Chinese strategy is called "cost innovation," wherein the company uses low costs to offer specialty products at dramatically lower prices, turning itself into a volume business. In addition, cost innovation is not based on cheap wages but on applying a new product and process innovation to low-end goods. In learning how to innovate, the companies rely on various channels, such as licensing and M&As of companies in Korea and Europe.

These observations on growing Chinese companies are in sharp contrast to the gloomy description of them in the 1990s by Nolan (2002), who pointed out that China did not have any company in the lists of the UK R&D scoreboard, Financial Times Global 500, and Business Week's top 100 brands and had only 10 companies in the Fortune Global 500 at the time of his study. China's later performance in these criteria reveals a radical change in the 2000s and 2010s. Table 5.4 shows that China has 23 companies in 2010, and 37 in 2015, listed in the Financial Times Global 500. In terms of the top 100 brands listed by Business Week, China had 15 companies in 2019, which is second only to the US (54) but more than Japan (2) and Germany (8). Most impressively, its number of Fortune Global 500 companies increased to 46 in 2010 and 119 in 2019, which is almost the same as that of the US (121), surpassing all the major European countries and Japan (52).

Nolan (2002) and Zeng and Williamson (2007) treated different samples of companies in their studies; thus, the right assessment of the performance of Chinese companies may lie somewhere in between. However, the increasing

---

[6] This information is particularly true for the 2000s according to two books entitled, ndustrial Map of China, published in Chinese in 2004 and 2005.

number of success stories and the abovementioned figures serve as a powerful counterargument against the belittling of the Chinese companies. They also provide evidence that Chinese companies do not remain simply as low-end or OEM producers. At present, they are not only upgrading to manufacturing higher end brand products but also leapfrogging to emerging technologies, as demonstrated by the case of BYD, a global producer of rechargeable batteries for electric vehicles.

5.4.3 Broader Dimensions: State Activism, Firm-level Strategies, and the Size Factor

Catching-up performance at the firm level is inextricably linked to the policies implemented by the government. Over the years, the Chinese government implemented a series of policies to enhance science and technology capabilities. The historic "open door policy" declared in the late 1970s was also aimed at gaining access to foreign technology and foreign management methods. China periodically announced the main directions of the reform through the decisions of the State Council and of the Central Committee of the party, particularly the March 1985 Decision on the Reform of the Science and Technology Management System and the May 1995 Decision on Accelerating Scientific and Technological Progress.[7] President Hu, since his inauguration in 2003, has emphasized the so-called "indigenous innovation" (*Zizhu Chuangxin*), which inevitably necessitates larger investment in the knowledge base. Since then, the Chinese government has supported innovation led by Chinese firms with in-house R&D.

These initiatives are intended to consolidate the national innovation system of China. While these initiatives have been translated into aggregate-level changes highlighted by the increase in the national R&D-to-GDP ratio, college enrollment ratio, scientific publications, and so on, they have also affected firm strategies. Essentially, the elements of specific policies are present in all the three key components constituting the Beijing model. First, parallel learning, which is linked to the policy of trading market for technology, appeared in several policy documents. Second, the origin of URE promotion dates back to the 1995 "joint resolution" by the State Council and the party. Third, international M&As and going global specifically originated from the 16th Party Congress decision in 2002.

Such state activism affecting firm-level strategies falls within the Asian tradition shared by the neighboring economies. In this sense, we can find several commonalities among Asian strategies that can be summed up as the "BeST (Beijing–Seoul–Tokyo) consensus" (Lee and Mathews 2010). The BeST consensus

---

[7] IDRC and the State Science and Technology Commission of China 1997, *A Decade of Reform: Science and Technology Policy in China*, IDRC: Canada.

Table 5.4 Number of global companies by country, 2000–2019

		2000	2004	2007	2010	2015	2019
Financial Times Global 500 (rank by market capitalization)	US	218	231	184	163	209	n/a
	Japan	77	55	49	42	35	n/a
	China	–	–	8	23	37	n/a
	India	3	2	8	16	14	n/a
	Korea	5	3	6	6	4	n/a
	Germany	20	19	20	19	18	n/a
	France	26	28	32	27	24	n/a
	UK	46	42	41	32	32	n/a
No. of companies in UK R&D Scoreboard	US	133	294 (115)	509 (123)	n/a		
	Japan	83	154 (76)	220 (57)	n/a		
	China	–	2 (1)	7 (3)	n/a		
	India	–	–	7 (0)	n/a		
	Korea	1	9 (6)	21 (9)	n/a		
	Germany	19	54 (26)	83 (27)	n/a		
	France	21	36 (22)	58 (22)	n/a		
	UK	14	41 (16)	75 (16)	n/a		
Business Week's list of the world's top 100 brands	US	n/a	58	52	n/a	48	54
	Japan	n/a	7	8	n/a	5	2
	China	n/a	–	–	n/a	15	15
	India	n/a	–	–	n/a	1	3
	Korea	n/a	1	3	n/a	1	1
	Germany	n/a	9	10	n/a	6	8
	France	n/a	8	9	n/a	4	5
	UK	n/a	5	6	n/a	5	3
Fortune Global 500	US	179	189	162	139	128	121
	Japan	107	82	67	71	54	52
	China	10	15	24	46	98	119
	India	1	4	6	8	7	7
	Korea	12	11	14	10	17	16
	Germany	37	34	37	37	28	29
	France	37	37	38	39	31	31
	UK	38	35	33	29	29	17

Source: http://money.cnn.com/**magazines/fortune/global500/; http://specials.ft.com/ln/specials/global_ft500004.htm;

http://www.businessweek.com/interactive_reports/best_global_brands_2009.html;

http://specials.ft.com/ln/specials/global_ft500004.htm; Business Week's lists of the top 100 brands are from BRANDZ for the years 2015 and 2019.

Notes: The numbers inside the paranthese in the row on R&D Scoreboads are the number of firms from each country which belongs to the top 300 by R&D expenditure.

identifies private firms and the public developmental agency as the two primary vehicles for latecomer development. However, the specific implementation process has several distinctive Chinese flavors that are associated with its size. For instance, the tremendous bargaining power associated with its size is an important factor in the trading market for technology strategy, and international M&A strategy is also related to the size of cash power of big corporate sectors. To a lesser degree, the initial success of the UREs is associated with the availability of a large population of educated human capital at lower cost that can also take advantage of the agglomeration economy in college locations.

In any case, one important factor in this regard is the interaction of size and openness, which brings in the power of market competition in the domestic economy (Zeng and Williamson 2007). Due to the strong inflow of FDI, the domestic market of China has been transformed into one of the most competitive markets in the world; thus, domestic firms surviving in this market cannot help but become highly innovative and competitive. Xie and Wu (2003) emphasized the fact that the huge market serves as the key incentive for local firms to invest in technological learning. Whereas smaller, newly industrialized Asian economies rely upon export markets, Chinese firms rely on the domestic market and compete within this market. These findings suggest that the Chinese model may not be applicable to other developing countries (Xie and Wu 2003). However, this assumption does not rule out the existence of common elements for catch-up in successful latecomers, that is, learning and access to foreign knowledge.

The Chinese government and firms have tried to obtain access to foreign and new domestic (academia) knowledge, but they can only do so with a better deal, probably owing to their size. However, other developing countries can also try other access channels better suited to their own conditions. Nowadays, countries, whether developed or developing, are all trying to tap more effectively the knowledge pool of the academia. Developing countries can also utilize other diverse channels to access foreign knowledge such as licensing, OEM, JVs, M&As, strategic alliance, and overseas R&D outposts. The experience of Korea and Taiwan shows that different channels can be relied upon depending on the level of firm capabilities (Lee 2005).

There are other important initiatives in larger latecomer economies such as China, Brazil, and India (Mathews 2008b). These countries are forging ahead in seeking a new development path powered not by traditional fossil fuels but by new alternative energy sources such as biofuels and other renewable energies. China is known to have great potential in this field and is already the third largest ethanol producer in the world (Mathews 2008b). Mathews argues that these new initiatives call for another "latecomer effect" type of industrial policy to boost these initiatives.

5.5 Summary and Concluding Remarks

This chapter took a Schumpeterian approach to examine the catch-up strategies in China. We focused on the strategies for learning and access to foreign knowledge base. The unique features of the Chinese economy were identified, such as forward engineering, acquisition of technology and brands by international M&As, and parallel learning from FDI to promote indigenous companies. These features make up the Beijing model as they have not been explicitly adopted by Korea and Taiwan.

These characteristics must be understood in a relative sense. For example, it would be more accurate to say that the Chinese are engaged in both reverse and forward engineering. However, our point is that during the early stage of their catch-up, Taiwan and Korea did not experience the emergence of UREs to the extent that China experienced in the 1990s and 2000s. In terms of parallel learning from FDI firms, that Taiwan also pursued this goal can be argued, although China is capable of relying on a stronger bargaining power in its negotiations with MNCs. The sheer size of its economy and its attendant cash power enable it to utilize this strategy on a much larger scale.

In general, these strategies are expected to help China achieve a "compressed catch-up" or compressed development (Whittaker et al. 2020) and to avoid some of the risks involved. By following the East Asian sequencing rather than the Washington Consensus, China avoids the risk of the "liberalization trap," where premature financial liberalization leads to macroeconomic instability (Bresser-Pereira, Araújo, and Peres 2020). Thus, the current Beijing model seems to be a natural extension of the earlier gradual approach to system transition responsible for China's early success.

We also discussed the challenges involved in the Beijing Consensus, such as the difficulties in enhancing design capabilities. With all the challenges faced by China, we can conclude that the Chinese industry will not remain simply as a low-end OEM economy but will rise to the status of high-end or brand producers, as shown by many successful cases and other indicators. If we broaden our perspective beyond the firm-level analysis, we can see that there are more challenges, apart from the possibility of the middle-income trap, that China needs to overcome, such as rising inequality, unemployment, and corruption. Chapter 9 deals with these issues. Thus, a more thorough and broader analysis should be conducted in future research, which should also focus on the longer term challenges of sustainable growth and the tension between political authoritarianism and economic prosperity. Given these limitations, this chapter contributes a comparative analysis of the firm-level institutional basis of China's technological catch-up from the theoretical perspective of Schumpeterian economics.

6

Catching-up and Leapfrogging in Key Manufacturing Sectors

A Comparison with Korea[1]

6.1 Introduction

The literature on economic catch-up by latecomers has increased over the past decades. Japan provides an early example of the catch-up phenomenon, which can be traced back to the pre-war period (Johnson 1982). Amsden's research (1989) was a pioneering work on catch-up during the post-war period and analyzed Korea as the next Japan by attributing the so-called Korean miracle to an industrial policy similar to that of Japan. This finding was in contrast to the market-oriented or compromising view of the East Asian catch-up as proposed by the World Bank (1993). Lin et al. (1996) discussed China as another example of an economic miracle.

This chapter focuses on the micro-foundation of the economic growth in China. Specifically, we examine the catch-up process of indigenous firms in four sectors, namely, mobile phones, telecommunications systems, automobiles, and semiconductors. Despite the diverse performance and catch-up patterns that these sectors show, this study aims to find out the similarities and differences across sectors and sort out stylized facts about the catch-up pattern in China in comparison with that of Korea.

The present study adopts the Schumpeterian model of technological leapfrogging and catch-up introduced in Section 1.2.2 of Chapter 1 (see Figure 1.4). The model is based on the sectoral systems of innovation (SSI) framework of Malerba (2004). The SSI framework applied in the catch-up context implies that catch-up dynamics can be explained by referring to the ease and difficulty associated with the particular nature of technological and market regimes and then analyzing how actors, such as firms and governments, respond to exploit the potentials by deploying diverse strategies (e.g., variants of leapfrogging) and at the same time try to overcome the limits imposed by the regimes. Details of dynamics diverge, and such divergence reflects the heterogeneity of sectors as well as the responses

---

[1] This chapter is a re-writing of an article, Keun Lee, Xudong Gao, and Xibao Li (2016), "Industrial Catch-up in China," *Cambridge Journal of Regions, Economy and Society*, 10(1), 59–76.

China's Technological Leapfrogging and Economic Catch-up: A Schumpeterian Perspective. Keun Lee, Oxford University Press. © Keun Lee 2021. DOI: 10.1093/oso/9780192847560.003.0006

by the actors. In particular, our focus is on the leapfrogging thesis of Perez and Soete (1988) that the shift in generations of technologies could be a window of opportunity for latecomers to forge ahead with the quick adoption of new technologies.

This framework is applied to each sector, and each catch-up episode is explained as an outcome of the interaction of the technological and knowledge regimes and the responses by the actors. Specifically, we consider how the huge market size and strong bargaining power of China affect the access to foreign technology. Thus, we investigate the role of market segmentation as a nurturing ground for indigenous firms. Second, we consider the technology cycle time of sectors as an important element that reflects the double-edged nature of the frequent generation changes in technologies. Short cycles could provide latecomers with a high chance of catching up only when the latecomers have accumulated a certain level of technological capability. Otherwise, frequent changes in technologies could hinder them from catching up by truncating their learning processes (Lall 2000). Third, we consider the role of the Chinese government because of its paramount importance and complexity.

Sections 6.2, 6.3, 6.4, and 6.5 analyze four sectors in China by describing their catch-up performances and then explaining these according to the proposed framework. Section 6.6 summarizes the key findings and concludes the study by identifying generalizable catch-up strategies.

6.2 Mobile Phone Industry

6.2.1 Catch-up Performance

In the early 1990s, all mobile phones sold in China had been either imported or manufactured by multinational corporations (MNCs). The three largest mobile phone vendors, Motorola, Sony Ericsson, and Nokia, dominated the Chinese market upon their entry (Lee et al. 2009). The Chinese mobile phone industry underwent a series of ups and downs since its catch-up process began in the late 1990s. In 2003, the local brand makers took over half of the domestic market. However, their dominant position was not maintained for long. From 2003, Chinese indigenous firms began to lose their shares to foreign vendors, such as Nokia and Samsung (Lee et al. 2009). The share of indigenous makers in the domestic market in the late 2000s or in the 2G era remained approximately one-third or less (Table 6.1). However, they quickly regained their momentum afterward, at the onset of the 3G era when "smartphones" dominated the market. About 80 percent of the mobile phones sold in China in 2014 were domestic brands (Table 6.1). Several leading domestic vendors emerged during the catch-up process, such as Huawei and Xiaomi. However, Chinese vendors

Table 6.1 Chinese mobile phone market

Year	Units of sales (million)	Share of domestic vendors
2002	62.5	36.5
2003	73.8	52.9
2004	78.7	44.3
2005	88.1	36.7
2006	119.3	31.3
2007	148.1	32.5
2008	160.4	33.2
2009	161.1	33.1
2010	195.2	33.8
2011	249.9	37.5
2014	388.8	78.3

Source: China Center of Information Industry
Development Consulting (2015).

continue to receive only a small share of the total profits because they tend to produce for the low-end segments or sell their products at low prices to win the price wars against other vendors. Therefore, the sustainability of Chinese firms remains questionable.

6.2.2 Explaining the Catch-up

Technological and Market Regimes
The mobile phone industry underwent two generation changes over the 1990s and 2000s. First, the shift from analog phones (1G) to digital phones (2G) during the 1990s resulted in the growth of Nokia. Second, Apple initiated the shift from feature phones (2G) to smartphones (3G) in 2007. Chinese indigenous firms began their catch-up upon entering the digital age in 1998, skipping the first-generation analog phones but focusing on digital phones.

The production method of mobile phones is highly modularized. The knowledge embodied in hardware can be easily accessed by latecomers through outsourcing (Lee et al. 2009). However, the designs of mobile phones changed rapidly in the early 2000s, and new features or parts were frequently integrated into these products. Chinese firms had to master architectural knowledge and find a qualified supplier to incorporate new designs and features. The high frequency of innovation in both exterior designs and features presented a challenge for indigenous firms, which could partly explain why these firms soon lost their shares to MNCs in the early 2000s. The situation however changed in 2005 when MediaTek, a Taiwanese firm, offered a turnkey solution for phone makers, which significantly lowered the entry barrier for new firms (Zhu and Shi 2010). The advent of smartphones provided Chinese firms with new opportunities. Component innovation became the focus of new product development in the 3G era; thus, cost competition was critical. Indigenous vendors regained their momentum.

The turbulent catch-up history of these indigenous firms can be further understood by investigating market regimes. Chinese firms began to produce phones under their own brands in the late 1990s, a period when mobile phones were regarded as luxury goods. MNCs, such as Nokia and Motorola, focused their marketing efforts on high-end markets in large cities. This strategy helped domestic firms penetrate low-end segments in small cities and towns. The importance of these low-end segments increased as mobile phones gradually turned into standard consumer goods. However, customers in this low-end market have low brand loyalty because they frequently replace their handsets for newer ones with additional features and often try new brands. Thus, the low-price advantage of indigenous firms is important because most customers are unwilling to spend large amounts on products that are quickly outdated.

Another distinguishing feature of the Chinese market is its size and segmentation; the low-end market is large enough to become a harbor for indigenous firms (Liu 2010). Therefore, competition among domestic firms is intensified and drives the firms to engage in technological learning and innovation. The sizable low-end market also enables local firms to achieve a certain economy of scale, which is an important element in price wars. The technological capabilities that indigenous firms accumulate from this market segment have provided them with a foundation to compete with their forerunners in the high-end market since 2010. Moreover, the large distribution channels built by these indigenous firms cannot be easily imitated by MNCs.

Role of the Government and Firms

The government played a mixed role in the mobile phone industry. It previously implemented certain regulatory rules. In 1996, the Ministry of Posts and Telecommunications (MPT) separated communication services (SIM cards) from handset production, and mobile phones became independent goods that consumers could purchase from any vendor. The detachment of mobile phones from services significantly reduced the effect of operators on the consumers' choice of handsets and attracted many indigenous firms into the sector (Zhu 2005). The MPT implemented a licensing system to limit the number of firms that could enter the sector to maintain its control over the industry. This rule created an entry barrier and limited the number of incumbent firms. Before the licensing system was lifted in 2003 and rescinded in 2007, the Chinese government issued only 49 licenses, including those for CDMA and GSM systems.[2] A total of

---

[2] CDMA and GSM represent different standards in wireless telecommunication.

13 MNCs and 24 indigenous firms were allowed to sell mobile phones in China (Zhu 2005). The indigenous entrants came from multiple sources, which included successful TV makers, such as TCL, Haier, and Panda. These firms had no previous experience in making mobile phones; thus, they turned to original equipment manufacturers (OEMs) in other countries or unlicensed MNCs for necessary core components or technologies. Chinese vendors usually sourced their technologies from the same foreign providers (Liu 2010). Thus, these vendors produced similar models that could only be distinguished through their prices. The turnkey solutions that were offered by MediaTek in 2005 even attracted *Shanzhai* (illegal) vendors into the market and drove the government to rescind the licensing system and open the sector to all firms in 2007. The market has become more competitive since then.

What are the strategies that local firms adopt to catch up in the cell phone market? Similar to those in other consumer goods industries (Liu 2010), local firms overcame entry and survival barriers by targeting low-end markets. The same phenomenon was observed in the 3G era, when indigenous firms began to provide affordable smartphones, engage in technological learning, launch new products more frequently than their foreign peers, and improve their products according to the feedback of their consumers. As a whole, the Chinese vendors developed 3,694 models in 2012, which accounted for 94.6 percent of the new models launched in China that year.[3] This strategy further allowed local firms to dominate the market in more segments.

The successful catch-up of indigenous firms in the 3G era has been largely attributed to their flexible and effective marketing strategies. Several firms, such as Huawei and ZTE, have established favorable relationships with major operators (Fan 2010a). Huawei and ZTE took the opportunity and became the major supplier of customized handsets with increasing market shares, when China Mobile, China Unicom, and China Telecom competed with one another for new subscribers in the early development of 3G wireless communication. Lenovo collaborated with the operators and made full use of its distribution channel in its personal computer business to penetrate the mobile phone market. As a new entrant to the industry, Xiaomi used online communities as its distribution channel, and these communities helped the firm to penetrate the market successfully.

Summary

Easy access to knowledge and high modularity in the cell phone sector facilitated the entries by Chinese firms into the low-end segment of the market. The short-cycle nature of technological changes eventually helped indigenous firms against foreign firms whose exclusive superiority in technologies were often disrupted.

---

[3] Information is from the website of the China Academy of Telecommunication Research of MII: http://www.catr.cn/kxyj/qwfb/zdyj/.

Table 6.2 Changed market share (%) of indigenous firms and MNCs in telecom system industry in China

Company name	TD-SCDMA	TD-LTE
Ericsson	• 2009: 4.4 • 2010: 5	• 2013: 11
Alcatel-Lucent		• 2013: 11
Nokia Siemens Networks	• 2009: 6.8 • 2010: 8	• 2013: 11
Datang	• 2009: 20.6 • 2010: 19.5	• 2013: 9
ZTE	• 2009: 34.9 • 2010: 22	• 2013: 26
Huawei	• 2009: 18.6 • 2010: 28.5	• 2013: 26

Source: http://news.mydrivers.com/1/273/273554.htm;

http://www.c114.net/topic/1120.html; http://guba.eastmoney.com/news,600198,17474510.html.

Note: MNCs include Ericsson, Alcatel-Lucent, and Nokia Siemens Networks. Indigenous firms include Datang, ZTE, and Huawei.

Therefore, indigenous firms fully exploited the potential implied by the technological regimes without much government support.

6.3 Telecommunications System Industry

6.3.1 Catch-up Performance

In the 1980s, no domestic Chinese firms were capable of supplying advanced telecommunications equipment, such as telephone switches (Mu and Lee 2005). MNCs dominated the Chinese telecommunications equipment market from the 1980s to the 2000s (Editing Committee 2008); however, the situation changed dramatically by the 2010s. Indigenous firms have progressed in their market and technology catch-up in the telephone switch market. These firms captured a small percentage of the market during the 2G era (5–10 percent) and successfully overtook MNCs during the 3G era. The market share of local firms in TD-SCDMA systems exceeded 85 percent.[4] Table 6.2 shows the market share of indigenous firms and MNCs in 2009 and 2010. For instance, in TD-SCDMA, MNCs (Ericsson, Alcatel-Lucent, and Nokia Siemens Networks) had less than 15 percent of the market share. Indigenous firms' strength in the domestic market led to the

---

[4] TD-SCDMA is a China-developed standard in wireless telecommunication. See Gao (2014) for more.

expansion into the foreign market, and Huawei surpassed the Swedish Ericsson in terms of global sales revenues in the 2010s (Joo et al. 2016).

In the early stage of the technological catch-up, indigenous firms were able to catch up in mature technologies, such as fixed-line digital switches and 2G wireless technologies (GSM and CDMA) (Fan 2006; Liu 2010; Shen 1999). Domestic research on digital switches began in the mid-1980s, and the turning point was at the end of 1991 when Great Dragon successfully developed the HJD04 digital switch, the fastest digital switch in the world at that time. The price of imported switches and switches from joint ventures (JVs) dropped dramatically as a result of the successful development of the HJD04 switch. Then, in the later stage, indigenous firms developed new technologies, such as Soft switch, SCDMA, and SDR, and even international technological standards, such as TD-SCDMA, TD-LTE, and TD-LTE Advanced (Fan 2006; Gao 2014; Gao and Liu 2012). TD-SCDMA, which was mainly developed by Datang Telecom Technology and Industry Group, was accepted as one of the three international standards by the International Telecommunication Union in May 2000. TD-LTE Advanced became one of the two international standards for 4G wireless communications based on TD-SCDMA.

6.3.2 Explaining the Catch-up

Technological and Market Regimes

The earlier catch-up by Chinese firms in fixed-line telephone switches was possible because they were mature technologies with predictable technological trajectories; thus, access to foreign technologies was possible (Chapter 2 of this book). Consequently, the Chinese firms were able to follow the given technological trajectories or path, skip some stages along the path, and rely on local universities, research institutes, and internal R&D capacities. In terms of the market regimes, the existence of segmented markets was a favorable condition for latecomers to utilize the low-end market or rural market as their initial nurturing ground, whereas MNCs ignored this market in the 1980s and the early 1990s (Fan 2006; Liu 2010).

The fast-changing (short-cycle) nature of technologies has now become one of the important sources for the technological catch-up and leapfrogging in the era of wireless technology, in contrast to the era of fixed-line telecommunications (Lee et al. 2012). This difference had to with the fact that the Chinese firms had learned and accumulated a certain level of technological capabilities during the fixed-line era (Lee et al. 2009, 2012). Therefore, the frequent emergence of new technologies and standards became a window of opportunity for the catch-up in new markets, as the thesis of leapfrogging implies. The key battleground is the technological standards in the new generation of wireless communication; who obtains recognition of their standard in which market is decisive in determining market competition (Gao and Liu 2012).

Role of the Government and Firms

Given the initial policy of opening the domestic market to foreign firms, indigenous firms had to focus on the low-end market in the 1980s and early 1990s. The Chinese government offered support to help local firms capture some of the market share after the firms developed their own fixed-line digital switches. For instance, the ministry organized two coordination meetings to encourage the use of domestically produced switches in 1996 and 1999, and these two meetings were the turning points for indigenous firms in replacing the MNCs (Mu and Lee 2005).

After the successful catch-up in fixed-line switches, the government became more confident and ambitious in emphasizing indigenous innovation in the era of wireless telecommunications with the case of the indigenous standard of TD-SCDMA for 3G as the main example (Gao 2014). The final outcome was the successful rise of the indigenous standard despite the complicated course of the full story. One of the key factors was the strategy adopted by indigenous firms to overcome latecomers' disadvantages. People did not believe in the reliability of TD-SCDMA in the same way that they trusted the internationally established standards of WCDMA and CDMA2000. Indigenous firms, especially Datang, took proactive actions to promote TD-SCDMA as an example of the new policy line of the so-called "indigenous innovation" of the Hu Jintao leadership (Gao 2014). Datang also decided to share its proprietary technology with other members and actors in the TD-SCDMA Alliance to facilitate the development of the TD-SCDMA value chain. The government also offered support to TD-SCDMA standards (Gao 2014) through signaling (e.g., the National Development and Reform Commission strongly supported the setting up of the TD-SCDMA Alliance), financial support (e.g., RMB 700 million was allotted to facilitate collaboration among member firms of the Alliance), technical service (e.g., the Ministry of Industry and Information Technology organized the MTNet test to verify the reliability of the TD-SCDMA system to be deployed as a stand-alone network rather than as a complement to WCDMA), and administrative order (e.g., the government requested service providers to test and verify TD-SCDMA in 2005 and finally asked China Mobile to adopt this standard in January 2009).

Summary

Stable trajectories and less frequent innovation of technologies of the fixed-line telecommunications system facilitated entry and catch-up by the Chinese firms,

Table 6.3 Market share (%) of domestic brands in China's automobile market

Year	Passenger cars	Sedans
2007	40.5	26.4
2008	39.9	25.9
2009	44.3	29.7
2010	45.6	30.9
2011	42.2	29.1
2012	41.9	28.4
2013	40.3	27.5
2014	38.4	22.4
2015	41.3	

Source: Statistics released by China Association of Automobile Manufactures at http://www.caam.org.cn.

which started from the low-end segment of the market. Later, in the wireless system era, for the indigenous firms with much enhanced technological capabilities, frequent generation changes in the standards served as a window of opportunity; they even tried to influence the government policy in their favor.

6.4 Automobile Industry

6.4.1 Catch-up Performance

Some statistics indicated that more than 30 percent of new passenger cars in the world were made in China in 2015, and China has become the largest car producer and market in the world. Foreign car makers that have manufacturing facilities in China may have contributed to this growth. However, the performance of China's domestic brands was also impressive, as shown in Table 6.3. Indigenous firms that produced passenger cars maintained a market share of around 40 percent in the 2000s. Several indigenous car makers also established their brands in specific segments. For instance, seven among the top 10 bestselling sport utility vehicle (SUV) models were produced by indigenous firms in 2015, and Greatwall, Chery, and Changan were among the most popular SUV makers in the Chinese market.

Nevertheless, foreign firms still maintained a dominant position in China's sedan segment. Table 6.3 shows that the market shares by indigenous brands declined from 30 percent in 2010 to 22.4 percent in 2015. Almost all bestselling sedans in China are made by foreign JVs, such as GM, Toyota, and Volkswagen. In sum, it can be said that indigenous firms have achieved moderate success in their catch-up.

6.4.2 Explaining the Catch-up

Technological and Market Regimes
The technological regime of the automobile industry has been characterized as less science-based and has a stable trajectory and low frequency of innovation (Lee and Lim 2001); the industry had no radical innovations in the last several decades at least before the arrival of electric or hybrid engines. Moreover, reverse engineering can be performed, given that the production of automobiles merely involves the assembly of parts and components. The whole industry is gradually being disintegrated vertically, as automobile production becomes increasingly modularized. Architectural knowledge, which was crucial in vehicle production, is no longer considered highly important. Moreover, component knowledge has become increasingly accessible. These changes in the technology regime have significantly reduced the entry barriers (Gao and Liu 2012), with the examples of Chery and Geely, which are two leading indigenous firms. Both of them relied upon global outsourcing for body design and major components from international suppliers (Lee et al. 2009).

The market regime for passenger cars in China is similar to that of typical consumer goods in that the market of these cars tends to be segmented into high and low ends. The existence of a large low-end market provides a haven for indigenous firms. This feature also explains why indigenous firms are relatively successful in the small-size SUV segment because many Chinese customers in the low-end market are more willing to buy spacious and multifunctional vehicles than sedans, which are limited in terms of multifunctionality. Similar to other consumer goods markets, indigenous firms introduce new models more frequently than their multinational counterparts by incorporating feedback from their customers. These firms frequently test and improve their ideas in the market to learn quickly. They launched more than 170 models in the four years from 2003 to 2007 (Lee et al. 2009).

However, market condition is not always favorable to indigenous firms. On one hand, the harsh competition in markets open to all global players has driven down the average price of passenger cars. On the other hand, foreign firms, mainly their JVs, have begun to penetrate the low-end market (Shang and He 2016). Indigenous firms face an increasingly unfavorable demand condition after the cancellation of consumer subsidies on small cars and the implementation of restrictions on new car registration in several large cities (Ma and Ye 2013). Thus, until mid-2010s, market shares by domestic brands failed to increase at a rapid rate and even stagnated or declined in some segments, such as sedans (see Table 6.3). This slowdown is also associated with the nature of the technological regime of this sector, which features a high degree of tacit knowledge. This posed long-term difficulties in closing the final gap with forerunning firms, as in the case of Hyundai Motors versus Toyota (Jung and Lee 2010).

Role of the Government and Firms

The initial policy of the central government was to promote JVs with MNCs rather than promoting indigenous firms, and it expected technology transfer to happen. However, this "trading market for technology" strategy has been ineffective in the automobile sector, although successful in the telecommunications system sector (Chapter 2). The government regulated the sale prices of cars in the domestic market, imposing high tariff on imported cars, and only nine firms in China, including three JVs, were allowed to manufacture passenger cars by the end of the 1980s and in 1990s (Yu 2006). Though the government was supportive of JVs, hoping for technology transfer, the technological capabilities of Chinese firms (mainly state-owned enterprises) remained far behind those of their foreign partners at the end of the 1990s (Yu 2006).

Finally, China became a member of the World Trade Organization (WTO) and lifted both entry restrictions and price regulations in the automobile industry in 2001. Indigenous private firms, such as Chery, were allowed to enter the industry but without support from the central government. Moreover, the central government changed the policy line and prohibited the formation of new JVs after realizing the ineffectiveness of JVs in facilitating the catching-up of local firms (Chu 2011). However, in conflict with the central government, with limited capability in coordination across the nation (Eun and Lee 2002; Luo 2006), local governments refused to follow the policy change of the former and they allowed some foreign automobile firms to establish new or additional JVs. Almost all of the big names in the industry had established their JVs in China by the end of 2008. The growth of indigenous firms was stalled for a while because MNCs and their local partners also began to enter the low-end market after developing a solid position in the high-end market. Indigenous firms eventually built their capabilities through global outsourcing and even acquired foreign companies; Chery recently established a JV with Jaguar Land Rover to further enhance its brand reputation and technological capabilities. Geely improved its technological learning through a merger and acquisition with Volvo.

Summary

Stable trajectories and less frequent innovation are the features of the technological regime of automobiles, which facilitated entry and catch-up by Chinese firms in the low-end segment first. However, government policy in the early period was geared toward promoting JVs and not indigenous firms. Indigenous firms emerged only in the later period, after the WTO entry. Their potential was eventually recognized by the central government. Therefore, the catch-up potential implied by the technological regimes has been exploited even without consistent government support by late-entry indigenous firms that performed well in low-end segments but not in high-end segments, which involve a high degree of cumulated skills and tacit knowledge.

6.5 Semiconductor Industry

6.5.1 Catch-up Performance

By the end of 2014, the revenue share of the Chinese semiconductor industry had increased to more than 20 percent of the world market (PWC 2016). The Semiconductor Manufacturing International Corporation (SMIC), a public firm with three Chinese state-owned enterprises as major shareholders, was the fifth-largest chip foundry in the world, and two Chinese integrated circuit (IC) firms, HiSilicon and Spreadtrum, were among the top 10 fabless IC suppliers in 2015 (IC Insights 2015). Despite the rapid increase in the volume of the semiconductor industry, China has remained highly dependent on other countries for a large share of its chip consumption. Chips have been the top imported product to China for many years in a row. None of the indigenous firms is listed among the top 10 IC suppliers in the Chinese market (PWC 2016). In the fabless IC sector, the sales revenue of HiSilicon (or Spreadtrum) is less than one-fifth that of Qualcomm, the leading fabless firm in the world (IC Insights 2015). The same can be observed in the IC fabrication sector. The sales revenue of the Taiwan Semiconductor Manufacturing Company (TSMC), which is the leading foundry business in the world, is 10 times larger than that of SMIC. This finding suggests that the Chinese semiconductor industry requires further improvement. The limited achievements of the Chinese IC industry can also be observed when the wafer fab capacities of China are compared with those of other countries (PWC 2013: 23). In 2012, China had a high proportion of small wafer sizes (5 inches or less) and mature process technologies (0.7 μm or bigger). However, its capacities in large wafer sizes (8 inches and 12 inches) and leading-edge process nodes (0.06 μm or smaller) were significantly lower than the worldwide average. Further, capacities of the factories in China are somewhat outdated; TSMC started volume production of chips at the 28 nm process node in 2011; by contrast, SMIC began to use its 28 nm process node in the beginning of 2014.

6.5.2 Explaining the Catch-up

Technological and Market Regimes
The semiconductor industry can be divided into memory chip and the application-specific IC (ASIC) segments. In general, the degree of embodied technological knowledge in memory chips is higher than that in ASICs because the former depends on large-scale generation-specific production facilities. Tacit knowledge is important in both segments to manage these facilities efficiently and stably, increase operating ratios, and increase the productivity of the facilities. In the memory chip segment, appropriability requires a company to lead

markets swiftly to recoup revenues as quickly as possible because of the short product life cycles. In other words, new and next-generation products must be produced rapidly. Moreover, new facilities must be built for future generations to increase the productivity of fabricating wafers with larger diameters. Although highly sophisticated technologies are not easily accessible, mature or outdated production technologies are often available upon licensing, as observed in the case of the Korea in the past (Lee and Lim 2001). However, leading companies tend to dominate patent portfolios to restrict latecomer companies from acquiring recent technologies. Given the oligopolistic structure of the semiconductor market, competition among semiconductor manufacturers is highly intensified, and intellectual property rights lawsuits are frequently filed. Technological and organizational knowledge in the semiconductor industry is highly cumulative, at least within the same generation of technologies. The cumulativeness of the learning process renders first-mover advantages as critical in the industry, and it stipulates a "success-breeds-success" process of the evolution. The organizational capabilities of the incumbent leaders improve over time; therefore, the industry increasingly focuses on and demonstrates a typical "Schumpeter Mark II" pattern of innovation (Malerba 2004).

In summary, the technological regime of IC manufacturing is characterized by a low level of accessibility (with some exceptions in the mature production technology in memory chips) and a high level of appropriability for the incumbents, which are unfavorable for Chinese latecomers in catching up with their foreign forerunners. Therefore, unless access to foreign knowledge and designs is arranged as in the case of the Korean firms' entry in the 1980s (Lee and Lim 2001), Chinese firms may suffer from late entry and can hardly catch up with their forerunning counterparts. According to the 1996 Wassenaar Arrangement, the home countries of leading IC companies in the West restricted the export of leading-edge IC fabrication technologies to Communist countries such as China. Thus, Chinese firms could hardly obtain the key equipment with the latest technology from upstream suppliers. At best, the level of technology that these firms could import was one or two generations behind their global competitors, and this limitation significantly slowed their pace of learning (Chapter 5).

The market regimes of the semiconductor industry are quite different from those of typical consumer markets and are generally not as favorable as those of the mobile phone industry. In memory chips, low-end markets cannot be explicitly distinguished from high-end ones, especially for general-purpose chips. Therefore, low-end markets cannot be leveraged by indigenous firms.

Roles of the Government and Firms

When China opened its door to the outside world in the late 1970s, its semiconductor industry was significantly behind the world frontier. Hence, the Chinese government began to rebuild this industry by importing foreign technologies. However, the Wassenaar Arrangement (or the Coordinating Committee for Multilateral Export Controls) strictly controlled the export of technology and prevented Chinese firms from obtaining the latest technology. During the 1990s, the Chinese central government launched national projects to facilitate the catching-up process of their local firms (Rho et al. 2015). The first project, called "Project 908," was initiated in August 1990, with the aim of constructing a 6-inch wafer line. However, the process level achieved by this seven-year project was already several generations behind the world frontier. Therefore, the Chinese government launched its second project in 1996 and intended to establish an 8-inch wafer line in Shanghai. The project ended up with the establishment of a JV with NEC of Japan. Since 2000, the Chinese government has adopted a series of tax incentives and measures to support indigenous firms (Yu 2008), as an increasing number of overseas Chinese entrepreneurs began to return to China and establish IC firms. Other promotion policies include credit support and R&D expense super-deduction for income tax purposes. The Chinese government has become aggressive in recent years. Nonetheless, the full effect of the new initiatives is not realized yet or still undeveloped to assess, and it depends on the firm-level responses.

The leading firms in the global IC industry have several different business models (Wang and Lai 2013). Some firms, including Intel and Samsung, have their own chip design and manufacturing processes and are the so-called integrated device manufacturers (IDM). Other firms either adopt a fabless model and focus on chip design or take a foundry approach and focus on chip fabrication. The IDM model is clearly intensive in terms of capital investment and technology innovation. State-supported projects in China attempted to adopt the IDM model in the early stage, but none succeeded. Drawing from this lesson, almost all Chinese indigenous firms followed the model prevalent in Taiwan and focused either on fabless firms or on foundries. A very few of these firms are IDMs (Chen 2014). Another strategy that many Chinese IC design firms follow is targeting the ASIC market. The ASIC segment does not rely on the actual leading-edge technology, but market knowledge is decisive for firms to develop ASICs. To some extent, latecomers, like SMIC, find entering the ASIC segment easier than penetrating the segment of memory chips.

Summary

Frequent innovations, ever-increasing size of required capital investment, and uneven access to foreign technologies characterize the technological regime of IC chips, particularly memory chips. Combined with the lack of segmentation of markets, these features imply high entry barriers against latecomer firms in China. Thus, the catch-up has been slow, although the Chinese firms have the potential in relation to huge market sizes.

6.6 Summary and Concluding Remarks

6.6.1 Summary

The catch-up performance in the four sectors in terms of market shares is summarized in Table 6.4. The market share trend of indigenous cell phone makers has been very volatile, characterized by quick catch-up, retreat, and recent regaining of the catch-up. By contrast, the telecommunications system sector initially exhibits a slow catch-up through the path-following strategy and then displays a rapid catch-up through path creation. The automobile sector is characterized by a steady catch-up with medium speed or slower than that of the IT sector. Finally, the semiconductor sector has the most modest performance of catch-up thus far.

This study explains the varying records of market catch-up by referring to the different technological and market regimes. We consider the diverse elements of the technological regimes, such as modularity, degree of embodied technical change, tacitness of knowledge, knowledge accesses, and frequency of innovations. As summarized in Table 6.4, easy access to foreign technologies from developed countries (mobile phones vs. semiconductors), high degree of modularity (mobile phones vs. automobiles and semiconductors), and frequent changes in the generations of technologies or short cycle times of technologies (mobile phones and telecommunications systems vs. automobiles) generally help latecomers catch up. More importantly, sectors with a high degree of tacit knowledge (e.g., automobiles) tend to show a slower speed of catch-up than the manufacturers of telecom equipment with a high degree of explicit knowledge.

In particular, in the market regimes, market segmentation (or the existence of low- and high-end segments) seems to play an important role as seen in all the three successful cases of cell phones, telecommunications systems, and automobiles, in contrast to the slow catch-up in IC chips without such features. This finding implies that one of the most difficult challenges faced by latecomers is the identification of the initial entry point or niche market. It also indicates that Chinese firms managed to achieve initial success from a low-end market in segmented market conditions (e.g., telecom equipment and mobile phones) as well as markets protected by the government (e.g., telecom equipment). Conversely, latecomers in markets with no such segmentation (e.g., memory chips) find entering the sector to be difficult. This difficulty is one of the reasons behind the slow progress of Chinese firms in the memory chip sector (Rho et al. 2015).

A tricky point in this condition is the double-edged nature of the technological regimes featured with rapid technical changes or short technical cycles. In mobile phones and telecom equipment, the short cycle times of technologies and frequent changes provided opportunities for latecomers, whereas the frequent generation changes interfered with the Chinese effort to catch up with the ever-moving forerunners in IC manufacturing. Therefore, the difference must come

Table 6.4 Summary of the catch-up in four sectors in China

	Mobile phones	Telecommunications systems	Automobiles	Semiconductors
Market catch-up	Very rapid (path: up-down-up)	Steady, then accelerating	Steady; modest speed	Most slow
Role of the technological regimes	Easy access to knowledge; high modularity helped catch-up	Fixed; easy access, predictable wireless: uncertain and short cycle	Stable trajectory; easy access to knowledge	Frequent innovations; knowledge access uneven; low appropriability for latecomers
Role of the market Regimes	Market segmentation (low-end first) helped	Market segmentation helped	Market segmentation (low end first) helped	No segmentation
Role of the firms	New entries and innovative marketing	Rise of indigenous firms; firms pushing government	From JVs to indigenous firms; diverse models with lower prices	Still weak indigenous firms
Role of the government	Early: mixed roles; later: not much active involvement	Consistent promotion of local products and standards (wireless)	Early: promotion of JVs; restricted entry of indigenous firms; later: promotion of indigenous firms	Early: some support of JVs; hesitant; recent: became aggressive
Interaction of the regimes and the actors	Firms under competition exploiting the potentials implied by the technological regimes without much government activism	Indigenous firms exploiting the potentials of the technological regime with consistent government support	Early: ineffective government /lost opportunity; later: firms exploiting the potentials of the technological regimes	High entry barriers implied by the technological regimes not overcome by either firms or government

Source: Author.

from the level of initial absorptive capacity (or the initial gap) and from the degree of lateness in entry by latecomers. For instance, the Chinese entry into the IC chip market was relatively late than their entry into the mobile phone market. Another reason for the difference in catch-up may have been the degree of market openness to foreign firms. When a market is less open to foreign competition, local firms may have more time to develop capabilities even in the short cycle-based sectors. Lee (2013) clarified that short cycles provide latecomers with some chance of catching up only when they have already accumulated certain absorption capabilities. Otherwise, the frequent changes in technologies become an additional barrier against catch-up. Therefore, sectors with short-cycle technologies follow the leapfrogging strategy to target and jump to the emerging or next-generation technologies, as exemplified by the TD-SCDMA standard. However, given the intrinsic risks involved in leapfrogging, the government played a key role in the TD-SCDMA case, and the firms had to persuade the government to take the role.

The above cases suggest that the technological regimes are not the only paramount determining factor; the final outcomes are affected by the roles of actors, including firms and governments. Despite having a similar regime of rapid technical changes, the wireless telecommunications sector in China has succeeded in catching up in contrast to IC manufacturing. In these comparable cases, one of the main differences between the sectors is the different roles of the government. Chapter 3 of this book and Lee, Mani, and Mu (2012) argued that the Chinese government has been timely and consistent in implementing its supportive role in the telecommunications sector; however, this was not the case with the semiconductor sector in China during its early days, when the government was not confident and thus inconsistent (Chapter 4). The case of the early days of the semiconductor industry in Korea is an example of the manner in which the difficulty posed by the nature of the technological regime can be mitigated by the supportive role of the government in conducting joint R&D with private actors. In this sense, the government may indeed have a facilitating role, but this statement does not mean that it is a necessary condition, as shown by the case of cell phones, where the catch-up was successful even without much government activism. In the case of semiconductors, whether an even more committed government activism would have changed the course is doubtful.

Overall, the abovementioned stories are consistent with the main hypothesis of this study, that catch-up dynamics can be explained by the interaction of technological and market regimes with the responses by actors, including the firms and governments. Details of dynamics diverge, reflecting the heterogeneity of sectors. In some cases, the weight of the technological regime looms heavily without the government playing a significant role, whereas in others the proactive responses by the firms and government succeed or fail in overcoming the difficulties implied by the technological and market regimes.

6.6.2 Remarks on Generalization

The Chinese catch-up stories can now be compared with the earlier success cases in other economies, such as Korea and Taiwan. China is significantly larger than both these economies and is a more recent example of the catch-up phenomenon even after WTO imposed some restrictions on industrial policies. Thus, if any common facts or patterns are identified in both groups despite the high heterogeneity, then they may be considered as common essential ingredients for a successful catch-up.

First, an essential element for a successful catch-up is the promotion of the growth of indigenous firms by cultivating their in-house capabilities instead of passive reliance on foreign direct investment (FDI), as emphasized by Amsden (1989). FDI can be an important channel for learning foreign knowledge, but it tends to interfere with the eventual growth of indigenous technological capabilities. This situation is based on the comparable examples in the automobile sectors of China and Korea (e.g., Geely and Chery vs. Shanghai Volkswagen and First Auto Works in China and Hyundai Motors vs. Daewoo (a JV with GM) in Korea). The success of Taiwanese catch-up is also supported by the eventual rise of indigenous firms (Amsden and Chu 2003).

Indigenous firms should be developed because foreign firms tend to become increasingly reluctant to provide technology transfer or sell technology. Latecomer firms generally attempt to imitate forerunners by incorporating similar technologies in their early stages. However, to eventually succeed in later stages, latecomer firms should go beyond imitations to bring them to a new or different trajectory from those of the forerunning firms. Furthermore, foreign firms tend to stop the technology transfer when latecomer firms develop their capabilities. An example of this condition is the mobile handset sector in China. To take advantage of the large market, MNCs formed various JVs with indigenous firms to produce mobile phones in China. Nevertheless, in 2001, most MNCs stopped their JV collaborations after China joined the WTO. However, China's mobile phone sector regained catch-up despite the break-up with the foreign JVs. The same phenomenon was observed in Korea when Korean IC chip firms caught up with foreign firms, and the latter became increasingly reluctant to provide designs for chip production (Kim 1997; Lee and Lim 2001). This event was both a crisis and an opportunity because it forced Korean firms to develop their own chip designs.

Second, with regard to the choice of firms among the alternative catch-up strategies (e.g., path following, stage skipping, and path creating) described in Figure 1.3 in Chapter 1, the path-following strategy based on initial factor–cost advantages may serve best for the gradual catch-up of market shares. However, use of this strategy alone may not be enough to stage a rapid catch-up or to overtake the incumbents, which may require the leapfrogging (path-creating or stage-skipping) approach. In the path-following strategy, latecomers move along the existing technical trajectories of incumbents. However, incumbents tend to become increasingly reluctant to provide latecomers with technologies if the latter emerge as a competitive threat in the market. This situation denotes the time and the reason for latecomers to turn to the leapfrogging (path-creating or stage-skipping) approach, as observed in sectors in China and Korea. However, given the intrinsic risks in using the leapfrogging strategy, such as uncertainty in standard choice and (non-)existence of initial markets, identified by Lee et al. (2005), supplementary actions are often required by the governments.

Thus, a related observation can be put forward: the role of the government is important but not always successful, and it should be different across sectors. In high-tech sectors, the simple provision of tariff or the process of encouraging licensing or FDI may not be effective. Instead, public–private joint R&D or R&D subsidies or grants, as well as foreign–domestic joint R&D and scouting of foreign engineers, may be required, as demonstrated by the telecom and auto sectors in China and by the firms that produce IC chips, mobile phones, and digital TVs in Korea (Lee 2013: Ch. 7). This observation is consistent with that of Lee and Lim (2001), who stated that in sectors where innovations are infrequent and highly predictable, a successful catch-up may be possible largely through private initiatives along a path-following or stage-skipping strategy, whereas in sectors with technologies that are highly fluid and are facing high risks with large capital requirements, a successful catch-up may require public–private collaboration along a path-creating strategy.

The abovementioned observation about the success formula from East Asia can be contrasted with the opposite case in South Africa, where a government-backed initiative attempted to try leapfrogging by developing its own electric car called "Joule." According to Swart (2015), this state-owned company succeeded in developing road-worthy prototypes that incorporated locally developed battery, motor, and software technologies. However, the company had to close in June 2012, as the government decided to stop further funding required to start large-scale production of the electric car because of uncertainty of marketing success. In ex post sense, the cause for the failure was the lack of involvement of private firms that would play an important role in volume production and sales. Given this result, existing MNCs and local auto companies did not want this new company initiating a "disruptive innovation" to grow as another rival. The government should have formed from the beginning a private–public consortium, specifying that volume production would be done by the private actors.

Finally, if China's pattern varies from those of smaller economies, such as Korea and Taiwan, then some of the discrepancies can be explained in terms of the size difference and the associated complex interplay between the central and local governments. Given the large population of China, it is open to or flexible in adopting foreign capital, is less concerned about the foreign influence on the domestic economy, and, more importantly, can arrive at a better deal with foreign companies in transferring technology by adopting the so-called "trading market for technology" policy (Chapter 2). In the meantime, these Chinese attributes (e.g., open or flexible) often create difficulties for local firms in their competition against foreign firms, and the automobile industry is a good example. The government encouraged local firms to form JVs, which enabled MNCs to control their local partners. Conversely, the protected Korean market seemed to have greatly supported local firms. The peculiar nature of Chinese markets with several tiers of segmented market is an additional benefit for indigenous companies because low-end segments serve as their nurturing home, similar to the infant industry protection in Korea.

The decentralized nature of China's political and economic system (Xu 2011) must have restrained the implementation of coordinated industrial policies (Eun and Lee 2002). Some government agencies actively promote indigenous innovation, whereas some believe that FDI is more important than such an innovation. An example of this case is the complicated process of developing TD-SCDMA (Gao 2014). The inconsistency or conflict among governments critically affects the degrees and modes of access to foreign knowledge and thus shapes the pattern of the technological development of sectors. This inconsistent nature of government intervention is an important cause of the difference between China and Korea, but government actors in China have experienced learning over time, as discussed by Chu (2011) with regard to the automobile sector. For instance, with regard to wireless telecommunications standards, the earlier position taken by the Chinese government was more "market oriented," such that diverse standards were allowed to co-exist in markets without explicit prioritization by the government (Gao 2014). The government switched to a policy stance that prioritized indigenous standards over foreign-originated ones only in the later stages.

7

Catch-up in the IT Service Sector and the Role of the Government in China[1]

7.1 Introduction

Numerous case studies of catching-up at sector or firm levels have been conducted in the literature. A specific theoretical framework was provided by the so-called sectoral systems of innovations (SSI) concept in neo-Schumpeterian economics, which is also explained in Section 1.2 of Chapter 1 in this book. However, thus far, most of the SSI-based studies have been on manufacturing sectors. This chapter tries to analyze service sectors from the SSI perspective, in particular, the online game and applied software industries in China.

Several indigenous firms in software sectors in China have successfully caught up with Western incumbent firms in terms of market share. In the enterprise resource planning (ERP) software markets, Chinese firms have taken up substantial market shares, competing successfully against incumbent global giants, such as SAP and Oracle. In 2008, Chinese security software firms likewise were in the second and third positions in the domestic market. In the online game market in China, Chinese companies have been in the lead against foreign firms in terms of market share since late 2004. How did these Chinese software firms gain such extraordinary success in their domestic market? Although the success tends to be restricted within the domestic market, these firms have battled successfully against the existing world champions that exercise omnipotent power all over the world. Given the scarcity of studies on the successful catching-up in the software sector, this subject is worthy of study to sort out the factors that have enabled the emergence of the latecomer firms in the software industry.

The SSI concept is comprehensive and comprises several building blocks, such as (1) technological regimes; (2) demand and market regimes; (3) role of actors, including firms and the government; and (4) surrounding institutions. This chapter will analyze how these factors affected indigenous firms in China in their effort to catch up. As emphasized by Mazzoleni and Nelson (2007), the

---

[1] This chapter is a re-writing of an article, Jun-Youn Kim, Tae-Young Park, and Keun Lee (2013), "Catch-up by Indigenous Firms in the Software Industry and the Role of the Government in China," *Eurasian Business Review*, 3(1): 100–20.

acquisition of indigenous technological capabilities has become, and will continue to be, important for countries attempting to catch up.

This chapter will first specifically elaborate on what kind of strategy these Chinese firms adopted for their catch-up and how well-fitted these strategies were in terms of technological and knowledge regimes of the sectors. For the online game sector, which has characteristics that make copying easier (low appropriability), learning through imitation has been an effective catch-up strategy. On the other hand, for the applied software sector, its characteristics of high appropriability and high cumulativeness make both imitation and creation difficult, and thus, Chinese firms preferred mergers and acquisitions (M&As) as a means for quickly accessing third-party technology.

Second, this chapter focuses on the role of the government in providing support for the latecomer firms facing competition from foreign firms. It is related to the issue of infant industry protection, which is one of the classical arguments in industrial policy literature. The chapter elaborates the role of government regulation in nurturing indigenous firms against direct threats from incumbent firms. It will be shown that in both subsectors of the software industry, initial protection of indigenous firms and regulation against foreign firms are critical in earning time for learning by indigenous Chinese firms. Thus, this work suggests this role of the government as another "artificial" window of opportunity for catching up.

In what follows, Section 7.2 discusses the related literature and the theoretical framework of this chapter. Sections 7.3 and 7.4 elaborate the process of catching up in two sectors, respectively, in terms of the theoretical framework. Finally, Section 7.5 summarizes the findings and presents several lessons learned from the study.

7.2 Role of the Government in Catch-up

Lundvall (1992), Rosenberg and Nelson (1994), and Porter (2003) state that the existence of competence gaps among countries is due to the different national innovation systems followed in each country. Porter (2003) suggested a framework explaining the competence gaps among industries and nations. His framework delineated the fact that a national innovation system has several sub-innovation systems (sectoral innovation systems). Therefore, technological innovation needs to be studied at both the industry and national levels. Catch-up studies emphasizing national and technical factors have tended to overlook the dimension of "products." Vernon (1966) and Utterback and Abernathy (1975) created the "product life cycle theory" by introducing this dimension (i.e., "product"). However, the product life cycle also has a theoretical limitation in that it emphasizes only the firms' efforts but ignores those exerted by the government, universities, and public institutions meant to initiate catch-up. Aside from the firms' efforts in building their technological capabilities, interventions of various factors, such as external knowledge and networking with related industries and capital powers, are necessary for firms to move on to the upper level and absorb advanced technologies in a more effective manner.

In this vein, Section 1.2.2 in Chapter 1 of this book introduced the Schumpeterian model of technological leapfrogging and catch-up, which is a comprehensive framework that simultaneously considers technology, market, and institutions, which includes the role of the government (see also Figure 1.4 in Chapter 1). It suggests that the way innovation and hence catching-up are performed in each industry is closely related to the technological regime of the industry concerned. Though firms that belong to one sector have common characteristics, they are heterogeneous in terms of learning processes and capabilities. Learning and access to foreign knowledge are quite critical for latecomers in building up their technological capabilities; however, learning and building up take time, which entails the requirement of surviving long enough to ensure that learning can be completed. However, if the latecomer firms face direct attack from incumbent firms, they would not survive. As such, some form of infant industry-type protection is necessary before these firms learn fully. Here comes the possible role of the government or regulation in nurturing indigenous firms against direct threats from incumbent firms.

The market protection effect of infant protection in Korea by import tariffs against imported goods has been confirmed in some studies, such as Shin and Lee (2012), which finds that the effect of protection by tariffs tends to show up not in terms of total factor productivity but in terms of the increase in export shares. Similar examples include POSCO in the steel-making industry in Korea and other high-tech industries in Korea and Taiwan (Lee and Lim 2001; Mathews 2002), as well as Huawei in the Chinese telecommunications industry, discussed in Chapter 2 of this book. Actually, Chapter 1 (Section 1.2.1) elaborated that changes in government regulation or intervention is considered the third kind of window of opportunity for leapfrogging and catch-up, in addition to the technological window of emergence of new, often disruptive, technologies and the second window of demand changes including business cycles (Lee and Malerba 2017). An example is the intellectual property rights (IPRs) regulatory system in India, which provides asymmetric protection for Indian firms in their growth in the pharmaceutical industry (Ramani and Guennif 2012).

This chapter shows how the Chinese government's programs to create the initial market and provide various support policies and systems have affected the technological catch-up of the country's latecomers. In the case of online games, it restricted foreign firms from conducting direct marketing (so-called publishing of games) to Chinese people. In the case of Chinese application software firms, particularly ERP firms, an exclusive procurement policy was established that encouraged the use of indigenously developed software.

7.3 Online Game Industry

7.3.1 Technological Regimes of the Industry

The online game industry is one of the digital content industries and involves knowledge from diverse fields. In general, appropriability tends to be low in this industry as an online game can be easily imitated. Online games also tend to evolve continuously after the initial publication. They may evolve into a new form and grow like an organism through continuous upgrading after being launched on the market. In online games, repairing patches have to be applied to various bugs, and large-scale but routine updates are executed on an almost-daily basis. As such, the strategy of maintaining the level of customer satisfaction by combining major and minor innovations is essential. Interaction with game players is important to successfully execute such continuous innovation.

Given that continuous innovation is critical to extending the life of an online game, securing in-house R&D capabilities is an important asset and should be fully exploited as an entry or imitation barrier to other rival firms. For instance, "Free Style" (JC Entertainment) tried to prevent unauthorized reproduction of its source code by using server security technology and protecting its IPRs via registration of the trademark. Efforts to keep increasing the "gaming value" (entertainment value) by continuous modification is also very important.

The technological regime of the online game industry described above implies that entry by latecomers is not difficult given the low appropriability and that a late entrant can try to create its own gaming value by subsequent modification of games. These phenomena are what have occurred with Chinese firms, as will be explained in the following sections.

7.3.2 Process of Catch-up

Rapidly growing market and infrastructure

In 2005, the market size of the Chinese online gaming industry was only USD 7 billion (RMB 48 billion). In 2008, it increased dramatically to USD 29.3 billion and grew to USD 45.5 billion in 2009. In comparison, the market sizes of the Korean and Japanese online gaming industries were smaller at USD 15.46 billion and USD 8.26 billion in 2008, respectively (NIPA 2007). According to market research conducted by International Data Corporation (IDC), the number of paid subscribers of Chinese online games in 2008 reached 49.4 million, recording a 22.9 percent increase from 2007. IDC forecasted that in 2013, the annual growth rate of subscribers would be 13.9 percent, and the total number of subscribers would be 94.5 million, 60 million of whom would be paid subscribers.

One infrastructural factor that affected the rapid growth of Chinese online game firms was the widely popular "PC or internet cafés" where people could come and use PC facilities on a fee basis. In 2008, 317,000 such cafés sold online game coupons published by Shanda Entertainment for users in China. Without the collaboration between PC cafés and online gaming industry firms, online games would not have been diffused at such a high speed in China. The number of Chinese PC cafés grew very quickly in 2001 and reached over 0.2 million in 2002. Their emergence is important in many ways. First, they enabled high-speed internet service to diffuse quickly. Second, they provided gamers with excellent education fields, in which beginners quickly learned many game skills because they were physically located in one place (Stewart and Choi 2003). Third, they provided online gaming industry firms with the new profitable business model of selling a pre-paid user card (called PPCard) for game players in PC cafés.

Catch-up process: original equipment manufacturers → publishing → learning by imitation → developing

Since 1988, China has been regarded as a major site for outsourced production of multiuser dimension or domain (MUD) games by global game companies, mainly from the US. During this time, the representative games produced in China included Disney's *Donald Duck Advance*, *Rayman 2*, *Ninku*, *Namco Gallery*, *Konami Collection*, *SpaceNET*, *Football 2000*, *Dragon Quest*, and *Pokemon*. Chinese firms played the role of original equipment manufacturers for US and Japanese game companies at the time. With the advent of online gaming, a new business model (i.e., the developer–publisher division model) appeared, in which Korean, Taiwanese, Japanese, and US firms were responsible for developing online games and then Chinese firms were in charge of publishing or marketing them to customers (see Table 7.1).

The emergence of this business model was a result of the confluence of interests of the two parties. For developers, who were leaders of the game market, alliances with local partners were desirable because the leaders had limited knowledge of the characteristics of local users as well as of the local distribution and market structure. On the other hand, for Chinese companies, offering publishing and operating services through alliances with industry leaders was a better choice than independently developing online games because they used to be short on technical capabilities and the horizontal network for product development. Therefore, this developer–publisher model was favorable for both Chinese firms and industry leaders who wanted to enter the Chinese market.

The next part of the Chinese online game firms' catch-up process is learning by imitation. As previously explained, latecomers find it easy to gain entry into the online market by imitating the market leaders. Imitating activities in this industry consists of two types: (1) the operation of illegal servers, in which imitators copy the source codes of publishers' servers without permission and then operate their

Table 7.1 Main developers and publishers in the Chinese online gaming market

Publisher	Developer (nationality)	Year launched	Name of the game
Shanda	Wemade Entertainment (Korea)	2001	2 Mir's Legend
The9	Webzen (Korea)	2002	MU Online
9you	T3 Entertainment (Korea)	2004	Audition
The9	Blizzard (US)	2005	World of Warcraft
Tiancity	Nexon (Korea)	2005	Kart Rider
Shanda	NHN Games (Korea)	2006	Archlord
Shanda	Wemade Entertainment (Korea)	2007	Changchun Online
Shanda	NCsoft (Korea)	2007	AION
Tencent	SmileGate (Korea)	2007	CrossFire
Tencent	Neople (Korea)	2008	Dungeon & Fighter

Source: Restructured based on the Game Industry White Book (KOCCA, NIPA 2003 to 2008).

server using the stolen source code, and (2) the distribution of online games containing copied graphics and contents from developers. Korean firms that entered the Chinese online gaming market as developers and collaborated with Chinese firms (e.g., Shanda and The9) incurred significant losses owing to the Chinese publishers' piracy and distribution of imitation products (see Table 7.2).

Companies in the Chinese online gaming industry gradually increased their technical capabilities by publishing and imitating in terms of understanding and operating with the source codes. They also entered into, and accelerated, the independent development of game contents. According to Table 7.3, in 2003, the number of online games developed by Chinese companies was zero; however, the number dramatically increased from 62 in 2004 to 286 in 2008 (KT Business Research Center 2008).

Strategies of Chinese firms

Developing a single online game takes at least three years, with great uncertainty involved in the success probability of a new game. The reason for this uncertainty is that the success of any online game relies on playing up customer's emotions, which are difficult to predict. For instance, WEBZEN's early work *Mu* was extremely successful, but the company's succeeding projects, *Sun* and *Huxley*, were not. NCsoft's work, *Tabula Rasa*, failed to replace its popular first work, *Lineage*. Therefore, even leaders pursue a strategy of developing several or a large number of games together.

Chinese developers adopted this multiple development strategy. They also secured new online game contents through M&As or by raising funds for the development of a multiple number of online games. Shanda adopted the strategy of outsourcing and providing funds to several small studios that developed online games and later gained property rights to the online games developed. This process resulted in Shanda's *Project 18*. Giant Network also bought game designs and

Table 7.2 Major pirated games published by Chinese game firms

Pirated game		Original game	
Name of the game	Local firm (China)	Name of the game	Developer (Korea)
Crazy Kart	Shanda	Kart Rider	Nexon
Kart Racer	88 joy	KartRider	Nexon
QQ Tang	Tencent	Crazy Arcade	Nexon
Super Dancer	9You	o2jam	Nowcom
Dancing Star	9You	Audition	T3
Hot Dance Party	Perfect World	Audition	T3
East Fantasy	BLTech	Elsword	KOG
Crazy Guitar Online	H-ONE	Guitar Hero	Activision
Petrix	Magic Grids Networks	Paperman	Cykan Entertainment
Aurora Blade	IGG	Ragnarok	Gravity
Magical Land	Shanda	Creamph	Wemade
The World Of legend	Shanda	Legend of Mir	Actoz
Dungeon & Dragon	Shanda	Dungeon & Fighter	Neople
World of Fighter	The9	Dungeon & Fighter	Neople
Ghost Fighter	Shanda	Dungeon & Fighter	Neople
Joyful Journey West	The9	Maple Story	Nexon
Mu X	The9	Mu	Webzen
Extreme Basketball	9You	Freestyle	JC Entertainment

Source: Restructured based on the Game Industry White Book (KOCCA, NIPA 2003 to 2008) and *Chosun IIbo* (October 6, 2009).

Table 7.3 Number of online games developed by Chinese firms, 2002–2008

Year	2002	2003	2004	2005	2006	2007	2008
Number	0	2	62	192	218	250	286

Source: Restructured based on the Game Industry White Book (KOCCA 2003 to 2008) and iResearch (2006, 2007, 2008), "Research on China Online Games."

contents from small companies, according to "Win@Giant." These outsourcing efforts resulted in doubling the number of Chinese online games launched in 2008 compared with the previous years (NKIIPA 2009). By 2006, Shanda had launched an average of two new online games per year. In the late 2000s it began introducing one new online game per month and planned to launch seventeen online games simultaneously per year (Korea IT Industry Promotion Agency, NIPA 2009).

The export of online games developed by Chinese companies radically increased. In 2007, these accounted for approximately USD 71 million, marking a 28.6 percent increase from the previous year. In 2008, 15 Chinese online game companies, including Perfect World and King Soft, exported 33 online games to

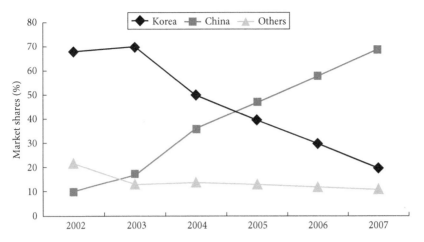

Figure 7.1 Change of the Chinese domestic market share between Chinese and Korean firms

Source: Drawn using data from the Game Industry White Book (KOCCA 2009; NIPA 2003 to 2008).

Korea, North America, and Vietnam. Although the Chinese domestic market used to be dominated by Japanese and Korean online games, it has been conquered by Chinese online games. As shown in Figure 7.1, in 2008, Chinese online games had a domestic market share of about 75 percent (KOCCA 2009).

Chinese firms, such as The9 and Tencent, increased their market shares and produced a platform of newly launched games. They also developed their own games based on the large amount of capital earned by publishing contents.[2] Although Korean online games had occupied 70 percent of the Chinese market until 2003, they had only a 20 percent market share in 2007 (see Figure 7.1). Meanwhile, Chinese games gained approximately 70 percent of the domestic market in 2007. With regard to the Chinese domestic market share of online games in 2008, Shanda (18 percent) and The9 (18 percent) jointly ranked first and Tencent (14 percent) and NetEase (12 percent) garnered second and third ranks, respectively (iResearch 2008; KT Business Economics Research Center 2008).

7.3.3 Role of the Government

Korean online games dominated the Chinese market in the early 2000s. At the time, the Chinese government inaugurated the "Committee of Examining Games" to impose regulations on game contents. The General Administration of Press and Publication, the government entity in charge of granting permits,

---

[2] Information from the website of this company: http://www.the9.com/en (July 20, 2009).

increased the level of regulations related to publishing foreign games in the domestic market. It used various tactics, such as pointing out inappropriate contents or citing cultural and religious reasons, to postpone the issuance of permits. In addition, although foreign companies may have previously obtained permits for a certain online game, a new permit for the updated game was required if the game had been updated since its initial sale. Moreover, as previously explained, online games in China were mainly diffused through PC cafés. However, the Ministry of Culture did not allow foreign companies to operate PC cafés. Furthermore, even if Chinese firms pirated foreign games, foreign companies could not actively sue them because they were not certain whether they would obtain a publishing permit for the next updated version if they make noise in China. Even if they pursued legal options, foreign firms were not successful in copyright litigations in China because Chinese law does not have clear criteria for plagiarism of online games as the law does not regard online games as written works.

In sum, asymmetric and obscure regulations by the government provided local Chinese firms with a favorable environment for catch-up by allowing them to imitate and learn from foreign firms. Recently, the Chinese government reinforced its support for Chinese game firms by granting national publication funds. It also announced plans to support exporters of online games, nurture online game human resources, and prepare an overseas road show together with Chinese online game companies.

7.4 Applied Software Industry

7.4.1 Technological Regimes of the Industry

The applied software industry consists of support software and business software. Support software refers to application development, security, memory, and system management software. Business software pertains to enterprise management software (EMS), industrial software, and personal software. The applied software industry is dominated by global leaders such as Microsoft (MS), SAP, and IBM. For example, SAP's world market share accounts for over 50 percent of the enterprise software market. Given that applied software companies that hold high market shares also enjoy large economies of scale in production and marketing, the applied software market has high entry barriers. One key competence required in applied software is the capability for vertical integration, given that the functions of applied software are often to integrate hardware with peripheral software (e.g., system software and other engaging software) in a vertical structure. A significant element is the interconnectivity between suppliers and users on the vertical lines.

Applied software is characterized by a short life cycle. In the case of ERP, which is the largest segment in the applied software industry, the system's life cycle is three to five years, which is shorter than that of other software. Applied software continues to evolve in terms of upgrading solutions and functions corresponding to the improvements in information and communication technology. Therefore, the opportunity of applied software businesses can be said to be high, but the risks and turbulence are also high. Thus, the emergence of new or sudden entrants with an initial but short-lived success is often seen in this market.

The enterprise software industry has a higher appropriability compared with other industries. Merely looking at the user interface will not grant an understanding of the architecture that integrates the complex business processes. Installing the same applied software in a different firm is impossible. In terms of the property of the knowledge base, applied software products involve a large amount of tacit and firm-specific knowledge. For example, ERP has a cross-sectoral difference in production methods, such as mass production versus flow production. Therefore, if local companies can acquire more context-specific knowledge about a certain market (industry) compared with global leaders, they would have opportunity as entrants in the market.

7.4.2 Process of Catch-up

Record of catch-up and learning

In the early 2000s, the applied software market in China was dominated by foreign firms. The hierarchical structure based on compatibility was a source of entry barriers. All aspects of the applied software, such as applied, memory, and system maintenance software, had to be compatible with the system software, at the time dominated by leading foreign firms, such as IBM, MS, and Oracle. Thus, competing against the products of these leading firms was difficult for Chinese firms with new products. However, some segments among the broadly defined applied software markets were different, especially the security software and ERP software markets. Hence, several indigenous firms emerged. Chinese firms succeeded in differentiating their products by satisfying local-specific requirements and by entering the market early. Chinese security software firms, such as Rising and JiangMin, started from the PC security software business but extended to network security software. In 2008, they successfully competed with the global firm Symantec (see Table 7.4). In the ERP market, Chinese companies (UFIDA and KingDee) held more market shares than SAP and Oracle, as shown in Table 7.4.

In the field of security software, the development of security vaccine is extremely important. The competitiveness of a vaccine depends on its ability to analyze hacking patterns and then build a library of virus configuration files. The

Table 7.4 Share of security software (2008) and ERP (2005) in the Chinese market

Rank	Security software		ERP (financial management)	
	Name of the firm	Market share	Name of the firm	Market share
1	Symantec	16.6%	UFIDA	28.6
2	Rising	10.8%	KingDee	19.5
3	JiangMin	9.6%	LangChao	9.5
4	TrendMicro	8.1%	JinSuanPan	7.3
5	CA	7.3%	SuDa	6.8
6	Others	47.6%	BoKe	4.4
7			SAP	3.4
			Others	11.1

Source: Drawn using data from CCID (2009), "Chinese Software Industry Annual Report," and Sino Link Securities (2007).

Chinese security software market used to be dominated by global firms, such as Symantec and TrendMicro, both of which entered the local market in 2000. However, the products that the global firms delivered were standard security software developed for global IT environments rather than for China-specific environments. Meanwhile, local firms, such as Rising, Jinshan, and JiangMin, all of which started from the PC security software business in the early 1990s, took advantage of the language differences in developing "Chinese Security Software" by analyzing the hacking patterns of local hackers, the evolutionary patterns of malignant codes, and the attack methods of viruses. By tailoring their products to the Chinese market, these firms were able to distinguish their products from those offered by global firms. Another of their advantages was the rapid response to local customers; they were able to solve PC and network security problems faster than global firms did because they knew the behavior of local viruses and hackers thoroughly.

Another field in applied software industry in which local firms have achieved a successful catch-up is ERP. The implementation of an ERP system is based on best practice, which is created by utilizing knowledge of unique production methods and system integration. The involved knowledge is tacit rather than explicit and is difficult for competitors to imitate.

In the 1980s and 1990s, China and Chinese firms did not follow international Generally Accepted Accounting Principles (GAAP) but its own GAAP based on socialism. Only from the late 1990s did it take a gradual road of changing its GAAP in several phases to conform to international standards until it joined the World Trade Organization (WTO) in November 2001. This gradual transition of the Chinese accounting system deterred global leaders from entering the Chinese market. During that time, about 300 Chinese firms (e.g., Beijing Case Software,

Beijing Kexiwang, Beijing North Star ERP, and Hejia ERP) developed finance software and entered the market successfully, resulting in Chinese firms gaining over 97 percent of the market share in the Chinese financial accounting software industry (CCID 2009).

This gradual transition period provided Chinese firms an opportunity to build their technological capabilities and also enter the ERP market. In 1997, local firms held a measly 9 percent share of the Chinese ERP market, a figure that increased to 62 percent in 2006 (Figure 7.2). Meanwhile, the market share of global leaders was 91 percent in 1997 but decreased to 38 percent in 2006. The market position of Chinese firms underwent a 180-degree change in a span of 10 years (NIPA 2007).

Given that the applied software industry has characteristics of high cumulativeness, high appropriability, and frequent appearance of new technologies, latecomers must acquire technologies by gaining access to external knowledge. Chinese ERP firms acquired new technologies through M&As. For instance, UFIDA acquired ERP technology in manufacturing business through an M&A of Hankang Software (Taiwan) and IFS (Sweden). More M&A cases are reported in Table 7.5. Another ERP company, KingDee, bought 90 percent of Beijing Case Soft in 2001, which gained ERP technology in the manufacturing business from TCL (Hong Kong). It also acquired a 25 percent stake in Asia21 Cybics HK Technology in 2002. These M&As helped Chinese firms gain knowledge over ERP platforms that were previously implemented by leading firms.

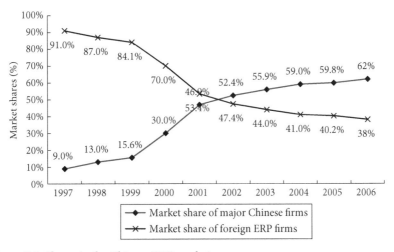

Figure 7.2 Shares in the Chinese ERP market

Source: Drawn using the data from CCID (2001–2006), "Chinese Software Industry Annual Report," and UFIDA (2001–2006).

Table 7.5 UFIDA's M&As and acquired assets

Announced	Stake (%)/Cash (USD)	Acquired firm	Assets (technology and market)
2001.11	Cash (20 million)	Hankang ERP (Taiwan)	ERP system of manufacturing business
			Human resource of development
2002.1	Stake (75)	IFS (Swedish)	ERP solution of electric power and aerospace business
			Enterprise asset management (EAM) technology
			The fifth ERP developer in the world
2002.6	Cash (1 million)	ENTENA (US)	Finance management
2002.8	–	Shenzhen Shuowang	Human resource planning
2002.12	–	Beijing Anyi Software	The first-place rank in the Chinese e-government market
			The fourth-place rank in the Chinese financial ERP market
2003.8	–	Beijing Fengfu	Enterprise accounting solution
2006.11	Stake	Beijing Lotus	Financial management solution (FMS) technology
2007.1	Stake (66.6)	Fidatone (US)	3G mobile business solution
2008	Cash (2 million)	Shanghai Tian Nuo	Real estate management solution
2008.10	Stake (100%)	Fang Zheng Chun Yuan	E-government solution
2008.10	Cash (7 million)	Turbo CRM	CRM for service sector
2009	Cash (0.3 million)	Taizhou Zhiyoun SW	Knowledge management
2009	Cash (0.15 million)	Tong Chung Eng	–
2009	Cash	Xinghongjia Tech	–
2009	Cash	Hanyi SW	–
2009.5	Cash (1 million)	Maite Technology	Management for product life cycle
			DB management (PDM)
2009.9	Cash (2 million)	Shanghai Heng Ju	Networking management
2009.9	Cash (1 million)	Shanghai Ha Jiu	Networking management
2010.6	Cash (6.2 million)	Ying Fu Si Wei	ERP for auto industry

Source: UFIDA (2000–2007), "Annual Report."

7.4.3 Role of the Government

In the catch-up by local firms in China's applied software industry, the government promotion and regulation program played a critical role in creating and protecting the domestic market.

In 2002, the Ministry of Science and Technology announced the "informatization project for the manufacturing industry" right after China joined the WTO. This project selected about 2,000 firms across China and supported them in establishing their information infrastructure. This project provided Chinese software firms with the initial market. In 2003, the Chinese government announced the Law of Governmental Procurement, which included regulations requiring all government organizations to buy Chinese software with a target software localization ratio. Given that the public sector is a large market accounting for 14 percent of the total applied software, the law had a positive effect on Chinese software firms. Since 2003, most government organizations have chosen local products except for operation and system software.

The government played another key role through the process of software authentication. In the case of anti-virus products, the Chinese government required software companies to verify whether their software can detect both local and foreign viruses effectively. Foreign firms were not able to collect virus samples diffused in local areas, and most of the foreign anti-virus software applications were graded as poor. Therefore, foreign companies had a disadvantage in the anti-virus software market. Several types of Chinese certifications (e.g., Certification of the Ministry of Public Security of PRC, Certification of China IT Security Evaluation Center, and Certification of the People's Liberation Army) were involved in security software, and several certifications could only be issued to Chinese firms (Korea Information Security Agency 2006).

7.5 Summary and Concluding Remarks

This study on catching-up in China's IT services sector focused on two aspects. The first is about how latecomer firms have been able to learn from and gain access to foreign knowledge bases and thereby acquire their own innovation capabilities. The second is the role of the government and regulation in the process of catch-up.

Regarding the first aspect, this chapter finds that indigenous software firms in China selected different learning and catch-up strategies in different technological regimes. For the online game sector where imitation is easier than in other sectors and incremental innovation is more important than radical innovation, Chinese firms learned initially by handling the publishing (or distributing) of games developed by foreign firms, then imitating them, and even pirating them occasionally. Eventually, they secured in-house game development capabilities by imitating global leaders' products and then started developing their own products. Next, for the applied software sector where imitation was difficult, Chinese firms chose to obtain third-party technology through M&As rather than trying in-house development by themselves, and then they differentiated their products from those of global leading companies by taking advantage of local specificities embedded in their products.

In general, IPRs are critical in the business of the two aforementioned segments. Despite the entry barrier effect of IPR protection, the latecomer firms discussed in this chapter were shown to circumvent the barrier to entry and learning and to acquire their own innovation capabilities. However, such learning and acquisition would not have led to commercial success without government regulation against foreign companies, such as business restriction in online game and exclusive procurement for indigenous products in applied software (ERP and security software). Such restrictions against foreign companies were a critical constraining factor against them in expanding their share in the Chinese market. In this sense, this study underscores the significance of the government and regulation in "artificially opening" windows of opportunity for latecomers, although the process often involves "unfair" business practices from the incumbent point of view. Such intervention had led to a more competitive market structure than monopoly by a few (foreign) companies.

The two factors of success, namely, advantage from China-specific contents and asymmetric protection by the government, are also applicable, in varying degrees, to the three platform business giants of the so-called BAT (Baidu, Alibaba, and Tencent). These three have emerged as the vital firms leading China into the era of the 4th Industrial Revolution, and their status and businesses tend to correspond to Google, Amazon, and Facebook in the US. Wang (2012) and Meng et al. (2008) also underscore the importance of local knowledge for firm performance and success in e-commerce and platform business. They point out that while the technology involved in e-commerce consists of two components, technical aspects and non-technical aspects, the entry barriers to the former continue to decrease, and firms increasingly compete on their ability to understand and adapt to local markets. In this sense, these firms represent more business model innovations adapted for the Chinese context than technological innovations (Chakravarthy and Yau 2017); however, they keep evolving from the former to the latter direction and recently to a combination of both types of innovations as they keep embracing artificial intelligence in their new platform businesses (Jia et al. 2018).

In sum, this chapter provides two lessons to strategists and policy-makers in latecomer economies. First, in different sectors with different technological regimes, latecomer firms and the government have to choose different sector-specific firm strategies and government policies and thereby overcome the latecomers' disadvantages. Second, the initial protection of domestic markets and firms may be essential in the early stage because latecomers have limited resources and need time to learn. However, after acquiring their own in-house R&D capabilities, policy-makers may switch to a new institutional regime, thus allowing fairer competition with foreign companies. These points are consistent with the observations of Lee and Lim (2001), who found that the roles of the government were also different in different sectors in Korea. In the automobile sector, where knowledge access and learning were not particularly difficult, government intervention was in the form of market protection (e.g., tariffs) only, whereas in memory chips and telecommunication equipment, where knowledge access and R&D were more difficult and risky, the government was directly involved in co-sponsoring and conducting joint R&D with private firms. In other words, when access to foreign knowledge is not difficult, the necessary intervention can be merely the protection of the initial market in the form of entry limit or exclusive procurement, and it does not have to be in the form of sharing R&D cost or activity itself.

8

Huawei's Leapfrogging to Overtake Ericsson[1]

8.1 Introduction

The telecommunications system industry was long dominated by several Western firms. In particular, the industry was led by the Swedish telecommunications giant Ericsson, followed by Siemens, Nokia, Motorola, Alcatel, Nortel, and Lucent. In the early 2000s, the industry faced some decline in market demand because of the IT bubble burst. Although many incumbents suffered, Huawei, a private Chinese firm founded in 1987, successfully entered the global market and achieved rapid growth. It has accelerated its market shares since the mid-2000s, and in 2012, it finally overtook the long-standing industry leader Ericsson in terms of annual revenue.

Huawei's catch-up is distinct from those of typical Chinese firms in that it is not a state-owned but a private firm. Moreover, its success seems to have more to do with technological competitiveness than with low-cost labor. Huawei was ranked first globally based on the number of international patent filings through the Patent Cooperation Treaty (PCT) in 2008. Its portable wireless access device, "Femtocell 2.0," won an iF Design Award and a Red Dot Design Award in 2009, and its optical distribution network access terminal box, called PIVOT, won a Red Dot Design Award in 2010. Fast Company ranked Huawei fifth among the world's 50 most innovative companies in 2010.

The Chinese government played a part in Huawei's accumulation of technological capabilities through the "trading market for technology" policy, which allowed China to gain access to fixed-line telephone switching technologies via foreign direct investment in the 1980s (Chapter 2 in this book). In the 2000s, the Chinese government's support for TD-SCDMA as a third-generation mobile telecommunications standard helped Chinese telecommunications equipment firms to establish indigenous innovation capabilities (Chapter 6 of this book; Liu and Dalum 2009; Yu 2011). However, not all Chinese firms were as successful as

---

[1] This chapter is a re-writing of an article, Si Hyung Joo, Chul Oh, and Keun Lee (2016), "Catch-up Strategy of an Emerging Firm in an Emerging Country," *International Journal of Technology Management*, 72(1/3): 19–42.

China's Technological Leapfrogging and Economic Catch-up: A Schumpeterian Perspective. Keun Lee, Oxford University Press. © Keun Lee 2021. DOI: 10.1093/oso/9780192847560.003.0008

Huawei; ZTE, China's second-largest telecommunications equipment firm, has remained behind Huawei and the major incumbents (Kang 2014). Such situation indicates that the role of the Chinese government's policy was an important but not a primary factor in relation to Huawei's catch-up.

To explain Huawei's successful catch-up, its innovation strategies must be examined. The existing research has emphasized Huawei's intensive internal R&D, strategic R&D alliances, and R&D globalization (Yeung 2005; Huang 2006; Zhu 2008; Sun 2009; Zhang 2009; Zhu et al. 2009; Athreye and Chen 2010; Gao 2011; Fan 2010b). Since the 1990s, Huawei has invested more than 10 percent of its revenue in R&D and globalized its R&D by entering India, Sweden, and the US, among other countries. In 2000, it started establishing strategic R&D alliances with Texas Instruments, IBM, Motorola, Lucent, Intel, and Sun Microsystems and joint ventures with NEC, 3COM, Siemens, and Nortel. Intensive internal R&D, R&D globalization, and strategic R&D alliances have undeniably contributed tremendously to Huawei's technological competitiveness. Given the heavy investment in R&D, a question emerges regarding the result of the enormous amount of R&D as well as Huawei's specific innovation strategies.

This study focuses on the technological details of Huawei's catch-up strategy and raises the key research question of whether Huawei has caught up and finally forged ahead by using technologies similar to or different from those of the forerunning incumbent. Using similar technologies implies that the latecomer simply attempts to imitate, whereas using different technologies indicates the pursuit of creating new technologies and taking a different technological path or trajectory from the incumbents. This contrast between similar and different technologies is interesting in terms of the literature on technological catch-up. Traditional or early studies, such as Lall (2000), Kim (1980), Westphal, Kim, and Dahlman (1985), and Hobday (1995), observed that the latecomers tried to catch up with advanced countries by assimilating and adapting the incumbents' more-or-less obsolete technology. A contrasting view was expressed by Lee and Lim (2001) and Lee (2013): the latecomers do not simply follow the advanced countries' path of technological development; rather, they sometimes skip certain stages or even create their own path that is different from those of the forerunners.

However, we have not found studies that quantitatively analyzed whether a latecomer firm catches up with forerunners in market share by relying on similar or different technologies. Moreover, no method has been suggested for such analysis. This study suggests an assessment method using patent citation data and applies the method to the case of Huawei versus Ericsson. Our choice of these two companies is not arbitrary because our objective is to compare a leading company and a latecomer firm that eventually overtook the leading company. Thus, our analysis is different from that of Kang (2014), who compared Huawei with a state-owned Chinese company, ZTE. Other latecomer firms that are also increasing market shares in diverse speed may exist, but they are not the target of our comparison. We choose only such a case of catch-up where overtaking in terms of market share is completed, so that we may find out the necessary conditions of a successfully completed catch-up.

This chapter uses the data of patent applications that Huawei and Ericsson filed in the European Patent Office (EPO) between 2000 and 2010. The related citation data are used as well. Our analysis shows that Huawei's consistent accumulation of technological capabilities, rather than its cost advantage, has been the crucial factor in its successful catch-up. Furthermore, its catch-up is a result of its eventual success in creating its own technological trajectory, although it started by imitating the forerunner by integrating the same or similar technologies in the early stages.

Joo and Lee (2010) compared the patent citation data of Samsung and Sony to examine the diverse aspects of technological catch-up. Similarly, we define and measure various patent-based variables, including the way in which they validate the comparability of the two rival firms in terms of the firms' patent portfolio. However, Joo and Lee (2010) did not include an explicit research question as to whether the latecomer (Samsung) had been catching-up with the forerunner (Sony) by developing the same or different technologies. As explained in Section 8.3, this study uses three explicit criteria, namely, quality of their patents, mutual citations, and self-citations, to answer this research question. First, we examine the quality of the two firms' patents (measured by the average number of received citations) to determine whether the latecomer's patent quality catches up with or even surpasses that of the forerunner. Second, we examine the mutual citations between the two rival firms' patents to determine the degree of reliance on each other as source of knowledge. Third, we also examine whether the two firms rely on the same sets of knowledge from a third party in their invention activities by measuring the "indirect dependence" between the two firms using the common citation ratios. Fourth, we examine the rival firms' degree of self-citation to assess the extent to which the latecomer firm has become independent of external knowledge sources and has become self-reliant on its own knowledge base (Lee 2013; Ch. 5).

The remainder of the chapter is structured as follows. Section 8.2 provides a brief overview of Ericsson and Huawei and then describes Huawei's catch-up in the global telecommunications equipment market. Section 8.3 discusses the data, methodology, and the hypotheses of this research. Section 8.4 analyzes Huawei's technological catch-up with Ericsson based on the three criteria to verify our key hypothesis. Section 8.5 addresses two additional aspects of comparison, namely, citation lags and citations in non-patent literature. Lastly, Section 8.6 summarizes the findings and provides the concluding remarks.

8.2 Huawei versus Ericsson

8.2.1 Basic Profiles of the Two Firms

Ericsson

Ericsson has been the undisputed world leader of the telecommunications equipment industry since the 1990s. Essentially, the history of Ericsson is also the history of the global telecommunications industry. The company was founded in 1879 by Lars Magnus Ericsson as a telegraph equipment repair shop in Stockholm, Sweden. In 1880, Ericsson started manufacturing its own telephones and delivered its first telephone switch in Gävle, Sweden. The Swedish domestic market was limited, and Televerket, the Swedish operator, provided all locally required equipment via its own equipment manufacturing division, Teli. Consequently, in as early as the nineteenth century, Ericsson reached out to the international market and won its first major foreign contracts in Norway and Russia in 1881. By 1900, it had produced 50,000 telephones and employed 1,000 people globally.

Ericsson introduced several significant innovations, such as the 500-point rotating switch in the 1920s, the 500-point crossbar switch in the 1950s, and the AKE 13 SPC (stored program control) switch in the 1960s. The 500-point rotating switches, which accommodated approximately 100 telephone systems (350,000 lines), were produced in the 1930s. Sales continued to rise during the 1940s and were sustained until the 1970s (Ericsson 2014). Production of the 500-point crossbar switch began to exceed that of the 500-point rotating switch in the early 1960s, with cumulative production of the crossbar switch reaching one million by 1971. With the success of the 500-point crossbar switch, Ericsson became one of the major international telecommunications equipment manufacturers; in 1970, it had 50,000 employees in 26 different companies in 15 countries (Fridlund 2000). AKE 13 was the world's first multiprocessor SPC switch with modular software architecture. AKE switches were not commercially successful because they were expensive and their technological capacity was limited; however, these switches laid the foundation for Ericsson's technological breakthrough in the 1970s—the AXE switch.

In 1970, Ericsson formed a research joint venture with Televerket and started to develop digital switches. In 1977, it launched the AXE switch, which elevated its status to one of the global leaders of the telecommunications equipment industry. AXE switches were easily adjustable to different regional landline telecommunications systems, and the cost was lower because of its innovative modular architecture. In 1989, Ericsson was ranked the fourth largest supplier of landline telephone switches with a 13 percent global market share (Ericsson 1989). AT&T (US), Northern Telecom (Canada), and Alcatel (France) held larger market shares than Ericsson at the time; however, most of their sales were from the well-established domestic markets rather than the competitive international market.

In addition, Ericsson had been deeply involved in mobile cellular technology since the 1970s. During the commercial development of mobile cellular technologies in the 1980s, the flexible architecture of the AXE switch enabled Ericsson to cope successfully with various first-generation cellular mobile telecommunications technical standards, such as Nordic Mobile Telephony, Advanced Mobile Phone System, and Total Access Communication System. In 1989, Ericsson became the unrivaled leader in mobile telephony systems, holding 40 percent of the world market (Ericsson 1989).

In the 1990s, Ericsson led the advancement of telecommunications technologies, expanded its business, and maintained its dominant position in the rapidly expanding mobile infrastructure market. In 1999, it held the majority (27.6 percent) of the global mobile infrastructure market (Gartner 2001). In 2000, it was ranked the second-largest telecommunications equipment provider with a revenue of USD 29.26 billion, closely following Nortel (formerly Northern Telecom), which posted USD 29.80 billion in revenue.

Huawei

Huawei was established in 1987 by Ren Zhengfei, a former People's Liberation Army (PLA) communications officer, and five fellow PLA members with a starting capital of RMB 20,000 (about USD 3,000). It started from scratch in the city of Shenzhen (Xu and Girling 2004). The firm used to be a telecommunications equipment distributor with a barn on a Shenzhen farm as the office, from which the founders sold telephone switches imported from Hong Kong.

In 1990, Huawei decided to take the risk of transforming itself into a telecommunications equipment manufacturer by using in-house R&D, rather than joint ventures with multinational firms, which was the strategy of typical Chinese manufacturers. However, it had neither telecommunications equipment knowledge nor sufficient money for such development. Its five researchers experienced repeated failures and the company was forced to reinvest all its profits. However, by using reverse engineering on an imported switching device and networking equipment, Huawei developed HJD48 (a 512-line telephone switch) in 1991. Its cost advantage allowed it to gain access to the rural Chinese market, a market that was neglected by multinational firms.

Huawei expanded its efforts to develop a large-capacity digital switch by recruiting engineers who had experience and knowledge of developing the HJD-04 system (the local Chinese digital switch) at Jurong (Great Dragon), a state-owned company. In 1993, Huawei achieved a breakthrough when it launched C&C08, a program-controlled public digital switch system with a switching capacity of 2,000 lines. It started to deploy the C&C08 to the small cities and rural areas in which it had built close customer relationships. In 1995, it

upgraded the C&C08 system to accommodate 10,000 lines and thereafter penetrated the major city market, which at that time was dominated by multinational
firms and joint ventures. Huawei increased its market share rapidly by rolling out
an aggressive marketing campaign and taking advantage of the Chinese government's support as exemplified by its "buy local" policy and preferential loans.[2] In
1998, it became the largest digital switch supplier in China (Mu and Lee 2005).

From the mid-1990s, Huawei established domestic R&D centers in Beijing and
Shanghai, through which it extended its R&D into access equipment, optical
transmission, data networks, and wireless networks, thereby transforming itself
into an end-to-end solution provider. It expanded its product line to include
High-capacity Optical Networking and Enabling Technologies (HONET), integrated access network, and synchronous digital hierarchy (SDH) optical transmission equipment in 1996, data communication equipment (routers) in 1997, and
GSM mobile communication systems in 1998. However, the Chinese mobile communication market remained dominated by multinational firms; local Chinese
firms, including Huawei, held less than 5 percent of the market share until 1999.

In 1996, Huawei began to reach out to the international market, starting with
Hong Kong and extending to emerging and developing countries and regions,
such as Russia, India, South Africa, and Latin America. Its international market
revenues were sluggish during the first few years, but surged from the late 1990s,
reaching USD 120 million in 2000. Despite these changes, respective sales comprised less than 5 percent of its total.

To cope with the challenge of the increasing complexity and inefficiency as a
result of the rapid growth of the business and organization, Huawei declared the
so-called Huawei Basic Law and conducted business and R&D process reengi-
neering from the mid-1990s. To achieve long-term sustainable growth, Huawei,
with IBM's assistance, prepared an advanced management system, which incorporated integrated product development and integrated supply chain (Fan 2010b).
With remarkable growth momentum, it posted sales of USD 1.93 billion in 2000,
hiring 15,000 employees (Yu et al. 2004). Nonetheless, this equaled just one-
fifteenth of Ericsson's sales.

8.2.2 Huawei's Sales Exceeding Those of Ericsson

The telecommunications sector investment experienced a sharp decline with the
bursting of the IT bubble in the early 2000s. The Organisation for Economic

---

[2] The Chinese government started to impose tariffs on imported telecommunications equipment
and extended Huawei 3.9 billion RMB (yuan) in buyer's credit from the China Construction Bank and
RMB 3.5 billion RMB of revolving credit from the Bank of China and the Industrial and Commercial
Bank of China (ICBC).

Co-operation and Development (OECD) member countries cut their investment in telecommunications infrastructure by almost 40 percent over two years from USD 241 billion in 2000 to USD 150 billion in 2002 (OECD 2013), which had the ripple effect of a severe downturn in the telecommunications equipment industry.[3] The downstream industry's drastic slowdown resulted in the decrease of the total sales of telecommunications equipment of major firms by more than 30 percent from 2000 to 2002 (Gartner 2005, 2006, 2007, 2010).[4] Nortel, Ericsson, and Lucent (formerly AT&T's telecommunications equipment branch), whose main business area was landline/mobile telecommunications infrastructure, lost more than half of their telecommunications equipment sales during this period.

To address this slowdown, and survive, major firms in the market embarked on mergers and acquisitions from the mid-2000s to achieve economies of scale. Alcatel, a French firm with a 108-year history, and Lucent Technologies, a 137-year-old US firm, officially announced their merger in April 2006. The combined Alcatel-Lucent was established in December 2006. In June 2006, Nokia and Siemens agreed to launch a new joint venture by merging their telecom equipment arms and formed Nokia Siemens Networks (NSN) in April 2007. Moreover, Nortel, which had posted USD 29.8 billion in sales in 2000, the world's highest, filed for bankruptcy protection in January 2009 and sold its LTE and CDMA business divisions to NSN in June 2009. In 2011, Motorola was split into Motorola Solutions (the telecommunications infrastructure branch) and Motorola Mobility Holdings (mobile phones), with Motorola Mobility taken over by Google. Excluding Cisco, the main business of which is data communication equipment, and NEC, which had a large established domestic market, Ericsson was essentially the only survivor of the industry turmoil in the 2000s.

Figure 8.1 compares the annual sales of Huawei and Ericsson. Ericsson witnessed a drastic 40 percent drop in sales from 2000 to 2002.[5] From the mid-2000s, its sales improved; it recouped its global telecommunications infrastructure investment and has recently showed considerable growth. However, owing to its overwhelming sales growth in China's domestic market, Huawei was able to

---

[3] Telecommunications equipment includes landline/mobile telecommunications infrastructure (e.g., switching systems and base transceiver stations), user equipment (e.g., mobile phones) and enterprise network infrastructure (e.g., routers, hubs, and modems).

[4] "Major firms" refers to the telecommunications equipment manufacturers that posted at least USD 10 billion sales in telecommunications equipment as of 2000. These are Nortel, Ericsson, Nokia, Lucent, Cisco, Motorola, Alcatel, Siemens, and NEC.

[5] The main reason for Ericsson's sales drop in the early 2000s was the downturn in the telecommunications infrastructure industry; however, a portion of this decrease can be attributed to the spin-off of its mobile phone division. Ericsson spun off its mobile phone division in 2001 and conducted business through Sony Ericsson, a joint venture with Sony, since 2001. According to Ericsson's annual report, mobile phones accounted for 20.5 percent (SEK 56.3 million) of its total sales, and equipment systems (telecommunications infrastructure) accounted for 70.9 percent (SEK 194.1 million) in 2000. Sales for equipment systems declined by 4 percent to SEK 187.8 million in 2001 and by 30 percent to SEK 132.0 million in 2002.

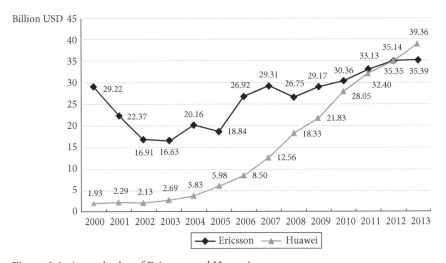

Figure 8.1 Annual sales of Ericsson and Huawei

Note: Ericsson's annual sales are obtained from the Compustat Global Database. Huawei's annual sales are from its annual reports (Huawei 2004, 2006, 2007, 2008, 2011, 2012). Its annual sales for 2009 and 2010, which are reported in terms of Chinese yuan, are translated into US dollars using the closing exchange rate on December 31 of each year.

overtake Ericsson finally in terms of annual sales in 2012.[6] In the early 2000s, the Chinese telecommunications industry, particularly mobile telecommunications, continued to expand despite the global slowdown.

Nevertheless, Huawei's initial success was mostly in fixed-line market and less so in the Chinese mobile telecommunications market. Although it made significant strides in the GSM value-added service market (e.g., its short message center and mobile intelligent network), it was nowhere near breaking into the GSM core infrastructure market, which had been dominated by multinational firms, including Ericsson. In addition, it missed the opportunity to participate in the new domestic CDMA market, which forced it to look to the international market. Fortunately, its R&D and its international market efforts in the late 1990s started to pay off from the early 2000s. In 2003, Huawei won the dual-band GSM network contract from MegaFon, the largest wireless operator in Russia, and Etisalat's UMTS network contract in the UAE, the first UMTS network project in the Middle East and the Arab world. It also built the world's first automatically switched optical network (ASON) for Telemar and Oi in Brazil. In the early 2000s, Huawei made inroads into the European market, and in 2001, it built optical transport networks for PfalzKom in Germany and Neuf in France.

---

[6] Unlike Ericsson, Huawei's mobile phone business is internal. In 2012, the mobile phone sales contributed 22 percent of Huawei's total sales.

To push forward with its global expansion, Huawei undertook radical organizational restructuring in the mid-2000s. After failing to obtain the British Telecom supplier certification in 2003, it commenced a series of painstaking reforms, transforming its hierarchical, functional structure into a multidimensional matrix structure (Fan 2010b). It became more flexible and more capable of responding swiftly to the global market demand. To finance its business expansion and to address the increasing cost-consciousness of customers, Huawei obtained credit lines in 2004—USD 10 billion from the China Development Bank and USD 600 million from the Export-Import Bank of China. It was further supported by Sinosure's export buyer's credit insurance.

In 2004, Huawei finally entered the first-tier international market—Europe's third-generation mobile network—when it beat Ericsson to win the Telfort WCDMA contract in the Netherlands. The cost-saving advantages of its products, rather than their low cost, stood out for Telfort. Its unique and innovative solution, a distributed base station system, allowed Telfort to upgrade its existing base stations with WCDMA technologies instead of building new ones (Fan 2010b). With Huawei, Telfort could not only save one-third of the total cost of ownership for the network but also sidestep the environmental issues that had impeded its rapid deployment. In 2005, Huawei was selected as one of the priority suppliers of British Telecom for its 21st Century Network program. With its successful entry into the first-tier market, its 2005 overseas revenue exceeded its Chinese market revenue for the first time. In the following year, it was awarded the largest GSM network contract in the southern hemisphere by Brazil's Vivo and a WCDMA network contract by the world's largest mobile operator, Vodafone. It also entered the US and Japanese markets. In 2007, Huawei ranked eighth on the list of the top 10 telecommunications equipment manufacturers for the first time.

Finally, Huawei rose to a leading position in the fourth-generation mobile technology era and delivered one of the world's first LTE networks for TeliaSonera of Norway in 2009. It emerged as the world's second-largest provider of telecommunications infrastructure in 2009, rapidly narrowing the gap with the global leader, Ericsson. Huawei ultimately topped Ericsson in terms of annual revenue in 2012, and in 2013 it increased its revenue leadership, achieving USD 39.36 billion in revenue, compared to Ericsson's USD 35.39 billion.

8.3 Data, Methodology, and Hypotheses

8.3.1 Patent Data and Making Sense of Comparison

Indicators based on R&D expenditures, patent statistics, and new product introductions, or a combination of these indicators, among others, have been widely used to measure a firm's technological capabilities (Schoenecker and

Swanson 2002). Given that patents and patent citations provide detailed information on the inventions and cover a relatively long period as well as virtually all fields of technology (Griliches 1990), they have been accepted as a reliable, though not perfect, source of information to measure firms' technological capabilities (Narin et al. 1987; Patel and Pavitt 1997). Hence, we analyzed the patents and related citations of Huawei and Ericsson for our study (European patents from 2000 to 2010).

The results of patent analysis may vary greatly depending on the data employed. Hence, we built an appropriate patent data set. First, patents filed by Huawei and Ericsson with various national authorities were obtained from the PATSTAT database, which was created by the EPO. The total number of patents from 2000 to 2010 show that both firms filed a majority of their patents with three common national authorities, namely, EPO, the United States Patent and Trademark Office (USPTO), and the Chinese State Intellectual Property Office (SIPO). These national authorities report patent statistics to the PATSTAT database (Table 8.1). Huawei filed the most patents with SIPO, followed by EPO and USPTO, whereas Ericsson filed the highest number with EPO, followed by USPTO and SIPO.

Huawei exceeded Ericsson in terms of the number of patents filed at all three patent offices: SIPO in 2001, USPTO in 2007, and EPO in 2008. The results provide strong evidence that Huawei's technological catch-up with Ericsson is real and not a spurious result from biased patent data. However, Huawei's technological strength could be overestimated based on Chinese patents owing to its home country advantage and underestimated in terms of US patents because of its low business presence in the North American market.[7] Thus, European patents were used, rather than Chinese or US patents, for further analysis to ensure objectivity of the analysis of the two firms' technological strength.

Establishing that these two companies are similar enough to be compared is necessary; that is, confirming that Huawei and Ericsson compete in similar technological areas is vital. Otherwise, the comparison would not make any sense (Joo and Lee 2010). This essential prerequisite process can be conducted by comparing the technological characteristics of the two companies. Given that the level of competition between the two firms tends to increase when they rely on increasingly similar sets of technology (Podolny et al. 1996), the level of technological similarity of the two firms' patent portfolio was analyzed using the measures of technological proximity (Jaffe 1986); the specific formula to measure this is explained in Joo et al. (2016). Technological proximity takes a value between 0 and 1. The more similar the two firms are in their technological specialization, the higher is the value that proximity takes.

---

[7] In 2009, Huawei's sales in the North American market were USD 408 million, which is less than 2 percent of its total sales according to a report published in 2010 in the Magazine, BusinessWeek.com.

Table 8.1 Patent filings of Huawei and Ericsson registered at EPO, USPTO, and SIPO, 2000–2010

	Patent office	2000	2001	2002	2003	2004	2005	2006	2007	2008	2009	2010	Total
Huawei	EPO	3	28	37	62	85	219	563	647	627	90	3	2,364
	USPTO	1	4	12	54	56	96	226	314	448	528	75	1,814
	SIPO	181	452	1,004	1,480	2,098	3,484	5,668	4,523	3,402	666	n.a.	22,958
Ericsson	EPO	871	766	606	431	521	523	618	658	378	16	2	5,390
	USPTO	890	616	272	333	489	406	231	288	230	95	7	3,857
	SIPO	601	193	248	254	353	379	443	299	91	n.a.	n.a.	2,861

Source: Author's calculation based on the PATSTAT database 2010 September edition.

The technological proximity of Huawei and Ericsson at the International Patent Classification subclass level is calculated to stand at 0.912. This value is high and suggests that the two firms compete fiercely in similar technological fields. The average technological proximity among US manufacturing firms within the same sector is 0.75 (Jaffe 1989), and the technological proximity between Samsung and Sony, two major competitors in the global electronics industry, is 0.98 (Joo and Lee 2010). Thus, we can say that comparing these two companies is sensible given the high degree of technological proximity of the two companies.

8.3.2 Main Hypotheses and Measurement

The patents and related citations of Huawei and Ericsson were analyzed to investigate whether a latecomer catches up with its forerunners by developing similar or different technologies compared with those by the forerunners. The main hypothesis of this study is that Huawei has caught up with Ericsson in terms of market shares by developing different technologies.

This contrast between the similar versus different technologies can be discussed using the literature on technological catch-up. Early literature (Lall 2000; Kim 1980; Westphal, Kim, and Dahlman 1985; Hobday 1995) observed that the latecomer tends to catch up with the advanced countries by assimilating and adapting the latter's obsolete technology. This is consistent with the product life cycle theory (Vernon 1966). However, an emerging view (Lee and Lim 2001; Lee 2013) points out that the latecomer does not simply follow the advanced countries' path of technological development but sometimes skips certain stages or even creates its own path that is different from those of the forerunners. This observation is consistent with the idea of leapfrogging (Perez and Soete 1988); some latecomers may be able to leapfrog older vintages of technology, bypass heavy investments in previous technological systems or stages, and make pre-emptive investments in emerging technologies to catch up with advanced countries in new markets.

Several studies have confirmed leapfrogging or path creating through case studies in East Asia (Lee et al. 2005; Mu and Lee 2005). However, studies that have quantitatively analyzed whether laggards successfully catch up with forerunners based on the same or different technologies are rare. Similarly, studies that have suggested a method to assess whether the technological path of the laggard is the same or different from the forerunners have not been found.

In this study, four criteria were used to assess whether the technologies were the same or different. First, the quality of the two firms' patents, which is measured by the average number of received citations, was examined to determine if the latecomer's patent quality catches up with or even surpasses that of the forerunner. Second, the mutual citations between the two rival firms' patents were examined to establish the extent through which they rely on each other as their source of knowledge. For instance, if Huawei's patents cite many Ericsson patents, then Huawei is imitating and relying on Ericsson. Third, we address the question of whether the two firms rely on the same sets of knowledge from third-party firms in their invention activities, and thus measure the "indirect dependence" between the two firms using the common citation rates suggested by Mowery et al. (1998). This common citation rate measures the similarity of two firms' knowledge sourcing (or impacts) at a more micro level. Fourth, the two rival firms' degree of self-citation, which can measure their self-reliance on their own knowledge base, was examined (Lee 2013: 109–20). This study focuses on the latecomer's degree of self-citation to assess the extent to which it becomes independent of external knowledge sources and self-reliant on its own knowledge base.

The catching-up process has a dynamic nature. Hence, this study's grand hypothesis is that the latecomer firm may imitate the forerunner by incorporating the same or similar technologies in its early stages but should be able to create new or different technologies from the forerunner firm to achieve an overtaking. The logic behind this idea is simple. If a latecomer continues to follow the same path as its forerunner, the latecomer would always remain behind the forerunning company, unless it runs much faster than its target, which is not easy. Thus, an alternative for the latecomer is to explore a short-cut or a different path. Lee (2013: xxi) observed that "just trying to emulate or replicate the practices of the forerunning economies is not enough, and catch-up realizes only if you take a different path."

The present study also investigates whether Huawei relies more on recent or old technologies than the incumbents by examining the latter's citation lags and whether the former relies more on scientific knowledge than the latter in terms of their patents' citation in scientific literature. These two aspects were verified by an analysis using a large sample of firms in Park and Lee (2015), and this study does a similar job for the case of these two comparable firms. A possible hypothesis is that the latecomer would rely more on scientific literature when catching-up because science literature is not protected by any intellectual property rights forms and is freely available for use. Thus, the latecomer has a reason to explore fully useful knowledge from scientific commons in its catch-up efforts.

The latecomer may try to rely less on old technologies protected by patents, which indicates continued reliance on the incumbents. Such attitude is also desirable to avoid any possible patent dispute with the incumbents. Thus, the latecomers have a reason to explore a technological trajectory that is less connected to existing technologies. Thus, their citation pattern will be geared more toward recent patents. The average cycle time of their patent portfolio would be shorter than those of the incumbents. This hypothesis is interesting given that some studies (Park and Lee 2006; Lee 2013) found that the latecomer countries tend to specialize in short cycle technology-based sectors. These studies are concerned with across-sector specialization, whereas the present study explores the twisted question of whether a latecomer firm's patent portfolio would show a shorter average cycle time than those of the incumbents in the same sector.

8.4 Catching-up with Similar or Different Technologies

8.4.1 Is Huawei's Technology of Higher Quality than that of Ericsson?

Not all patents are equal. The distribution of patent quality, technological impact, and the economic value is highly skewed. Few high-quality patents are available, and most patents have low quality. Therefore, quality, not quantity, counts.

The quality of two firms' patents can be measured by the average number of citations received; the more citations a patent receives, the higher the consideration that it is valuable or worthy of use (Albert et al. 1991; Hall et al. 2005). When we measure and compare the average number of citations that the two firms' patents received, we find that Huawei has remained ahead of Ericsson in terms of the average number of citations received since the early 2000s (Joo et al. 2016). Huawei filed its first European patent in 2000. It has outclassed Ericsson in terms of patent quality from the beginning and remained in the lead ever since.

This phenomenon may be partly attributed to the differences in patent strategies of Huawei and Ericsson, especially in the early 2000s. Huawei may have filed EPO patents for only a few of its high-quality inventions because Europe was not its home market and the cost of an EPO patent application was far greater than that of a Chinese patent application. By contrast, Ericsson may have filed EPO patents for most of its inventions because the European market was its home market.[8] Ericsson's patent strategy, which is filing a few good-quality patents and many low-quality patents, may have resulted in Ericsson's low average patent quality.

Notwithstanding the difference in the two firms' patent strategies, the result of this study provides some evidence that Huawei caught up with Ericsson in terms of patent quality no later than the mid-2000s. Huawei filed a comparable number of EPO patents as Ericsson from the mid-2000s but stayed ahead of Ericsson with respect to patent quality. Thus, Huawei filed as many quality EPO patents as Ericsson did.

Catching up with patent quality than patent quantity is more difficult for a latecomer. When a latecomer focuses on the practical implementation of an intellectual foundation laid down by its forerunners, it may be more successful in generating a large number of patents applications. However, doing so may restrain

---

[8] Table 8.1 shows that Ericsson filed EPO patents for most of its inventions, whereas Huawei filed EPO patents for only a few of its inventions in the early 2000s.

the latecomer from catching up with the quality of patents because the latecomer's developments would reinforce the economic and technological value of the basic principles invented by the forerunners. Thus, the catch-up in patent quality requires a latecomer to produce somewhat radical innovations, which is exactly what Huawei did.

The catch-up of patent quality can be achieved by taking a different technological path than the one taken by the forerunners or by taking the same path. Achieving both is rare because the two paths require a latecomer to adopt different and contradicting strategies and capabilities. If a latecomer tries to climb the same technological ladder after the forerunning incumbents, most of the important and valuable inventions on the current and higher steps are frequently preempted by the forerunners, which leaves the latecomer minimal chance. Thus, taking a bypass or a different technological ladder may allow a latecomer to circumvent such difficulties in catching up with patent quality. However, this would be a highly challenging and risky undertaking. In the former case, a latecomer often takes an exploitative innovation strategy by carefully selecting existing state-of-the-art technologies and focusing on refining and optimizing them to enhance efficiency. In the latter case, it needs to assume an explorative innovation strategy by deliberately taking the risk of uncertainties and searching wide sets of knowledge sources to discover a new breed of ideas (March 1991).

Developing similar or different technologies compared to the forerunning incumbents must have been an important decision for Huawei. Its patent quality catch-up shows that the company made a conscious decision at some point although what exactly this decision was is unclear.

8.4.2 Does Huawei Keep Imitating Ericsson? Mutual Citations

Latecomers usually start the technological catch-up by acquiring and assimilating forerunners' knowledge; subsequently, they make improvements or sometimes make innovations (Kim 1980). They are unlikely to sever their reliance on the forerunners' knowledge given that they do not have their own innovations. Hence, the latecomer's break from the forerunners' knowledge can be a good signal because such break signifies that the latecomer has its own innovations. The level of technological dependence between the catching-up firm and the leading firm can be analyzed by the degree of mutual citations (Joo and Lee 2010).[9]

Our measurement of this level of dependence suggests that Huawei is becoming less and less dependent on Ericsson.[10] However, negligible citations by

---

[9] The exact method for defining and measuring this variable is explained in Joo et al. (2016).
[10] Actual trend of this variable is in Joo et al. (2016). Huawei also cited the patents of other forerunners (Nokia, Lucent, Nortel, Alcatel, and Siemens). Its technological dependence on the other forerunners also showed a generally decreasing trend.

Ericsson have been found on the patents of Huawei, and Ericsson's technological reliance on Huawei has remained unchanged. Anyway, these results corroborate the argument that Huawei has taken a different path from Ericsson.

8.4.3 Is Huawei Having the Same Knowledge Sourcing and Impacts as Ericsson?

While mutual citations can measure the "direct dependence" between the two firms, we can also think of the "indirect dependence" between the firms by addressing the question of whether they rely on the knowledge from the same set of third-party firms in their invention activities. This idea of common citations between two firms is called the degree of technological overlap between the two firms, which was suggested by Mowery et al. (1998). This common citation rate measures the similarity of two firms' knowledge sourcing (or impacts) at a more micro level. This index measures the degree to which two firms' technologies are based on (citing) the same patents (knowledge sourcing aspect, called index A) and the degree to which two firms' patents are used (cited) by the same patents (knowledge impact aspect, called index B). Thus, the common citation rate (index A) measures the degree that both firms rely on a common pool of knowledge held by third-party firms, whereas the index B uses the citations received by the two firms and measures the degree that both firms have impacts on the same set of third-party firms.

It is calculated that the common citation index (A) measuring the degree of overlaps by these two firms in their knowledge sourcing is 0.045, whereas the common citation index (B) measuring the degree of overlaps by the two firms in their knowledge impacts is 0.026. This level of common citation rate is close to the average.[11] But it is very low compared to the common citation rate between Samsung and Sony, which is as high as 0.39 (citation made) and 0.32 (citation received) (Joo and Lee 2010), This implies that Huawei and Ericsson may not share the same knowledge sources, and their knowledge has had impact on different types of firms or innovations.

8.4.4 Is Huawei Getting Independent? Self-citations

A firm's ability to create new knowledge from its own knowledge base is an important aspect of its technological capability. Firms attempt to utilize their

---

[11] The average common citation rate between two firms randomly selected is between 0.01464 and 0.02413 (Mowery et al. 1998). The average common citation rate between pharmaceutical and biotechnology firms in in-vivo human therapeutics, which is a narrow area, is 0.0254 (Rothaermel and Boeker 2008).

internal knowledge base before relying on external sources because establishing in-house proprietary technologies is crucial to their technological competitiveness. The degree to which a firm is capable of drawing innovation from its own knowledge base can be measured by the ratio of self-citations of the firm's patents (i.e., citations directed to its own patents).[12] The higher a firm's technological capabilities are, the higher is its self-citation ratio (Lee 2013: 109–20).

In the meantime, if a latecomer follows a technological path with an industry-wide acceptance, it may become less dependent on each major forerunner's knowledge and become increasingly dependent on external knowledge sources by diversifying its knowledge sources. Hence, a latecomer's reduced technological reliance on each major forerunner does not directly imply that the latecomer has taken a bypass or a different technological ladder from the forerunners. Therefore, this reduced reliance needs to be further analyzed. Specifically, whether the latecomer has become less dependent on external knowledge sources as a whole or whether the latecomer has become more self-reliant on its own knowledge base should be investigated.

We, Joo et al. (2016), find that Huawei's self-citation ratio has been steadily increasing and eventually approaches that of Ericsson by the late 2000s. Thus, Huawei has become as self-reliant as Ericsson by increasingly developing technologies that are different from those of other firms, including Ericsson. The results support this study's argument that Huawei has been taking a different path from Ericsson.

8.5 Catching-up with More Recent and Scientific Knowledge

8.5.1 Huawei's Scientific Explorations (Citations in Non-patent Literature)

When a latecomer firm follows the technological ladder used by its forerunners, it tends to narrow its search space to locate the state-of-the-art technologies on which it can improve. However, a latecomer who takes a different technological ladder from its forerunners needs to challenge conventional dogma to create a de novo pathway. Given that the knowledge within or surrounding conventional dogma does not promote the questioning of conventions, the latecomer expands its search space widely to formulate unprecedented ideas and searches into a genuine principle. Therefore, a latecomer is more likely to conceive ideas from basic

---

[12] The self-citation ratio also reflects a firm's technological capabilities. The increasing self-citation ratio of Huawei can also be interpreted as Huawei's successful accumulation of technological capabilities.

research when it takes a different path and when it wants to stay away from patent disputes with incumbents.

The extent to which a firm draws ideas from basic research can be investigated by the number of citations directed to non-patent literature, most of which comprises scientific articles in academic journals. This extent reflects the proximity to basic research. The more ideas are taken from basic research, the more non-patent literature is cited.

Figure 8.2 provides the average number of citations directed to non-patent literature by the patents of Huawei and Ericsson. Huawei's patents had cited more non-patent literature than Ericsson's patents until recently. The result suggests that Huawei has been actively exploring basic research,[13] which is consistent with the idea that Huawei has been catching up by developing different technologies.

8.5.2 Huawei's Reliance on More Recent Technologies: Citation Lags

Backward citation lag measures how recent are the prior patents that a patent cites, whereas forward citation lag indicates how quickly a patent is cited by subsequent patents. The two indicators show how agile a firm is in assimilating new technologies to recreate them and how rapidly a firm's technologies are adopted for subsequent developments in the process of a technological catch-up.[14]

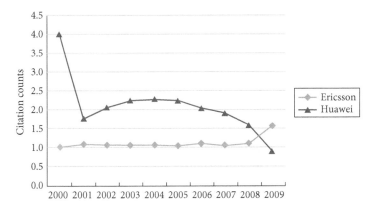

Figure 8.2 Average number of citations to scientific articles

Note: Using citations made to patents in PATSTAT and not EPO patents only.

[13] Exploring basic research is not an easy task, especially for a latecomer. Huawei may have been reaping the benefits of China's strong capabilities in basic research.
[14] A detailed explanation of how to define and measure these two variables is provided in Joo et al. (2016).

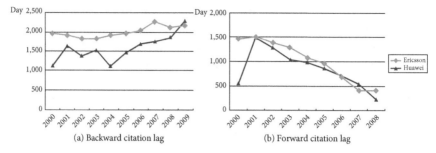

Figure 8.3 Backward and forward citation lags

Note: Using citations made to all the patents in PATSTAT and not EPO patents only.

Huawei had shown shorter backward and forward citation lags compared with Ericsson until recently (Figure 8.3). The results indicate that Huawei has focused on developing its technologies relying on more recent knowledge, which is consistent with the finding of Park and Lee (2015) with a bigger sample size. Though a bit different it can also be considered together with the finding by Park and Lee (2006) that the catch-up is more likely to take place in technological sectors with shorter technology cycles. A shorter backward citation lag shows that Huawei has been narrowing the technology gap with Ericsson by accelerating its technological progress with an up-to-date knowledge base. The shorter forward citation lag shows that Huawei's patents have had more immediate impact.

8.6 Summary and Concluding Remarks

This chapter raisesd the question of whether a latecomer firm catches up with a forerunning firm in market shares by using technologies that are similar to or different from those of the forerunners. It investigated the patents by Huawei and Ericsson and found that Huawei relied on Ericsson as a knowledge source in its early days but subsequently reduced this reliance and increased its self-citation ratio to become more independent. The results of mutual citations (direct dependence), common citations (indirect reliance), and self-citations provide strong evidence that Huawei has caught up with or overtook Ericsson by taking a different path.

Moreover, compared with Ericsson, Huawei developed its technologies by relying on more recent and scientific knowledge, and it utilized its technologies more quickly. The results of citations to scientific articles and citation lags show that Huawei has conducted extensive exploration of basic research and maintained up-to-date technologies to accomplish its technological catch-up. Overall, this study suggests that exploring a new and different technological path from that of the forerunners is a possible and viable catch-up strategy for a latecomer. The higher reliance on scientific articles by a latecomer, Huawei, makes sense because articles are free from intellectual property rights protection and litigations with incumbents, unlike patents. Also, a higher reliance on recent patents is consistent with the idea that a latecomer should try to minimize the reliance on old or existing knowledge (patents) owned by incumbents.

Moreover, Huawei's case re-confirms the hypothesis that a catch-up in technological capabilities tends to precede a catch-up in market shares, which was verified in the Samsung versus Sony case on consumer electronics by Joo and Lee (2010). Huawei overtook Ericsson in terms of both quantity and quality of patents before it did in terms of annual sales. In sum, the results suggest that Huawei's catch-up with Ericsson in the telecommunications equipment market is owing to not merely its cost advantage, the large domestic market, or the Chinese government's support but more importantly its technological strength and independence.

The present study contributes to the literature on innovation and catch-up studies in several ways. First, it is one of the first studies that used a quantitative method to assess whether a latecomer is taking the same or different technological path that its forerunners have taken. The lack of a proper yardstick has often impeded in-depth catch-up research. This study's method can be applied to other catch-up cases. Second, the study provides quantitative evidence that supports the assertion that a latecomer catches up with the forerunner and finally forges ahead by taking a different technological path from the forerunner. The argument should be further investigated using more cases before it can be applied generally. However, this study casts serious doubt on the idea that a latecomer can catch up simply by following the same technological path as the forerunner. Third, this study finds that some successful latecomer firms utilize basic research and up-to-date technologies more than the forerunning firm, which is contrary to the conventional impression. This idea, which also needs further investigation, suggests that a successful catching-up may happen quite differently from the expected. Strongly generalizable conclusions cannot be made based on a single case; however, this study has shed a new light on the process of a latecomer's innovation and catch-up.

PART III

PROSPECTS OF CATCH-UP AND LEAPFROGGING

9

Possibility of a Middle-Income Trap in China[1]

9.1 Introduction

Since the initiation of economic reform and the open door policy in 1978, China has achieved an impressive record of economic growth. Between 1978 and 2012, the GDP grew by nearly 10 percent and household income in urban and rural areas grew by 8 percent. By 2012, the GDP per capita had reached approximately USD 5,500, making China an upper middle-income country with its per capita income higher than 20 percent of the US (Figure 1-1B in Lee 2013). In 2020, reaching about 30 percent of the US per capita income but facing slowdown of growth even lower than 7 percent since the late 2010s, it is now subject to the possibility of the so-called middle-income trap (MIT), similar to other middle-income developing economies (Dollar et al. 2020). Several countries have attained middle-income status but have subsequently failed to achieve high-income status. Examples from Latin America include Brazil and Argentina, whose growth stalled in the 1980s and 1990s, respectively.[2] This chapter aims at assessing the possibility of China falling into a similar trap first by reviewing the literature to identify the relevant criteria and then by referring to the evidence available.

The MIT is a situation in which middle-income countries face a slowdown of growth as they get caught between low-wage manufacturers and high-wage innovators because their wage rates are too high to compete with low-wage exporters and the level of their technological capability is too low to enable them to compete with advanced countries (Lin 2012b; Williamson 2012; Yusuf and Nabeshima 2009; World Bank 2010, 2012). The risk of the MIT is not limited to select countries but is relevant to many countries in the world. The China Report by the World Bank (2012) compares the income levels of several countries (against that of the US) in 1960 with those in 2008. This analysis reveals that at least 30 countries have fallen into the MIT. Specifically, income growth is more

---

[1] This chapter is a substantially revised and updated version of an article, Keun Lee and Shi Li (2014), "Possibility of a Middle Income Trap in China: Assessment in Terms of the Literature on Innovation, Big Business and Inequality," *Frontiers of Economics in China*, 9(3), 370–97.

[2] See Lee and Kim (2009, Table 1) and Paus (2009).

China's Technological Leapfrogging and Economic Catch-up: A Schumpeterian Perspective. Keun Lee, Oxford University Press. © Keun Lee 2021. DOI: 10.1093/oso/9780192847560.003.0009

significantly slowed in upper middle-income countries or in countries with an income level of 20–30 percent of that of the US, which is the income level of China today.

Yao (2010) discusses the end of the Beijing Consensus, noting problems such as corruption, increasing inequality, and policy authoritarianism and warning against the possibility of China falling into the MIT. Many other studies have investigated the MIT in relation to China, such as Huang et al. (2013), Aiyar et al. (2013), Woo (2012), and Jankowska et al. (2012). Thus, examining the question of whether China will indeed fall into this trap should be an interesting task.

However, there is one difficulty—identifying the effective criteria for the assessment. Although several factors for economic growth and its slowdown are available, virtually no theory exists about why and how middle-income economies may be different (Aiyar et al. 2013). Aiyar et al. (2013) consider each factor and test its robustness by an econometric method. Following this idea, the present study develops its own criteria for this task by considering various factors and adopting only those verified as significant and robust determinants of economic growth in middle-income countries and those that are particularly relevant for China. For example, as discussed in Section 9.2, the literature finds political institution variables, such as democracy and the rule of law, important for economic growth in general and in low-income countries but insignificant in middle-income countries (Huang et al. 2013; Aiyar et al. 2013; Lee and Kim 2009). Hence, this study does not adopt this criterion to assess the MIT in China. Also, physical infrastructure or investment is significant for economic growth in middle-income countries (Aiyar et al. 2013), but China has been investing heavily in infrastructure and can be considered free from shortage of this factor. Hence, physical infrastructure would not be an interesting or meaningful criterion to assess the MIT in China.

As elaborated in Section 9.2, through a review of the relevant literature, this study identifies and justifies three criteria to assess the possibility of the MIT in China: (1) innovation and tertiary education, (2) big businesses, and (3) inequality. These criteria are all significant factors for economic growth in middle-income countries and particularly relevant for China (Lee and Kim 2009; Eichengreen, Park, and Shin 2013; Lee et al. 2013; Sylwester 2000; Jin and Lee 2013; Lee 2013). For instance, Lee and Kim (2009) find that basic institutions and primary and secondary education are significant factors for economic growth in low-income and lower middle-income countries, whereas innovation and tertiary education are significant factors in upper middle-income and high-income countries. Lee et al. (2013) find that having big businesses (e.g., Fortune Global 500-class companies) is key to becoming a high-income country, but many middle-income countries do not command a sufficient number of such companies and hence remain in the middle-income stage.

Certain variables may continue to be omitted but remain significant factors for economic growth in the middle-income stage of China. Despite this, this chapter has identified these factors from the existing literature involving a rigorous econometric method, after eliminating several other factors. This study is thus worthwhile on its own. The main findings and thus contributions of this study are that China is performing well in terms of the first two criteria of innovation and big businesses, but there is great uncertainty in the last criterion of whether China generates Kuznets curve-type dynamics of the growth–equality nexus.

The remainder of the chapter is arranged as follows. Section 9.2 discusses the criteria for assessment, and each subsection of Section 9.3 applies each of the three criteria to the case of China. Section 9.4 concludes the chapter.

9.2 Three Criteria to Assess Possibility of MIT in China

Considering that possibly diverse factors influencing economic growth exist, growth slowdowns could in principle be generated by numerous factors. Furthermore, as noted by Aiyar et al. (2013), virtually no theory explains why and how middle-income economies may be different. Thus, being agnostic about the causes of the MIT, Aiyar et al. (2013) consider as broad a range of factors as possible, such as demographic conditions; institutions; and industry and trade structures, including diversification, physical infrastructure, and macro-financial developments. They test whether each of these factors is particularly binding for middle-income countries. This approach may be a good start, and therefore, this chapter follows this line of direction in choosing the criteria to assess the possibility of the trap in China. Given that our goal is specific to China, we should also identify and justify criteria that are relevant or important to China.

In sum, the selection of criteria for assessment in this study is based on the idea that the criterion factors must first be binding for economic growth in a middle-income country by a well-established research method and must then be relevant and important to China. Furthermore, the relative rarity of the criterion in the literature would be more beneficial in terms of the degree of contribution. Therefore, this study uses the three criteria of innovation and high education, big businesses, and inequality. Before we discuss these criteria, we first discuss why this study does not consider other possible criteria, thereby justifying our own criteria.

One of the mostly widely considered variables in economic growth is "institution," and one may thus wonder why this variable is not considered in assessing the trap in China. In an increasingly larger body of research, institution is argued as an important factor for economic growth (Acemoglu, Johnson, and Robinson 2001, 2002; Rodrik et al. 2004). However, this variable has been criticized in terms of its robustness. For example, Glaeser et al. (2004) verified the robustness of human capital rather than institution. Another problem with the institution variable is that it can be measured in diverse aspects, such as rule of law, democracy, or political stability (order). These different aspects of institution may also be binding for only a particular stage of development. In this regard, certain studies find certain institutions unimportant for middle-income countries. Aiyar et al. (2013) find the rule of law an important factor for general growth slowdown but insignificant for middle-income countries. Huang et al. (2013) find the democracy variable to be insignificant for middle-income countries but political stability (order) to be significant for all income groups, from low-income to middle- and high-income groups. Lee and Kim (2009) find that political institution (checks and balances against rulers) is significant only for low- and lower middle-income countries, whereas for upper middle- and high-income groups, innovation and college education are significant. These studies suggest that neither rule of law nor democracy is particularly binding for middle-income countries, whereas political stability matters for every country. This finding may justify our omission of institution as a criterion to assess the MIT in China.

Other important factors may include the trade and industry structure and trade and financial liberalization. However, Aiyar et al. (2013) find that the significance of industry structure and export diversification variables disappear when they restrict the sample to middle-income countries, whereas they are all significant in the entire sample. Financial liberalization is problematic as Aiyar et al. (2013) find that a high level of financial inflow to GDP increases the probability of growth slowdown in middle-income countries, consistent with the episode of the liberalization crisis story observed in some countries. Huang et al. (2013) find the puzzling result that financial repression is negatively related to growth in middle-income countries but is positively related in high-income countries. However, a country such as Korea reached high-income status by the mid-1990s to join the rich-country club of the Organisation for Economic Co-operation and Development with a financial system that remained under government control and without external financial liberalization. The irrelevance of financial liberalization or privatization as a prerequisite for growth beyond the middle-income stage is also discussed by Rodrik (1996), who finds that the East Asian economies of Korea and Taiwan reached the high-income level without such liberalization, whereas Latin America embraced such liberalization but failed to sustain growth. On this ground, we do not consider financial openness as a to-be-met criterion in assessing China. We do not consider trade openness either because it is not robust for growth in upper middle- and high-income countries (Lee and Kim 2009). Further, China has already achieved a very high level of trade openness.

Given that we are now done with the variables of institution, industry and trade structure, and trade and financial openness, let us move on to consider several basic factors that can be identified from production functions, such as labor, capital, and technologies (innovation). Capital refers to physical infrastructure or investment share in GDP. This variable turns out to be binding for middle-income countries but not binding in general by Aiyar et al. (2013). However, the same study finds that China is free from this factor's influence because of its rather strong investment in physical infrastructure or a high share of investment in GDP. Labor refers to human capital, which is robust in general economic growth (Glaeser et al. 2004). However, when countries are divided into income groups, only higher education matters for upper middle- and high-income countries, whereas primary and secondary education matters for low-income and lower middle-income countries (Lee and Kim 2009). Eichengreen et al. (2013) also find human capital and innovation important, especially tertiary education, for upper middle-income countries. Given that China is already an upper middle-income country, this study considers this criterion of higher education and innovation for China.

This criterion of innovation and college education is most consistent with the original concern expressed by the term "MIT," because numerous studies consider the MIT to occur as middle-income countries get caught between low-wage manufacturers and high-wage innovators because their wage rates are too high to compete with low-wage exporters and their level of technological capability is too low to enable them to compete with advanced countries (Lin 2012b; Williamson 2012; Yusuf and Nabeshima 2009; World Bank 2010, 2012). In other words, the MIT phenomenon is a problem of growth slowdown because of weak innovation.

A World Bank (2005: 11) assessment of the reform decade of the 1990s also observes that growth-oriented actions, such as technological catch-up and the encouragement of risk taking, may be needed for faster accumulation and recognizes technological innovation as one of the most serious bottlenecks of growth in many countries, especially in the middle-income countries of Latin America. Lee and Mathews (2010) also compare the East Asian experience with the elements of the Washington Consensus to argue that the mixed results of the consensus are related to missing or neglected policies, such as technological policies and revolutions in higher education.

Figure 9.1A shows the R&D-to-GDP ratio of countries at different income levels. Although the figure seems to indicate a positive correlation between income levels and the R&D-to-GDP ratio, the ratios are largely flat among middle-income countries, or countries with per capita incomes between USD 1,000 and USD 10,000. In other words, the ratio does not increase proportionally with per capita income in this group of countries, suggesting that the flat relationship is a root cause of the MIT, as noted in Lee (2013) by the same graph.

A similar conclusion can be derived by examining the number of US patents filed by countries. In the early 1980s, when the income level of Korea was similar to those of Brazil and Argentina, the number of US patent applications by Koreans was approximately 50, within the range of other middle-income countries, such as Brazil and Argentina (Lee and Kim 2009; table 1). In the 1980s and 1990s, Korean applications increased rapidly to more than 10 times the average of other

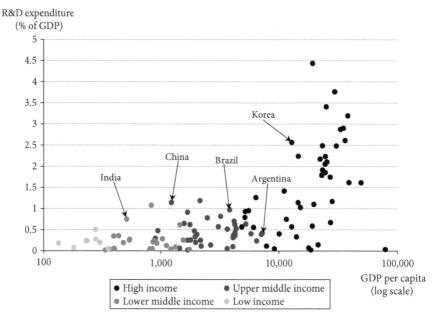

Figure 9.1A Ratio of R&D expenditure to GDP (2001–2005 averages)
Source: Author's calculation based on the data from the World Bank and UNESCO.

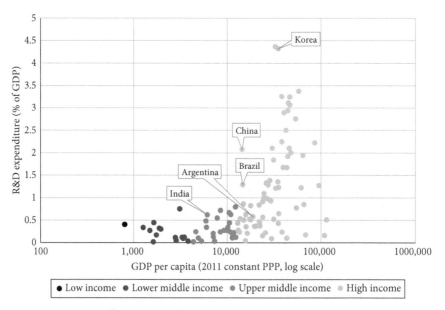

Figure 9.1B Ratio of R&D expenditure to GDP (2014–2018 averages)
Source: Author's calculation based on the data from the World Bank and UNESCO.

middle-income countries where incomes remained relatively flat. In 2000, Korea and Taiwan filed approximately 5,000 US patent applications, whereas other middle- or lower-income countries, including Brazil and Argentina, filed less than 500 per year (Lee and Kim 2009). In other words, the difference between the more successful Asian economies and the less successful Latin American economies (or the reversal of fortune between these two groups of countries) can be explained by the amount of priority given to the enhancement of long-term growth potentials, particularly innovation capabilities (Lee and Kim 2009; Lee 2013).

Although this study examines innovation and higher education as a factor for sustaining economic growth in middle-income countries, a factor of inequality also requires attention because excessive inequality may be detrimental to economic growth in the long run. Whereas the literature that follows the pioneering work of Kuznets (1955) has concentrated on the causal effect of economic growth on income distribution, the other stream of literature influenced by Kaldor (1955) emphasizes the opposite causal link from income distribution to economic growth. The most common arguments for a negative causality from income inequality to economic growth are summarized as follows (Jin and Lee 2013): (1) greater income inequality increases the demand for redistributive policies and hence distorts incentives for working and investing (Alesina and Rodrik 1994; Persson and Tabellini 1994); (2) in imperfect capital markets, a more unequal income distribution reduces opportunities for accumulating human capital and physical assets because more people are credit-constrained (Banerjee and Newman 1993; Fishman and Simhon 2002); and (3) worsening income inequality may lead to sociopolitical instability, thereby harming the investment environment (Alesina and Perotti 1996).

Given that cross-section regressions (Alesina and Rodrik 1994; Perotti 1996; Deininger and Squire 1998; Sylwester 2000) all found a negative relationship across countries between inequality and growth, and given that a fast economic growth in China has been accompanied by worsening income and regional inequality (Riskin, Zhao, and Li 2001; Li and Yue 2004), the current situation and trend of inequality in China should be assessed to judge the possibility of growth slowdown in China. Variant estimates indicate that income inequality has significantly increased in both urban and rural China. Inequality itself is an important aspect of the performance of an economy, let alone its possibly negative impact on growth. This is exactly the idea of the so-called Kuznets curve, that income inequality and per capita GDP have a relation in the form of an inverted U: income inequality increases over time while a country develops; when a certain income level is attained, income inequality begins to decrease. Thus, given that China aims to claim itself as a decent upper middle- or high-income country, inequality should be controlled as well.

Finally, the criterion of big business in assessing the MIT is quite new in literature. The only research that verifies by a rigorous econometric method the importance of big businesses in economic growth in and beyond the middle-income stage is by Lee et al. (2013). Their study finds that many middle-income countries command an insufficient number of big businesses, one of the reasons for their persistence in the middle-income stage. An alternative to big business is SMEs. The World Bank provided targeted assistance to SMEs in developing countries (Beck et al. 2005), such as more than USD 10 billion over 1998 to 2002 and USD 1.3 billion in 2003 (World Bank 2002, 2004). However, World Bank researchers Beck et al. (2005) fail to confirm a robust relationship between SMEs and per capita income growth when they control for endogeneity. They find certain positive but weak correlations without controlling for endogeneity and no significance when endogeneity is controlled.

Thus, given the evidence on the importance of big business and no evidence of SMEs, assessing China in this aspect would be interesting. China is one of the largest economies, second only to the US. As a large economy, it is expected to support numerous big businesses similar to the US and Japan. If China fails to generate a comparable number of big businesses, it is likely to be not a rich giant but a poor giant.

9.3 Innovation and Higher Education: Criterion One

As stated in the introduction, one criterion in assessing the ability of China to move beyond the MIT is whether the country is sufficiently innovative to achieve a certain level of technological capability backed up by an adequate emphasis on higher or tertiary education. In general, our answer to this question is that China appears to be performing well. In this regard, literature has already noted several unique features of the Chinese industry and firms in building technological capabilities and promoting industrial development. Chapter 5 of this book and Lee et al. (2011, 2013) note that unique Chinese features include the following three elements: (1) parallel learning from foreign direct investment (FDI) firms to promote indigenous companies; (2) an emphasis on "forward engineering" (the function of university spin-off firms) in contrast to the reverse engineering of Korea and Taiwan; and (3) the acquisition of technology and brands via international mergers and acquisitions (M&As). These three elements may be regarded as comprising the Beijing model because they have not been explicitly adopted by Korea and Taiwan (Lee et al. 2011). A brief summary of these three elements is given below.

Promotion of Indigenous Firms by Learning from FDI. China took advantage of its large market size to pressure foreign partners to transfer core technology to local partners. Thus, indigenous manufacturers emerged and competed directly with JVs in the mid-1990s, initially in rural markets and subsequently in urban markets. This process is called "parallel learning" (Eun et al. 2006). Although similar diffusion of knowledge also occurred in Southeast Asian countries, China was more successful in turning diffusion into the promotion of indigenous companies.

Promotion of Academy-Run Enterprises in Forward Engineering. China has successfully reared several national champion firms in high-technology sectors, and these firms have all been established by and affiliated with academic institutions. The direct involvement of academic institutions in industrial business is called "forward engineering" (Eun et al. 2006; Lu 2000). Forward engineering is a *top-down* mode in which creators (academic institutions) who already possess scientific knowledge process nascent knowledge until it can be applied to commercial uses. Forward engineering is an inherently Chinese characteristic that differentiates China from other East Asian countries..

Acquisition of Foreign Technologies and Brands by M&As. Since the mid-2000s, Chinese companies have actively invested overseas. One of their motivations is to acquire foreign technologies and brands, as evidenced by many M&As targeting foreign companies in the manufacturing sector. This strategy aims to save time for catch-up considering that building brands and technologies of one's own takes a long time and great effort.

Although the above is a qualitative account of China's success in technological learning and upgrading, many quantitative indications are also available as discussed below.

First, we can consider the R&D-to-GDP ratio, a basic measure of the innovation efforts of a country. China strongly pushed for considerable R&D expenditure and thus surpassed the 1 percent threshold ratio of R&D to GDP in 2000, earlier than the majority of middle-income countries in Latin America did.[3] The spending of China on R&D as a percentage of GDP, known as R&D intensity, more than doubled from 0.6 percent in 1995 to over 1.3 percent in 2003 (Figure 9.1A). This increase has accelerated since the 2000s and is now over 2.0 percent. Figure 9.1A shows that China is an outlier among middle-income countries with a high ratio of R&D to GDP. Further, several important points can be made by comparing Figure 9.1A (2001–2005) and Figure 9.1B (2014–2018). In Figure 9.1A, China just crossed the 1,000 dollar bar to join the lower middle income countries and its R&D-to-GDP ratio also just hit above the 1 percent benchmark, far higher than comparable economies. In Figure 9.1B, for the period 2014–2018, China's progress was impressive, crossing the 10,000 dollar line and recording R&D-to-GDP ratio higher than 2 percent, which is even higher than some of the high-income economies.

---

[3] From Lee (2011).

Because of this massive investment in R&D, China rapidly increased its flow of patents. The average growth rate of domestic invention patenting increased, from approximately 17 percent in the 1990s to approximately 49 percent in the 2000s (Table 4 of Lee 2010). The number of patent applications abroad (particularly in the US) also increased. The number of US patents filed by China reached more than 2,500 in 2010, greater than that of US patents filed by other middle-income countries (less than 300 patents per year) (Table 9.1). In terms of the growth rate of patents, China ranked first in the world in the 2000s, whereas Korea was the first in the 1990s. During the 10 years from 2010 to 2019 the number increased almost 10 times to reach 21,726, higher than Germany (21,074) and close to Korea (22,183), which is now ranked third after Japan.

Another important comparative criterion is whether China measures up to the three important yardsticks of technological catch-up (Lee and Kim 2010) followed by Japan, Korea, and Taiwan in the past: (a) whether resident patenting catches up with non-resident patenting in a host country, (b) whether regular invention patents catch up with utility model patents (petite patents), and (c) whether corporate patenting catches up with individual inventor patenting. Lee (2010) highlights that all three patterns of catch-up were observed in China in the mid-2000s. In terms of the number of patent applications, the share of domestic inventors outgrew that of foreigners in 2003, with domestic inventors filing more than 50,000 applications. In 2004, the number of regular invention patents exceeded that of utility model patents. In 2007, the number of patent applications by corporations exceeded that of applications by individual inventors, signifying the growing importance of corporate innovation.

In terms of the tertiary school enrollment ratio, China was at 3.4 percent in 1990, lower than that of the average of 13.5 percent of nine other middle-income countries in 1980. However, it reached 20 percent, close to the average of nine other middle-income countries, in the 2000s (Lee 2010). This remarkable progress can be explained by the revolution in higher education in the late 1990s and by the increase in the number of students who enter college (20 percent annually) since 1998. The emphasis on higher education is matched by the increasing publication of scientific papers. The number of Science Citation Index journal papers by Chinese authors increased 10 times, approximately 60,000 in 2005 from 6,000 in 1988, with the average growth rate rapidly increasing (Zhou and Leydesdorff 2006). The citation rate of papers with Chinese addresses for corresponding authors is also exponentially growing (King, 2004). Further updates into the 2010s about the publication is discussed in Chapter 5 by referring to Table 5.3 which shows that China is the top or above the US in the number of publication in key scientific fields.

Another important indicator of the technological strength of China is the cycle time of technologies measured according to the US patents filed by Chinese entities. Cycle time refers to the speed with which technologies change or become

Table 9.1 US patents granted to select economies, 1981–2019

Country	1981	1985	1990	1995	2000	2005	2008	2009	2010	2015	2019
US	39,218	39,556	47,391	55,739	85,068	74,637	77,502	82,382	107,792	147,593	175,633
Japan	8,389	12,746	19,525	21,764	31,295	30,341	33,682	35,501	44,814	53,382	54,602
Germany	6,304	6,718	7,614	6,600	10,235	9,011	8,914	9,000	12,363	18,765	21,074
Taiwan	80	174	732	1,620	4,667	5,118	6,339	6,642	8,238	12,270	12,161
Korea	17	41	225	1,161	3,314	4,352	7,548	8,762	11,671	18,362	22,183
China	2	1	47	62	119	402	1,225	1,655	2,657	9,957	21,726
India	6	10	23	37	131	384	634	679	1,098	4,589	7,406
Brazil	23	30	41	63	98	77	101	103	175	450	607
Malaysia	1	3	3	7	42	88	152	158	202	363	385

Source: US PTO.

obsolete over time and the speed and frequency at which new technologies emerge (Park and Lee 2006). A technology-based sector with a short cycle time relies less on existing technologies and can thus leverage the opportunities brought by new technologies. Lee (2013) argues that qualified latecomers have significant advantages in targeting technological sectors with short cycle times and specializing in these sectors because a short cycle of technologies implies that dominance by the incumbent is often disrupted and that new technologies always present new opportunities. Minimal reliance on existing technologies indicates low entry barriers and high profitability associated with few collisions with the technologies of advanced countries, minimal royalty payments, and even first- or fast-mover advantages or product differentiation (Lee 2013).

The technological development in Korea (Lee 2013) shows the increasing specialization of Korean industries based on short cycle times. The Korean economy began with labor-intensive (long-cycle technology) industries, such as apparel or shoe industries, in the 1960s. The economy then moved toward the short- or medium-cycle sectors of low-end consumer electronics and automobile assemblies in the 1970s and 1980s and then even further to the shorter cycle sectors of telecommunications equipment, memory chips, and digital TVs in the 1990s. Korean industries have kept moving into shorter-cycle technologies and have thus achieved technological diversification.

We can discuss the actual trends in the cycle time of technologies as calculated from the US patents held by selected economies, such as Korea, Taiwan, and China. For example, a value of eight as the average cycle time indicates that the average cycle time of patents is eight years (i.e., the patents held by Korea and Taiwan tend to cite eight-year-old patents on average) and that the related technologies are considered outdated or useless after eight years. Since the mid-1980s, Korea and Taiwan have shifted to technologies with increasingly short cycles. Therefore, the average cycle time of the patents held by Korea and Taiwan was shortened from eight to six or seven years by the late 1990s. This duration was two to three years shorter than the average cycle time of patents held by European G5 countries, the patents of which had had cycle times of 9–10 years since the late 1980s because of their strong performance in high value-added long-cycle sectors, such as pharmaceuticals and machine tools. Consequently, the patent portfolios of Korea and Taiwan completely differ from those of advanced countries. We consider the mid-1980s as an important turning point during which Korea and Taiwan achieved a sustained catch-up beyond the middle-income stage. Both economies reached the upper middle-income level during this period, and the GDP per capita of Korea reached 25 percent of that of the US. Since then, Korea and Taiwan have continued to increase their R&D expenditures, and their R&D-to-GDP ratio surpassed the 1 percent level. Along with upgrading their technological capabilities, these economies shifted to short cycle technology-based sectors, such as information technology products.

After achieving technological catch-up, the specialization of Korea and Taiwan had to either reach maturity or turn to long-cycle technologies. Figure 9.2 shows the trend of the normalized values of the average cycle time of technologies calculated from the patents registered in the US. It is shown that after both economies reached their bottom in the early 2000s, their technologies turned toward long cycles, such as biological or science-based technologies. China is following a similar path with about 10 years' lag, making a transition from short to long cycle technologies. Such strategy can be considered a "detour" because latecomer countries do not directly and immediately replicate the path and industries of advanced economies that specialize in long-cycle technologies, such as Germany, which tends to boast of technologies with much longer cycle times. Instead, those countries that successfully catch up initially moved first toward sectors with short-cycle technologies and then moved toward sectors with long-cycle technologies after reaching maturity. If you keep specialize in long-cycle technologies, as in Brazil in the figure, the economy would find it difficult to achieve commercial success given the high entry barriers and heavy competition with the advanced economies.

Therefore, an interesting measure of the prospects of a country beyond the middle-income stage is whether it has started to specializing in short cycle technologies along the curve of the cycle time of technologies. Figure 9.2 shows that

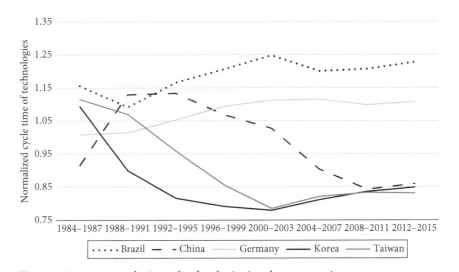

Figure 9.2 Average cycle time of technologies in select economies

Source: Figure 3-1 in Lee (2019); calculations using the raw data downloaded from the USPTO Patent Grant Red Book (Full Text, 1976~2016, http://patents.reedtech.com/pgrbft.php) after data mining and cleaning.

Note: The absolute values of cycle time of technologies are normalized by dividing by the world average so that the value of 1 may be the average of the cycle time. The (absolute) cycle times of technologies is measured by the mean backward citation, the time difference between the application or grant year of the *citing* patent and that of the *cited* patents (Jaffe and Trajtenberg 2002).

China realized such specialization in the early to mid-1990s, approximately 10 years later than Korea. The top 30 technologies in the US patents of China (Table 8.4 of Lee 2013) are similar to those of Korea and Taiwan from 1980 to 1995. The Chinese hold several patents for semiconductors, information storage, telecommunications, electrical lighting, electrical heating, X-rays, and computer hardware and software. The weighted average cycle time of Chinese technology from 2000 to 2005 was 8.07 years, closer to the Korean/Taiwanese average of 7.69 from 1980 to 1995 than to the Brazilian/Argentinean average of 9.26 in the same period (Lee 2013).

In sum, specialization into short cycle time-based technologies by China since the mid-1990s can be regarded as additional evidence of the progress of the country in terms of innovation. The growth engines of China have shifted from FDI, denationalization, and exports to innovation and exports.[4] Cross-province regressions reveal that whereas exports, FDI, and the reduction of the state sector were the important growth engines during the 1990s, knowledge and innovation have become more important in the period since the 2000s and that, among traditional policy variables, shares in exports remain significant but shares in foreign capital and state ownership have been insignificant for economic growth.

9.4 Big Businesses: Criterion Two

We now turn to the second criterion of whether China has produced a large number of big businesses. Economic literature notes the relationship between economic take-off and the rise of big businesses. Schumpeter (1934, 1942) and Chandler (1959, 1977, 1990) emphasize the significant influence of large companies in the US and Germany during the nineteenth and early twentieth centuries. Globalization has reinforced the importance of big businesses, and traditional SMEs may find independent survival difficult. Thus, the umbrella of networking under large companies creates outsourcing opportunities that increase national exports and thereby promote economic growth (Sanidas 2007; Hiratsuka 2006). Chandler (1990) also suggests that large companies facilitate the development of small companies by integrating them into complex mass production processes.

However, big businesses have their own limitations (Lee et al. 2013). Excessive dependence on (few) large firms may be counterproductive for economic growth. If large firms monopolize the markets in which they operate, their managers may not feel sufficient pressure to innovate, contrary to the expectations of Schumpeter. Large powerful companies can also lead to the adoption of policies that hinder growth (Grossman and Helpman 1994). In addition, market dominance by big

---

[4] Verified in Jin and Lee (2016) and Jin et al. (2008).

businesses and their absorption of excessive resources might become a barrier against entry by new SMEs. Whether dominance by large companies in a country affects economic growth positively or negatively is an empirical matter to verify.

Against this backdrop, Lee et al. (2013) confirm the significant and robust relationship between the number or sales of big businesses, such as of Fortune Global 500 firms, and national economic growth even after controlling for country size and endogeneity. The net effect of having one more big business is positive despite the negative effect of its dominant presence. Among latecomer countries, a few successful ones, such as China and Korea, have more big businesses than predicted by their country size, whereas other middle-income countries have fewer big businesses than predicted. Lee et al. (2013) run regressions of the number or sales of big businesses on country size as measured according to GDP to estimate residuals and find that many middle-income countries, such as Malaysia, Turkey, and Mexico, stay below the zero residual line, whereas many high-income countries stay above it (Figure 9.3). Several successful catching-up economies used to stay close to the zero line but move above it. Examples of these economies include the so-called BRIC (Brazil, Russia, India, and China), with China as the most outstanding economy. Figure 9.3 shows that China is far above the zero residual line, suggesting that it differs from other middle-income countries and has moved close to other successful catching-up economies, such as Korea, Taiwan, and other high-income economies.

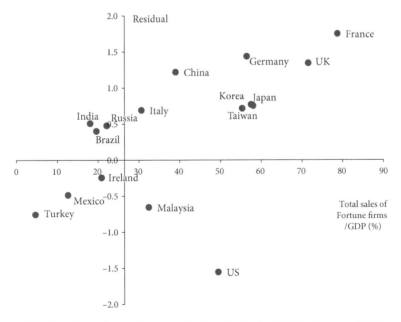

Figure 9.3 Location of countries in residual and sales-to-GDP ratio space, 2009

Source: Figure in Lee et al. (2013).

Table 9.2 Number of Fortune Global 500 companies and their total sales-to-GDP ratio in select economies, 1994–2018

Firm number (sales/GDP %)	1994	1997	2001	2005	2007	2010	2015	2018
US	151	175	197	170	153	133	134	121
	(41.8)	(48.0)	(57.5)	(54.2)	(55.0)	(52.7)	(46.5)	(45.7)
Japan	149	112	88	70	64	68	52	52
	(79.6)	(69.5)	(60.0)	(51.1)	(58.0)	(59.8)	(58.7)	(62.9)
Germany	44	42	35	35	37	34	28	29
	(41.7)	(49.0)	(64.0)	(59.2)	(62.6)	(58.3)	(55.7)	(51.8)
Brazil	2	5	4	4	5	7	7	8
	(5.3)	(8.9)	(11.1)	(13.1)	(15.6)	(17.4)	(20.0)	(21.1)
Russia	0	1	2	5	5	7	5	4
	(0.0)	(5.9)	(10.5)	(20.6)	(18.9)	(24.9)	(23.4)	(23.3)
India	1	1	1	6	7	8	7	7
	(2.5)	(3.5)	(4.4)	(14.4)	(17.9)	(17.5)	(12.6)	(14.0)
China	3	4	11	20	29	61	103	119
	(7.4)	(6.7)	(19.7)	(27.4)	(32.8)	(49.2)	(52.4)	(59.2)
Korea, Rep.	8	12	12	12	15	14	15	16
	(31.6)	(54.7)	(53.6)	(47.6)	(59.2)	(65.1)	(49.5)	(52.9)
Malaysia	0	1	1	1	1	1	1	1
	(0.0)	(11.0)	(19.1)	(32.1)	(35.5)	(32.3)	(21.1)	(17.4)
Taiwan	2	2	2	3	6	8	7	10
	(6.5)	(6.8)	(7.6)	(17.2)	(43.6)	(66.2)	(59.3)	(78.1)
Turkey	1	0	0	1	1	1	1	1
	(6.3)	(0.0)	(0.0)	(3.7)	(6.1)	(4.9)	(3.0)	(3.8)

Note: Current values of sales and GDP are used.

Source: Adaptation of the table in Lee et al. (2013); based on Fortune Global 500 (fortune.com/global500).

Thus, China is moving beyond the middle-income stage in terms of generating big businesses. Big businesses in China and their capabilities have rapidly increased. Table 9.2 shows a list of select countries and the number of their Fortune Global 500 firms. Japan has significantly declined since the mid-1990s, from 149 in 1994 to 52 in 2018, and the US since the 2000s, from 197 in 2001 to 121 in 2018. In contrast, the table confirms a strong rise of BRIC, with China in the lead. The number of Fortune Global 500 firms in China increased from 3 in 1993 to 20 in 2005, to 61 in 2010, and to 119 in 2018 (almost at par with US). China outranks Japan as second in the world in terms of the number of large firms, consistent with the fact that China replaced Japan as the second-largest economy in the world in 2010. Trends in the number of Fortune Global 500 firms in each country coincide with evidence of economic growth in these countries

(Lee et al. 2013). In terms of the number of Fortune Global 500 companies, China far surpassed all major European countries, such as France (39), Germany (37), and the UK (29), as of 2012. The gap with them became greater in 2019 as all these countries ended up having less than 30 companies.

Table 9.2 also shows the ratio of the total sales of these Fortune Global 500 firms to the GDP of each economy. Typically, these ratios range about 50 percent for most high-income economies, like the US (52.7 percent in 2010) and Japan (59.7 percent in 2010), whereas they tend to be less than 40 percent or even 30 percent for middle-income economies, like Brazil (8 firms with the ratio of 21 percent in 2018). The value of this ratio in China reached 30 percent in 2007, 50 percent in 2015, and recently 60 percent in 2018, close to that of Japan (63 percent in 2018). So, these numbers mean that China has generated a number of world-class companies in both absolute and relative terms comparable to other major advanced economies.

The only limitation of China used to be an insufficient number of large companies in the manufacturing sector. However, the share of manufacturing firms is rapidly increasing. Table 9.3 shows that the share of manufacturing firms in the Fortune Global 500 firms of China was 20 percent in 2003 but increased to 34 percent (25 out of 73) in 2011 and recently to 40 percent (48 out of 119) in 2018. This value is now close to that of Japan, which had a share of 43 percent with 29 manufacturing firms out of 68 in 2011. China now boasts of numerous successful manufacturing firms considered brand leaders in their sectors, such as Lenovo, Haier, Changhong, TCL, and Huawei (Lee et al. 2011). Several of these Chinese companies are not only leaders in the domestic market but also global players

Table 9.3 Number of Fortune Global 500 firms and numbers and share of manufacturing firms

	Total number	Manufacturing companies	Share (%)
China			
2018	119	48	40
(Out of the top 15, 12 firms are non-manufacturing firms.)			
2011	73	25	34
(The top 15 firms are all non-manufacturing firms.)			
2008	37	10	27
2005	20	4	20
2003	15	3	20
Japan			
2011	68	29	43
(Out of the top 15, 8 are manufacturing firms, including Toyota as the number one.)			

Source: Author; based on Fortune Global 500 (fortune.com/global500).

across a wide spectrum of industries. Many large firms in China are no longer simply low-end producers or original equipment manufacturers. These firms are upgrading into producers of high-end brands and leapfrogging into emerging technologies, such as renewable energy. Moreover, China is the only country that has generated world-class IT service companies that are counterparts to the so-called FANG (Facebook, Amazon, Netflix, Google) of the US, namely, Tencent, Alibaba, and Baidu.

9.5 Inequality: Criterion Three

Economic growth and income equality are the two primary objectives of governments across the world. China has successfully achieved rapid economic growth and thereby reduced substantially absolute poverty; population living under the poverty line has decreased from more than 50 percent in 1980 to less than 10 percent in 2001 (Ravallion and Chen 2007; table 10). However, the country has failed to achieve income equality as China, an egalitarian society 40 years ago, has experienced sharp increases in income inequality since the 1980s at least up to the mid-2000s (Li 2018).

The trend of income inequality requires separate examinations for urban and rural China. As a developing country, China has implemented separate economic and social policies for urban and rural areas, with apparent urban-biased features that have resulted in significant differences between urban and rural households in terms of income level, access to public services, and human development (Knight and Song 1999; Riskin et al. 2001; Gustafsson et al. 2008). Variant estimates indicate that income inequality has significantly increased in both urban and rural China. The Gini coefficient of China was 0.382 in 1988, 0.437 in 1995, 0.454 in 2002, and reached its peak of 0.49 around 2008–2009 and then declined to 0.42 in 2015 (Li 2018; Riskin, Zhao, and Li 2001; Li and Yue 2004). Estimates based on comparable data sets indicate that the Gini coefficient in urban China increased from 0.16 in 1978 to 0.34 around the mid-2000s and then has dropped a bit since 2010, and that in rural China increased from 0.22 in 1978 to 0.39 in 2009 and then dropped a bit in 2011 (Li 2018). Moreover, the income gap between urban and rural households showed a rising trend in the last decades to reach its peak of 3.3 times (urban-to-rural ratio) around the late 2000s and then declined close to 3 in the 2010s (Li 2018).[5]

The above figures indicate that the Gini coefficient for the entire nation is higher than those for rural and urban areas and it is because the income gap between urban and rural China is very large. In other words, one of the most

---

[5] The ratio of the income per capita of urban households to that of rural households increased from 1.8 in 1996 to 3.12 in 2011 in nominal terms (China Statistics Abstract 2012: 101).

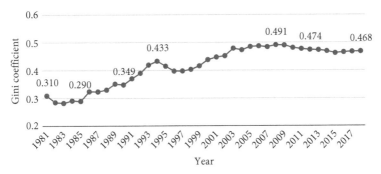

Figure 9.4 Gini coefficient in China, 1981–2018

Source: 2003–2018: CEIC (China Economic Information Center: https://www.ceicdata.com/ko);
1981–2001: Ravallion and Chen (2007)
2002: Gustafsson, Li, and Sicular (2008).

unique features of economic inequality in China, compared to other developing economies, is the heavy share of the rural–urban gap as its source. The related literature also attributes the significant income inequality in China to growing interregional urban–rural income inequality (Kanbur and Zhang 1999; Khan and Riskin 1998; World Bank 1997; Yang 1999). Moreover, the decomposition of income inequality shows that interregional income inequality is related to great urban–rural income inequality (Hussain et al. 1994; Kanbur and Zhang 1999; Tsui 1993). A Theil decomposition by Li and Yue (2004) shows that the urban-rural income gap represents over 40 percent of the overall income inequality in China, or 46 percent in 2002 and 51 percent in 2007. More importantly, although the level of within-rural or within-urban inequality is more or less flat, urban-rural inequality accounts for the absolute majority of the net increase of overall inequality.

In considering urban–rural inequality, we must account for rural surplus labor as an important condition that determines the inequality. The turning point concept proposed by Lewis (1954) predicts that the income gap between the urban and rural sectors will continue until the modern urban sector absorbs surplus labor in the traditional sector and that this turning point will narrow the gap. This conjecture has been confirmed in Korea (Lee 2010; Bai 1982). Korea also had rural surplus labor in the early 1960s, but its size was smaller than that of China. Thus, it had only a short period of worsening inequality caused by its small rural surplus labor force at its initial take-off period before or during the 1960s when several people migrated to urban areas for high incomes, whereas several others remained in rural areas as surplus labor. However, once the urban areas had fully absorbed the migrant workers from rural areas by the mid-1970s, when Korea is regarded to have reached the Lewis turning point, inequality soon declined. The

Gini coefficient of Korea increased from 0.32 in 1961 to 0.40 in 1972 but steadily decreased to 0.32 in 1997, the year of the Asian financial crisis.[6]

China faces a dualistic problem. The urban–rural income gap in China is primarily formed by the considerable amount of agricultural surplus labor, as confirmed by the econometric analysis by Jin and Lee (2016) using province panel data. The analysis reveals a robust and positive relationship between the initial size of surplus labor and the degree of urban–rural inequality. Thus, slow urbanization and the resulting slow reduction in rural surplus labor have widened the urban–rural income gap and thus increased overall income inequality.

Whether China has passed the Lewis turning point and has moved from a period of unlimited supply to an era of labor shortage has been a subject of heated debate (Zhang et al. 2011; Yao and Zhang 2010; Cai 2010; Zhao 2010; Das and N'Diaye 2013). Jin (2010) estimates the size of surplus labor in each province in the three major regions of China and finds that the eastern region already shows a shortage of labor or a lack of surplus labor, whereas an adequate size of surplus labor remains in the central and western regions. Jin and Lee (2016) find that the urban–rural income inequality is negatively associated with economic growth during the early reform period or the 1990s, but the effect of economic growth on the urban–rural income inequality has become insignificant or even negatively related during the late period or the 2000s when openness, higher education, and technology variables are controlled. This result can be considered evidence that the Kuznets hypothesis seems to have recently started working in China too, which must be an exciting news for the Chinese leadership if it is true.

Actually, Figure 9.4 shows that the Gini coefficient was 0.3 in the early 1980s, reached its peak of 0.49 or so in 2008–2009 but decreased to around 0.42 by 2015. These figures can also be regarded as some sign that China is following the Kuznets curve, with the gradual reduction of surplus labor and rising wage rates starting in coastal provinces. However, new sources of complications are emerging and will likely affect this prediction, such as the fact that inequality in China has been increasingly affected not only by income levels but also by differences in wealth (including financial and real estate assets), which have become a global phenomenon (Li 2018). Therefore, even if wage rates rise, inequality might not decrease as much as expected because of other new sources of inequality. Actually, the same figure shows that the national Gini coefficients of income inequality has increased again since 2015 to 0.468 in 2018 (Figure 9.4).

Notably, wealth distribution in China has become significantly unequal with rising income inequality since the mid-1990s. Chinese households had almost no private assets during the pre-reform era. The majority of private assets were also presented as household savings, which were small amounts in terms of per capita

---

[6] Source: WIDER DB (www.wider.unu.edu).

computation.[7] The inequality of wealth distribution was even lower than income inequality up to the 1990s. For instance, whereas the Gini coefficient of income inequality was 0.45 in 1995, that of wealth inequality was 0.40 (Brenner 2001). Since the mid-1990s, however, the inequality of wealth distribution has rapidly increased. The Gini coefficient of wealth distribution in China as a whole increased to 0.55 in 2002 (Li and Zhao 2008). Moreover, the inequality of wealth distribution rose rapidly in the 2010s because of rising income inequality and the fast rise of housing prices in urban areas. The Gini coefficient of wealth distribution reached 0.68 in 2010 (Knight et al. 2016).

In terms of expressing concentration of income, including wealth-based income, a better measure that has been used since Piketty (2014) is the share of the richest top 10 percent in the national income. Table 9.4 compares China with other economies in these shares. It is shown that the share of the top 10 percent in China has been higher than 40 percent since the mid-2000s, which is comparable to that in the US (45 percent), although lower than those in India (higher than 50 percent), Russia (higher than 45 percent), and Brazil (higher than 55 percent). One estimate is that the urban top 1 percent in China made 37 percent of its overall income from ownership of capital (e.g., investment income, rental income, and other property income) in 2007, which is comparable to the US figure of 35 percent in the 2000s (Milanovic 2019: 104).

It would also be interesting to compare China with some Asian economies that have smoothly moved to be high-income ones in terms of income inequality. South Korea and Taiwan are good examples in the comparison. These two

Table 9.4 Share (%) of the richest top 10 percent in pre-tax national income

	1980	1985	1990	1995	2000	2005	2010	2011	2015
Germany	31.9			31.8		38.5	39.7	39.0	
Korea	28.8	28.8		29.2	35.4	37.8	43.3	44.2	
Australia	24.2	24.9	26.1	27.4	29.7	30.0	30.1	29.9	
Brazil						55.1	55.6	56.6	55.3
China	27.2	29.5	30.4	33.6	35.6	41.9	42.6	42.9	41.4
India	31.5	34.8	33.5	38.5	39.9	45.5	52.2	54.5	
Japan	32.7	33.5	38.9	35.5	38.1	42.4	41.6		
Russian	21.0	22.4	23.6	42.4	48.2	47.4	46.8	48.1	45.5
Sweden	22.8	22.8	23.6	25.8	31.3	29.8	31.0	30.9	
Taiwan	23.4	27.1	29.4	28.8	31.3	33.4	36.4	37.6	
UK		32.7	36.9	38.5	41.0	41.6	38.1	39.2	
US	34.2	36.7	38.7	40.7	43.9	45.1	45.8	45.9	

Source: Downloaded from wid.world.

[7] The total bank savings of urban and rural households in 1978 was RMB 21 billion and RMB 22 per capita (NBS 2004).

economies had maintained a low level of income inequality before they became high-income economies.[8] According to Table 9.4, Korea and Taiwan maintained the share of the top 10 percent at lower than 30 percent in the 1980s and 1990s, although it has increased to a level higher than 30 percent since the 2000s. Such recent rise of inequality in East Asia has to do with financialization at the high-income stage, such as the increasing size of financial sectors, the increasing importance of dividends income, and financial globalization (Shin and Lee 2019).

In comparison, it can be said that one of the first causes of such rise of inequality in China is gradual financialization. But, there is also a systemic root cause—its nature as a state-led capitalism, which may be defined as the use of political power to achieve economic gains. The state capitalism in China rules the country by a combination of an efficient and autonomous state–party bureaucracy and a loose rule of law (Milanovic 2019: 91–96). While such state capitalism may bring in legitimacy through economic performance, the weak rule of law tends to bring in corruption, which would lead to more inequality (Milanovic 2019: 98–106). In this sense, it can be reasoned that inequality will remain a weakness of the Chinese economy in its effort to overcome the MIT. Similar corruption tendency was checked in Korea or Taiwan as their version of developmental states or state capitalism went through democratization and strengthening of the rule of law. This is one of the variables that assisted these economies to not fall into the MIT but realize the classical Kuznets curve of decreasing inequality in the later stages of catching-up development, in the 1990s. This might be where China would remain different from its neighbors for a while. It needs to pay more attention to the issue of income inequality.

9.6 Summary and Concluding Remarks

This chapter discusses the possibility of China falling into the MIT in terms of three checkpoints: innovation capability, big businesses, and inequality. Based on these criteria, our conclusions are as follows.

First, China has increasingly become innovative and thus differs from other middle-income countries. Second, it has many successful big businesses, that is, more than its size predicts. Thus, it differs from other middle-income countries, which have few globally competitive big businesses not only in finance, energy, and trading but also in manufacturing. Third, China faces some uncertainty in

---

[8] Even with rapid growth, the Republic of Korea's income distribution fluctuated in the 1960s. Later in the decade, the income gap began to widen until the mid-1970s, with the Gini coefficient reaching its highest level at 0.39 in 1976. The Gini coefficient, however, dropped by nearly 20 percent in 1996 to the level it was before the economic take-off (Li and Luo, 2008). The income gap in Taiwan narrowed considerably and remained stable for a long time in the 1950s and 1960s. In the late 1970s, the income gap began to widen but it has stayed at a low level since 1980s (Li and Luo, 2008).

terms of inequality. There are some signs that China's situation is following the Kuznets curve, as noted by some decrease of the Gini coefficient in the 2010s associated with the gradual reduction of surplus labor and rising wage rates. However, the Chinese are now facing new sources of inequality, such as wealth (including financial and real estate assets) and non-economic factors (including corruption) associated with its nature as a variant of state capitalism under the weak rule of law.

Finally, we suggest some policies for China to move beyond the MIT. First of all, this study implies that China should pay more attention to the third aspect, or equity, than the other two aspects. In this regard, as noted by Jin and Lee (2016) and Dollar et al. (2020), a more flexible approach in rural to urban migration should be one of the key policy agenda, in addition to providing broader access to education at secondary and tertiary levels. Also, given that China already has several big businesses, more than predicted by its size, and that too much reliance on a few big businesses might be detrimental to equity, it seems desirable to promote the SMEs. In terms of the first criteria of innovation, the best situation would be more SMEs getting active in innovation and thereby achieving upgrading from low-cost-based businesses to higher end goods and sectors.

10

Thucydides Trap, Global Value Chain, and Future of China

10.1 Introduction

Historically, the rise of a new power has always led to a mounting tension with an incumbent power. This tension between the old and new powers has been termed as the "Thucydides trap," named after an ancient Greek historian who wrote a book analyzing the Peloponnesian War, which was fought between the rising Athens and the incumbent Sparta. This trap refers to a situation where one great power threatens to displace another, and war is almost always the result. Allison (2018) found that in the past 500 years great powers have found themselves in the trap 16 times, and 12 cases have erupted into an actual war with catastrophic consequences. Currently, the same structural forces may propel China and the US toward a cataclysm of unseen proportions, even though both sides deny such a possibility.

Since 2017 or the Trump government in the US, the tension between the US and China have escalated, and the actions of the US toward China have not led to an actual war, but a trade war. The US imposed a 25 percent tariff on USD 34 billion of Chinese goods imported into the American market in spring 2018 and again on USD 16 billion imports in late August, which immediately led China to retaliate in a similar manner (Steinbock 2018). This was the beginning of the US–China trade conflict, which escalated in late 2019 until a compromise deal halted further escalation but is expected to continue under the Biden administration although Biden is known to support multilateralism.

Clearly, the US intends to stop China from growing into another superpower that would threaten American hegemony. Whether it will succeed or not is a vital question. Focusing on this question and on the impact of this trap on China, this chapter defines the Thucydides trap as a situation in which the US tries to cause China to stop expanding as an economic power. Relative economic power is measured as China's share in world GDP or its GDP relative to the US. This chapter aims to analyze whether China would fall into the trap. It also discusses the role of global value chains (GVCs) in this game as one of the key links between the Thucydides trap and the middle-income trap (MIT). Even before fully getting out of the MIT, China now has to face the Thucydides trap. This chapter argues that these double traps of China will also bring into surface the final trap of

China's Technological Leapfrogging and Economic Catch-up: A Schumpeterian Perspective. Keun Lee, Oxford University Press. © Keun Lee 2021. DOI: 10.1093/oso/9780192847560.003.0010

political democratization, which used to be a common challenge for every developmental state under authoritarian regime in Asia.

In this chapter, Section 10.2 compares the economic power of the two giant economies in terms of the recent trends of their GDP. Section 10.3 focuses on the GVC aspect of the trade war and examines the nature of Chinese participation in the GVC. The question is to what extent China has been building its own GVC and localizing intermediate goods that were formerly imported into its domestic production of final goods. Section 10.4 discusses the prospects of the Chinese economy, which is facing several challenges after engaging in the hegemony war with the US. Section 10.5 concludes the chapter with a brief summary.

10.2 Comparison of the Economic Size of the US and China: The Thucydides Trap

The influential book of Kindleberger (1996) on economic history, *World Economic Primacy*, considers the economic size and income level of a country as important aspects of economic performance. However, modern economics provides limited attention to economic size. This attitude in economics is in contrast to other social sciences, such as political science and international politics, which consider the economic size of a nation as an important variable, especially a variable of economic power. Cline (1975) also considered economic power measured by GDP of nations as one of the five key variables in the national power equation.

The economic size of a nation also matters because the size itself has many advantages. Alesina et al. (2005) argued that a bigger nation had many economic benefits, including economies of scale in the production of public goods, less external shocks, including foreign aggression, improved internalization of externalities from its borders, benefits from redistribution policy (Bolton and Roland 1997), and positive externalities in the accumulation of capital (Voigtländer and Voth 2006), human capital (Lucas 2002), and knowledge and technology (Galor and Weil 2000). Wrigley and Schofield (1989) verified these benefits from the historical evidence of the industrial revolution in England. Berry and Waldfogel (2010) argued that product quality increased with market size, and thus GDP size could affect the welfare of a country.

Although absolute size matters, relative size has its own implications. Von Hörnigk (1684) believed that the power and affluence of a country depended not on its own abundance or security but on its relative possessions compared with its neighboring countries. Kennedy (1987) asserted that the power of a nation in the global era, such as economic power and military strength, was always a relative norm. Relative size matters because international competition for scarce resources is widely observed. Scarce resources, such as physical capital, human capital, energy resources, and rare earth elements, possessed by one country cannot be accessed by other countries. This leads to rivalry among the countries competing for these resources.

This author's study, Park et al. (2019), verified the determinants of the relative economic size of a country econometrically, finding that the determinants of the share of each nation in world GDP differed from those of conventional economic growth measured by per capita GDP growth. Our study found that the determinants of the GDP share of each nation included the nation's shares in world population, investment, exports, R&D investment, and financial capital flows, and not conventional variables, such as educational enrollment or quality of political institution. Conventional openness (trades-to-GDP ratio) and political institution do not matter because they do not reflect economic rivalry. In comparison, a nation's share in world export can be an important determinant of its GDP share in the world because it is more closely related to international rivalry. In other words, variables that represent international rivalry and national shares of global resources well are significant determinants of the country size or national share of world GDP. Such finding is consistent with the reality that China has rapidly expanded in economic size not owing to improving political institution but owing to its increased share globally in exports, R&D, patent registrations, and inbound foreign direct investment (FDI).

Actually, simple calculations using the World Bank data (World Development Indicator) suggest that China's share in worldwide investment in fixed capital was larger (25 percent) than that of the US (20 percent) as of 2019 (it surpassed the US around 2010) and that the absolute amount of R&D expenditure (and thus its share in global R&D) is already close to that of the US. Also, China's share in world export is the same as that of the US at 10 percent. If we divide total exports into those in goods and in services, China lags behind the US in exports of services in world markets, with 5 percent by China and 15 percent by the US, whereas in goods export, China caught up with the US around 2009 to reach 12 percent in 2019, compared to about 9 percent by the US. These figures imply that China's catching up with the US is not just based on exporting low-end goods and fixed investment but also based on technological build-up represented by R&D.

Now let us turn to comparing the economic size of China versus the US to determine their economic power by assessing the trend of the relative size of GDP of the two superpowers. Using the International Monetary Fund (IMF) data released in October 2020 of GDP of G7 and other countries in dollar currency, Figure 10.1A shows that the relative size of GDP of the US in the world peaked in the early 2000s with the burst of the IT or dot-com bubble. The share of the US was as huge as 32 percent of the whole world in 2001, after which it decreased to 21.5 percent in 2011. This means the US share in the world GDP decreased by 10 percent points in 10 years or a 1 percent point decrease per year. However, since

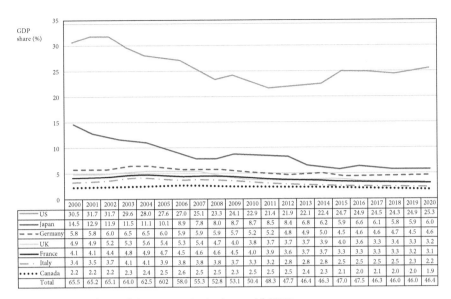

	2000	2001	2002	2003	2004	2005	2006	2007	2008	2009	2010	2011	2012	2013	2014	2015	2016	2017	2018	2019	2020
US	30.5	31.7	31.7	29.6	28.0	27.6	27.0	25.1	23.3	24.1	22.9	21.4	21.9	22.1	22.4	24.7	24.9	24.5	24.3	24.9	25.3
Japan	14.5	12.9	11.9	11.5	11.1	10.1	8.9	7.8	8.0	8.7	8.7	8.5	8.4	6.8	6.2	5.9	6.6	6.1	5.8	5.9	6.0
Germany	5.8	5.8	6.0	6.5	6.5	6.0	5.9	5.9	5.9	5.7	5.2	5.2	4.8	4.9	5.0	4.5	4.6	4.6	4.7	4.5	4.6
UK	4.9	4.9	5.2	5.3	5.6	5.4	5.3	5.4	4.7	4.0	3.8	3.7	3.7	3.7	3.9	4.0	3.6	3.3	3.4	3.3	3.2
France	4.1	4.1	4.4	4.8	4.9	4.7	4.5	4.6	4.6	4.5	4.0	3.9	3.6	3.7	3.7	3.3	3.3	3.3	3.3	3.2	3.1
Italy	3.4	3.5	3.7	4.1	4.1	3.9	3.8	3.8	3.8	3.7	3.3	3.2	2.8	2.8	2.8	2.5	2.5	2.5	2.5	2.3	2.2
Canada	2.2	2.2	2.2	2.3	2.4	2.5	2.6	2.5	2.5	2.3	2.5	2.5	2.5	2.4	2.3	2.1	2.0	2.1	2.0	2.0	1.9
Total	65.5	65.2	65.1	64.0	62.5	602	58.0	55.3	52.8	53.1	50.4	48.3	47.7	46.4	46.3	47.0	47.5	46.3	46.0	46.0	46.4

Figure 10.1A Share of G7 economies in the world GDP

Note: Drawn using the raw data from IMF data and estimates released in October 2020. GDP figures in current prices are used. World GDP is the sum of the top 100 economies.

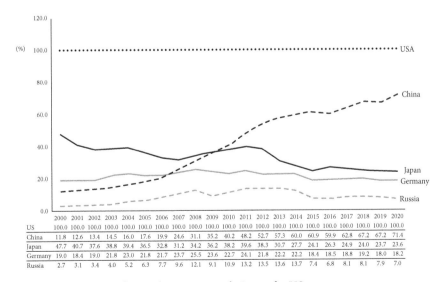

	2000	2001	2002	2003	2004	2005	2006	2007	2008	2009	2010	2011	2012	2013	2014	2015	2016	2017	2018	2019	2020
US	100.0	100.0	100.0	100.0	100.0	100.0	100.0	100.0	100.0	100.0	100.0	100.0	100.0	100.0	100.0	100.0	100.0	100.0	100.0	100.0	100.0
China	11.8	12.6	13.4	14.5	16.0	17.6	19.9	24.6	31.1	35.2	40.2	48.2	52.7	57.3	60.0	60.9	59.9	62.8	67.2	67.2	71.4
Japan	47.7	40.7	37.6	38.8	39.4	36.5	32.8	31.2	34.2	36.2	38.2	39.6	38.3	30.7	27.7	24.1	26.3	24.9	24.0	23.7	23.6
Germany	19.0	18.4	19.0	21.8	23.0	21.8	21.7	23.7	25.5	23.6	22.7	24.1	21.8	22.2	22.2	18.4	18.5	18.8	19.2	18.0	18.2
Russia	2.7	3.1	3.4	4.0	5.2	6.3	7.7	9.6	12.1	9.1	10.9	13.2	13.5	13.6	13.7	7.4	6.8	8.1	8.1	7.9	7.0

Figure 10.1B Sizes of several economies relative to the US

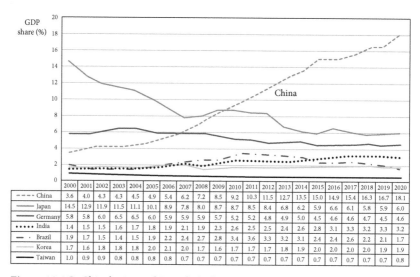

	2000	2001	2002	2003	2004	2005	2006	2007	2008	2009	2010	2011	2012	2013	2014	2015	2016	2017	2018	2019	2020
China	3.6	4.0	4.3	4.3	4.5	4.9	5.4	6.2	7.2	8.5	9.2	10.3	11.5	12.7	13.5	15.0	14.9	15.4	16.3	16.7	18.1
Japan	14.5	12.9	11.9	11.5	11.1	10.1	8.9	7.8	8.0	8.7	8.7	8.5	8.4	6.8	6.2	5.9	6.6	6.1	5.8	5.9	6.0
Germany	5.8	5.8	6.0	6.5	6.5	6.0	5.9	5.9	5.9	5.7	5.2	5.2	4.8	4.9	5.0	4.5	4.6	4.6	4.7	4.5	4.6
India	1.4	1.5	1.5	1.6	1.7	1.8	1.9	2.1	1.9	2.3	2.6	2.5	2.5	2.4	2.6	2.8	3.1	3.3	3.2	3.3	3.2
Brazil	1.9	1.7	1.5	1.4	1.5	1.9	2.2	2.4	2.7	2.8	3.4	3.6	3.3	3.2	3.1	2.4	2.4	2.6	2.2	2.1	1.7
Korea	1.7	1.6	1.8	1.8	1.8	2.0	2.1	2.0	1.7	1.6	1.7	1.7	1.7	1.8	1.9	2.0	2.0	2.0	2.0	1.9	1.9
Taiwan	1.0	0.9	0.9	0.8	0.8	0.8	0.8	0.7	0.7	0.7	0.7	0.7	0.7	0.7	0.7	0.7	0.7	0.7	0.7	0.7	0.8

Figure 10.1C China's rise and Japan's decline in world GDP shares

2011, its share in the world GDP has continued to increase to reach 25 percent in the late 2010s and has remained around that level until 2020. Such reversal of the formerly decreasing trend in the US is impressive, given that no other G7 country has shown such recovery. In the same period, or since 2000, the world GDP share of Japan, Germany, and the UK has continuously decreased from 14.5 percent to 6.0 percent, 5.8 percent to 4.6 percent, and 4.9 percent to 3.2 percent in 2020, respectively. Of course, the relative decline of the G7 countries was affected by the expansion of China.

Figure 10.1B shows that China's economy was as small as 12 percent of that of the US in 2000 but quickly became as big as 20 percent of the US share in 2006, 40 percent in 2010, and 60 percent in 2014. This means a reduction of 20 percent point gap within four years or 5 percent points per year. It is to be noted that the most rapid catch-up happened during 2006 to 2014, which was the period of the global financial crisis. It is not surprising that the economic crisis in the US helped China reduce the gap with the US quickly. However, in the late 2010s, with the recovery of the US economy, the catching-up rate slowed down. China's relative size to the US reached 60.9 percent in 2015, and then slightly declined to 59.9 percent in 2016, although it started to increase again in the next few years to reach 67.2 percent in 2018 and even 71.4 percent in 2020. Such a jump in 2020, although they are estimates, reflects the impact of Covid-19, which hit the US badly, whereas China boasted a V-shaped recovery to record even a positive growth rate in 2020. Again, this story of ups and downs of the catching-up story reflects the simple idea that catching-up is a game of chasing a moving target so that your slowdown is my catch-up (Lee 2019: 17–21).

Now, let us try to forecast when China will catch up with the US in economic size. A simple way is to extend the recent trend of catch-up. During the last five-year period, from 2015 to 2020, the gap closed by about 10 percent points, or China grew from 60 percent of the size of the US to 70 percent. If we extend this trend of 10 percent point reduction for every 5 years, then we can expect that it will take another 15 years for China to close the remaining gap of 30 percent points or it will catch up with the US by 2035. In comparison, if we extend the trend during the last 10 years of catching-up, or reducing 30 percent point gap in 10 years, namely, from 40 percent of the US in 2010 to 70 percent in 2020, we can expect that China will catch up with the US by 2030, or in 10 years or so, which is exactly the same as the old forecasts by Goldman Sachs and some new forecasts.[1]

Given the above estimates, one rough forecast can be that China will catch up with the US by the early 2030s. However, a simple catching-up in economic size does not necessarily mean a great change in power relations between the two superpowers. Although the US surpassed the Great Britain in economic size in the late nineteenth century, it took another 50 years for the US to open the era of Pax-America in the 1950s after World War II. Also, there still remains several uncertainties, such as future unfolding of the US–China relations under the Biden administration, political changes in China, and retreat of globalization and changing GVCs after Covid-19. Furthermore, China has yet to establish itself as not only an economic power but also a soft power. Thus, the US is expected to remain a superpower for several decades to come although its power and dominance might not be as uncontested as before.

Figure 10.1C contrasts the rapid growth of China and the sharp decline of Japan since 2000 in terms of their GDP share in the world. China's share in the world was approximately 15 percent in the mid-2010s and 18 percent in 2020. The figure shows that this size is almost similar to Japan's share in the late 1990s or 2000 (14.6 percent). Japan's share was as big as 70 percent of the US share in the late 1990s, which is close to that of today's China compared with the US. Hence, one might conjecture that China would also follow the Japanese path of decline in the last two decades from 15 percent to 6 percent or less of world GDP. Although China's economic growth rates themselves may slow down, such decline is not sure to happen because it is also affected by the relative economic performance of other countries, especially major G7 countries, which are badly affected by Covid-19.

Further, the Japanese collapse was triggered by the so-called Plaza Accord in 1985, which suddenly and substantially appreciated the Japanese currency (yen) by more than 200 percent in several years. The agreement among the major

[1] A recent forecast after the Covid-19 by CEBR in the UK is that China will become larger than US by 2028, which is five years earlier than its old forecast before the Covid-19. Also, see Steinbock (2018) for a related discussion on the old forecast by Goldman Sachs.

economies happened because Japan accepted the appreciation owing to the pressure from the US and other European economies. It gave in because it sided with the US militarily and was under the US protection in terms of nuclear weapons. However, China is a different military block country and will not accept such a big compromise, as shown by the dragged nature of the US–China trade deal by the end of 2019 during the Trump administration. Furthermore, the strength of the measures adopted by the US in the trade wars alone in comparison with that of the Plaza Accord is still unknown, and the Biden administration is taking a slightly different policy stance toward China.

Thus, although China might be different from Japan and not face a sudden fall, its current size to that of the US (70 percent) cannot be considered big enough either to stage a major challenge in global politics. In this sense, the aggressive position of the Chinese leadership since the mid-2010s seems to have arrived too early. For instance, the Central Foreign Affair Work Conference held in China in June 2018 observed that history is on China's side and the Chinese Communist Party's mission is to extend the strategic opportunity period for its growth (Chung 2019). Some political scientists are of the view that it should have kept the old foreign policy line of strategic modesty represented by the Chinese word *Taoguangyanghui* (韬光养晦: wait until you are equipped with enough power) longer, rather than quietly discarding it, together with the old tenet of "not seeking hegemony" and switching to the proactive diplomacy represented by *yousuozuowei* (有所作为: I will do what I am supposed to) (Chung 2019). The changes in China's foreign policy lines alarmed the US and have triggered the turnaround of the US position toward China to a more hawkish direction since the beginning of the Trump government. Actually, when the US under Trump introduced the 2017 National Security Strategy, China was termed as America's strategic "rival," even an "adversary" (Steinbock 2018).

Another factor to consider is the change in economic policy lines of the Chinese government after the 2009 global financial crisis. Seeing the weakness of Western capitalism during the global financial crisis, China dismissed it as its role model and instead decided to go for its own version of economic system. Such pride in the Chinese system has been further reinforced by the Covid-19 as China boasted the strong V-shaped recovery much faster than any other economies in the world. The Xi government brought back the old (the 1980s) slogan of "socialism with Chinese characteristics" as the so-called "new normal" (*xin changtai*) and declared that China will strive to "institutionalize" socialism with Chinese characteristics. Such institutionalization included giving up Deng Xiaoping's reform policy of the separation of the party from the enterprise management (*dangqi fenli*), in which the supreme leader in the management of the enterprise should be the manager (CEO) rather than the party secretary of the enterprise (Lee 1991). This change marked a reversal of policy to the Mao period, putting the party back as the leader of the enterprise over CEOs. Further, the Chinese government brought back the supremacy of state-owned enterprises (SOEs) over privately owned businesses (*guojin mintui*; state marches, private retreats), which is a significant reversal of the several decades long policy. Since Deng initiated economic reform and the open door policy, one of the core policies was privatization, which has actually been pursued during the last several decades.

The US and other Western powers expected China's entry into the World Trade Organization (WTO) to lead China toward becoming a proper market economy. As of the late 2010s, those countries realized that their expectation was wrong, as they saw China going backward. The new perception of the US is that without becoming a proper free and open market economy, China only took advantage of the WTO entry to gain access to the world market and further wanted to keep its own system, challenging the US hegemony.

Going back to the comparison of Japan and China, the sudden appreciation of the Japanese yen since the Plaza Accord caused trouble to many Japanese exporters and to the outbound relocation of factories out of Japan to the Southeast Asia. This change was huge in the Japan-led GVC as it spread to Asia and globally. However, with the stability of its currency, China has moved its GVC more in an inward-looking way or more localization of formerly imported parts and supplies into domestic production, which will be discussed further in the next section.

10.3 GVC as the Key Linkage between the Two Traps

Value chain refers to a series of value-creating activities that transform raw or intermediate materials into finished products; GVCs appear as such supply chains have become global in scope, and more intermediate goods are being traded across borders (Gereffi 2014; UNCTAD 2013; Baldwin 2011). Baldwin (2016) proposes that joining a GVC will help in the industrialization of latecomer economies because the production process has become a less complex one when the supply chain became less lumpy and less interconnected domestically. His main point is that building an entire value chain in a latecomer economy (such as what was done by Korea) is very difficult and risky, and such activity will not provide enough for the economy due to the limited market size of an emerging economy. He observed that unlike the failed "build strategy" in Malaysia, a successful case is the "join strategy" of the automobile sector in Thailand, where the Thai factories established by the Japanese firms (Toyota) only focused on the assembly and promotion of Thai component suppliers (Baldwin 2016: 250–254).

However, a more important issue is whether a narrow specialization in a specific value segment is powerful enough to free a country from the MIT (Lee 2019; Ch. 2). The World Bank (2012) defines the MIT as a situation in which a country's per capita GDP stays for several decades within the range of 20–40 percent of the US level. If we apply this criterion for purchasing power parity (PPP)-based GDP per capita, then Thailand has not escaped the MIT because its GDP per capita has not yet surpassed even the 30 percent level by 2018, and the same is true of China (Figure 1.1 in Chapter 1).[2] This can be said of Mexico as well, which has a very high level of participation in GVCs. The country's GDP per capita was 35 percent of that of the US in the early 1990s, or around the beginning of the North American Free Trade Agreement (NAFTA) period, but has continued to decline since then. Specifically, Mexico's GDP per capita stood below 33 percent in 2015. These cases indicate that the key issue in value chains is whether the amount of the domestic value added is high or low at each link (Gereffi 1999). In other words, while joining the GVC is necessary for learning and accessing foreign knowledge, the risk in being stuck in low value-added activities without making progress toward higher tiers in the value chains exists; consequently, the economy falls into the so-called MIT (World Bank, 2012; Lee, 2013). Hence, what matters more critically are who captures and how to capture the "bigger share" of the value in the GVC, and a battle for this position may occur among the involved key parties.

The degree of participation in GVCs can be measured by the share of foreign value added (FVA) in gross exports. FVA indicates how much percentage of a country's gross exports consists of inputs that are produced and imported from other countries. In other words, a higher (lower) value of FVA indicates further (or less) integration with the global economy through GVCs. This index can represent the degree of an economy's participation in GVCs, and at the same time, lower values of FVA correspond to more reliance on domestic value added in generating exports.[3]

Figure 10.2 shows the FVA estimation results for China since 1995. China's FVA peaked at 37 percent in the early 2000s and declined to 31 percent by the late 2000s and even further to less than 20 percent by the late 2010s. This trend of the sharp decline of FVA implies that China has recently been relying more on domestically made intermediate goods for its exports of final goods. It also suggests that as a successful catching-up economy, it is replicating the pattern of Korea with lags (approximately 15 years). Korea also experienced a decade-long decline in its FVA, which decreased by over 5 percent points, or from approximately 35 percent to 30 percent or lower, during its rapid catch-up period since the mid-1980s.

From the 1960s and 1970s, FVA in Korea continued to increase until the mid-1980s. In these decades, the country's participation in GVCs was through original equipment manufacturer-based exports, starting with labor-intensive goods, until reaching its peak in the early 1980s. FVA in Korea then started to

---

[2] Per capita GDP compares the living standard of people in different countries. Hence, the standard practice is to use the PPP based on exchange rates when one converts local currency-based GDP to dollar terms. PPP-based exchange rates reflect price level differences across countries and thus are different from exchange rates in markets.

[3] The figure of FVA and related discussion rely on Lee et al. (2018).

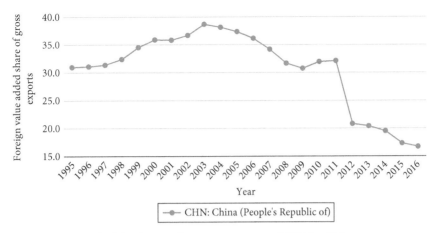

Figure 10.2 Trend of the degree of GVC participation (FVA) by China
Source: Drawing using the data from TiVA database of the OECD.

decline until the mid-1990s, as Korean firms localized formerly imported goods by domestic production. For instance, Hyundai Motors developed its own engines and thus stopped using the Japanese engines for its cars. Finally, FVA increased again after the country joined the Organisation for Economic Co-operation and Development (OECD), or in the 2000s, and Korean firms became globalized and relocated their factories abroad to look for cheaper wages. Specifically, its FVA peaked over 36 percent in 1980 and dropped to 28 percent in 1993, the year Korea became an OECD member. It experienced a rapid catch-up between the mid-1980s and the mid-1990s, but was facing the possibility of falling into the MIT from the early to the mid-1980s because of its rising wage rates and low value-added export structure. This dynamic, non-linear pattern of more GVC, less GVC, and then more GVC again suggests that Korea escaped the MIT by increasing the share of local value-added in its exports from the mid-1980s (Lee et al. 2018). I have checked if a similar pattern occurred in other Southeast Asian or Latin American economies and find no such case. After the launch of the NAFTA, Mexico has shown the highest degree of integration with GVCs but experiences no period of decline in its FVA to create local value chains.

The above discussion suggests that China is successfully moving out of the MIT by building its domestic value chain and reducing its reliance on foreign value chains dominated by other incumbent countries. This pattern is expected to be further reinforced after the US–China trade conflict and Covid-19. Such pattern at the aggregate level has been confirmed at sector level, too. Figure 10.3 shows the case of the transportation sector (automobiles). China shows a decreasing period from 45 percent in the mid-1990s to 30 percent in the late 2000s and finally even to less than 20 percent in the late 2010s, similar to that in the

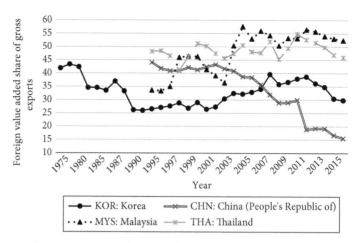

Figure 10.3 GVC participation (FVA) in the automobile sector in Korea, China, Malaysia, and Thailand

Note: Korea 1975–1993 FVA data are the estimation using the input–output table of Korea. Other values are from the OECD TiVA database version 2016 and version 2018 (1995–2011 data are from TiVA 2016 and 2012–2016 data are from TiVA 2018.

Source: Figure 4 in Lee, Qu, and Mao (2021) drawn by Mao.

mid-1970s to 1990s in Korea (Lee et al. 2021). Periods of decreasing FVA or increasing domestic value added are not clearly observed in auto sector in Thailand. FVA in Thailand had always remained high without a decreasing trend until the mid-2010s, which indicates no success in increasing domestic value added and no successful building of a local value chain.[4] Although not reported here, similar figures of FVA in the electronics sector show a sharper decline of this value for China from 70 percent or so in 2000 to 25 percent in 2015, reflecting more rapid and substantial localization in electronics than in automobiles.

The decreasing period of GVC participation is the period of localizing formerly imported products into domestic products. This process of localization usually begins for less difficult or low-end parts and moves to more difficult or high-end products. However, localization has limits when the target turns to more high-tech parts. This is why FVA values cannot go downward unlimitedly or stop going down around 25 percent depending upon products or countries. Thus, the localization drive tends to accompany the emergence of domestic (rather than foreign) flagship companies (e.g., Samsung and Hyundai in Korea; Huawei and BYD in China), which are leading firms carrying many suppliers in their network of global production and marketing. With the growth of such domestic flagship companies, latecomer economies may now seek to be integrated again into the GVCs, sourcing globally and establishing factories abroad. In this way, the FVA

---

[4] More details in automobile sectors in Asia are found in Lee, Qu, and Mao (2021).

starts to increase again. This process of increasing FVA again or reintegration with the global economy is caused by rising wage rates and outbound FDI (setting subsidiary factories abroad) or outsourcing of low-end goods and domestic focus on high-end goods. Flagship companies from Korea went along with localization (of some imported components and parts) and then globalization of production and marketing systems.

China is yet to enter the final stage of reintegration into GVCs after building a certain degree of domestic value chains. Or it is happening partly as China starts relocating some low-end chains abroad due to rising wage rates at coastal areas and is also trying to upgrade into high-end products and sectors. In a sense, its One Belt, One Road initiative is a move for such dynamic upgrading by globalizing the China-led GVC around the world or at key strategic locations. In the meantime, the US does not want China to succeed at upgrading into high-end segments or high-tech goods in order to avoid the situation in which it has to rely on China-led GVC for its supply chains for strategic goods like semiconductors and telecommunications systems. Then, an expected scenario is the decoupling of the US and China, and China will encounter some problems and delays in its plan to upgrade and scale-up China-led GVC. Disruption in China-led GVC will affect the possibility of China's prospects of growing beyond the MIT, which requires moving out of low-end segments and moving into high-end segments. In this sense, the GVC is one of the key linkage variables between the Thucydides trap and the MIT.

While China has achieved dynamic catch-up in mobile phone markets with the emergence of locally owned companies and built up domestic clusters in Shenzhen areas in South China, these companies still rely on foreign sources for high-tech parts. For instance, Xing (2019) shows that the share of FVA in mobile phone production in Chinese companies, such as Xiaomi and Oppo, is as high as 80 percent or more of their manufacturing costs. These companies still rely on Qualcomm (snapdragon CPU), Samsung (memory chips), and Sony (cameras). However, domestic value added is created at marketing and distribution stages than in the manufacturing stage, and the share of domestic value added increases to more than 40 percent of the retail prices of mobile phones (Xing 2019).

If we turn to semiconductors, the degree of catch-up by China is quite limited, as discussed in the preceding chapters (Chapters 4 and 6). Hence, the Chinese government set this sector as the key target for localization or indigenous innovation. However, the prospects are still uncertain after the onset of the US–China trade war. In other words, for semiconductors, China might not be able to adopt the Korean strategy of catching-up. At their early stage of entry and gradual catch-up, Korean companies, such as Samsung, produced memory chips using the production equipment and facilities imported from the Japanese company Sharp and based on circuit designs licensed from a microelectronic company in the US (Lee and Lim 2001). Samsung's strategy has been to rely on high-tech components, parts, and supplies from foreign sources but focus on enhancing production efficiency, such as yield rates. The strategy worked fine until summer 2019 when Japan imposed restriction of exports of such high-tech parts and supplies to Korea after the bilateral tension over history issues.

The number of supplier firms in these high-tech parts and suppliers is very limited, with just one or two firms, and the market is thus an oligopoly or even close to monopoly depending on the products. Thus, if these companies, like ASML in Netherlands, go under the control or influence of the US government, China's plan to localize the production of semiconductors will be affected and delayed until it finds an alternative way. An example of such a case already exists in the semiconductor sector;[5] Tsinghua Uni, a Chinese company representing the country's ambition of catch-up in this sector, declared bankruptcy in December 2020. Chinese efforts for localization will be further affected by the tightening of intellectual property rights protection by the US and the Western world against China.

Overall, the above discussion indicates a possibility of slowdown of China's US catch-up in high-tech sectors. However, such a slowdown does not mean a collapse, and the situation could merely mean a delay in catch-up. Or, it could be a partial decoupling involving some sectors like semiconductor, but not a comprehensive decoupling across boards, given that China has already achieved substantial catch-up in many sectors, such as electric cars and batteries, drones, wind turbines, and displays, etc., and the US relies on China for many consumer goods.

An estimate by a computable general equilibrium model by Wang and Yang (2019) is that traditional trade will be most affected by the trade war, but GVC-based trades will be less affected. Their study distinguishes simple and complex GVC-based trades, where the latter means trade involving products that cross international borders more than twice. Their study further finds that China will be affected negatively by increased tariffs on its products by the US. However, an increasing trade diversion will occur in terms of widening GVC-based indirect exports of made-in-China products via increased exports to the US by third countries adopting Chinese intermediate goods. Thus, when such indirect trade increases, the US might not succeed much in reducing China's export unless tariffs are imposed on the third countries that import intermediates from China. China is already the number one trading partner of most major economies in Asia and around the world, including EU economies. In other words, the US–China trade conflict would have trade diversion effects, such that third countries trading with the US may increase. Consequently, these third countries would

---

[5] The Chinese firm SMIC doing foundry business is trying to catch up with the leading firms, like TSMC (Taiwan) and Samsung (Korea), but it needs to purchase equipment, such as extreme ultraviolet lithography, abroad, from a Dutch company called ASML, which is almost a monopoly firm for that product. This company is recently reported not to have renewed the exporting license with SMIC.

import more from China as they increase trade with the US. Thus, the sum of China's direct and indirect trade with the US would not decrease very much to the extent that the volumes of such indirect or GVC-based trades increase (Wang and Yang 2019).

Furthermore, such protectionism and US–China trade war will damage US economy and industries, although the effects are different according to the sector and item. For instance, China has become an important supplier of parts and components for automobiles and sells to the US, Korea, and several other countries. Hence, increased tariffs on automobile products will negatively affect the final assembly production of cars in the US (Wang and Yang 2019). For example, auto manufacturer Tesla announced that the higher tariffs on Chinese parts pushed up costs for the company by USD 50 million in Q4 2018 (Erken et al. 2019). In the meantime, in apparels and electronics, China is a supplier of the final products to the US, and thus US consumers would be negatively affected by tariffs on Chinese products. This is the case with Apple, which ships components to China for the assembly of its products and reimports the final products for distribution on the US and the global markets. In these sectors, the indirect impact on Chinese firms is most likely significantly lower simply because US firms use China as a manufacturing hub and not the other way around (Erken et al. 2019).

Furthermore, whereas China's value-added exports of apparel and electronics to the US market may decline, China may increase its value-added exports to other third-country destinations as these countries increase their exports to the US. This kind of trade diversion also means change in the GVC, and Vietnam is already coming up as a place to host factories that are being relocated out of China. Actually, such kind of trade diversion was what happened to Japanese trade after the 1985 Plaza Accord, which appreciated the Japanese yen suddenly (Liu and Woo 2018). With the rapid appreciation of the yen, Japanese firms relocated their factories out of Japan to Southeast Asian countries, where they assembled the Japanese-brand products and exported to the US. The ultimate consequence was that Japanese trade surplus with the US decreased a bit but the overall trade surplus of Japan did not. This is because Japan increased its exports of intermediate goods to Southeast Asia, which increased their export to the US, and thus the US overall trade deficits did not decrease as it imported more from non-Japanese countries (Liu and Woo 2018).

In fact, China and the US are the biggest trading partners of each other. These countries are already coupled to each other deeply in GVC-based trade network. In addition, China buys US treasury bonds using the dollars it earned from exporting to the US market. In this sense, staging a trade war with China might be too late for the US because the two are already connected and chained to globalization (Farrell and Newman 2020). The US might not achieve much in terms of containing China just by means of tariffs and IPRs restrictions. The power of such trade measures cannot be comparable with those of economic sanctions, which have a direct effect. The remaining option for the US is to scale up the current trade war into an all-front major war that involves banking and financial flows and tightening restrictions of firm-level transactions by global companies with Chinese firms. The latter scenario is too risky for the global and US economy to be borne by US politicians and their government, especially by the new administration under Biden. For instance, the long term impacts of the US actions against Huawei is yet uncertain in telecom systems markets, different from handset markets, partly owing to the mixed responses by European countries, and Trump had to allow Boeing to sell its engines and other components to Chinese firms that build China-branded airplanes. However, the US still seems to look for whatever possible options to challenge China. One such measure applied by the US jointly with the EU and Japan is to tighten up the WTO rules regarding industrial subsidies.[6] But, global political economy is very complicated, and the EU and China reached a bilateral investment agreement during the last week of 2020 after seven-year-long negotiations. The EU needs the Chinese market for its economic growth, especially after the pandemic.

10.4 Mounting Challenges Facing the Chinese Economy

The Chinese economy was undergoing important structural changes around the onset of the global financial crisis in 2008–2009. These changes included a shift to more domestic consumption-driven growth away from investment-driven growth, inland province-driven growth away from coastal province-driven growth, and indigenous technology-driven growth away from FDI-driven growth. These strategies were not just slogans; instead, they exhibited specific indicators. For instance, the ratio of new FDI flow to GDP declined from 6.2 percent in 1994 to 1.5 percent in 2018. Economic growth rates were reversed between inland and coastal provinces, and the former recorded higher rates than the latter. Such a reversal was unexpected considering the situation during the last several decades. Furthermore, the Xi leadership is pushing hard to reduce the debt of local governments (Wong 2016). However, these reform efforts were all disrupted by the global financial crisis in 2008, US–China trade conflicts in 2018, and the onset of Covid-19 in 2020. The responses to these shocks took priority over the ongoing structural reforms.

To counterbalance the negative impact of these shocks, the Chinese government loosened up its policy regarding credit supply by commercial banks, and

---

[6] For some more information on this, please refer to the following site: https://ustr.gov/about-us/policy-offices/press-office/press-releases/2020/january/joint-statement-trilateral-meeting-trade-ministers-japan-united-states-and-european-union. Although this trilateral agreement does not mention the name of any country, this article is obviously targeting China.

went on to reduce interest rates and to loosen control over fiscal expenditure by local governments. These changes have resulted in rising debts of the corporate sectors and local governments, rampant shadow banking, and housing bubble again. For instance, the ratio of corporate debts to GDP decreased owing to reform from 108 percent in 2006 to 97.6 percent in 2008, but increased afterward to 122 percent in 2009 and then kept increasing to 160 percent in 2016 (Figure 10.4). After the peak in 2016, the rate dropped to 152 percent in 2018, but increased again to 155 percent in 2019, owing to the policy response to the US–China trade conflict.

The ratio of local government deficits to GDP was stable at approximately 5.4 percent in the mid-2000s, but jumped to higher than 8 percent after the onset of the global financial crisis in 2009 and kept increasing to reach even 10 percent in 2019 (Figure 10.5). Such increase in local government deficits results in fiscal deficits of the national government along with those of the central and local governments. Figure 10.5 shows that the overall national economy attained fiscal surplus in 2007 or before the global crisis, thereby offsetting local deficits by central surplus. However, the overall balance eventually turns into deficits, reaching 5 percent in 2018, as the deficits by local governments (higher than 10 percent of GDP) increase more than the budget surplus of the central government (5 percent or higher).

These worsening symptoms in the Chinese economy suggest that the policy response to external shock by allocating resources to the problem sectors has increasingly become a burden on the domestic economy and government budget. The former Soviet Union collapsed even without a hot war with the US but owing

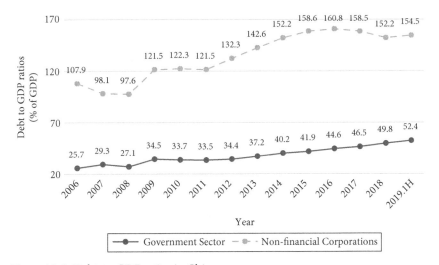

Figure 10.4 Debt-to-GDP ratios in China

Source: Drawn by the author using the data from the Bank for International Settlements.

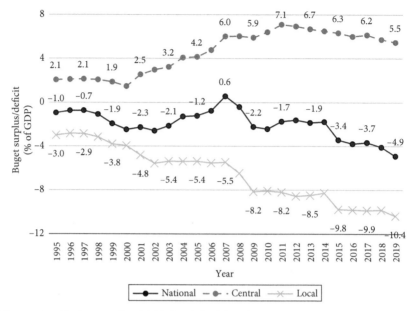

Figure 10.5 Budget surplus (+)/deficit (−) of the Chinese national, central, and local governments

Source: Drawn using the data from the China Economic Information Center (https://www.ceicdata.com/ko); the original source is the Ministry of Finance of China.

to the cold war and the associated burden of keeping up military expenditure. Fiscal imbalance is the main cause of the collapses of great powers in history (Hubbard and Kane 2013). Despite the double deficits (fiscal and trade), the US survives by continuing to print dollars. However, this strategy is not an option for China because the Chinese currency, Renminbi, is still limited as an international reserve currency and capital market is not open in China.

Such transmission of external shocks to domestic problems indicates the channels of reaction from the Thucydides trap to the MIT. Although the former trap will slow down China's catch-up with the US in terms of economic power, its repercussion on the MIT is disrupting the China-led GVC in Asia and the ongoing reforms. The rates of GDP growth in China had been slowing down to less than 6 or 7 percent even before the outbreak of the Covid-19 pandemic in spring 2020 (Dollar et al. 2020). The last 10 years have been a path of sharp decline from the peak of 14 percent in 2008 to 6.6 percent in 2018 (Figure 1.2 in Chapter 1). One of the consequences of this GDP slowdown is the slowdown of per capita income catch-up, vis-à-vis that of the US. Now, China has come close to the 30 percent level of the US per capita income; it was 29 percent in 2018 (Figure 1.1 in Chapter 1). However, its catch-up speed substantially slowed down, as can be seen from the slope of the graph, although Covid-19 has reversed the slowdown because the US is hit much more badly than China. Anyway the 30 percent level is similar to that of Brazil and is exactly at the middle of the 20–40 percent range, which is the World Bank's definition of the MIT for the upper middle-income countries.

Of course, the trend of slowdown of economic growth is affected by outside factors, domestic reforms, and changing priorities since the 2000s to rebalance the economic structure, as well as demographic changes including aging and environmental constraints (Dollar et al. 2020). However, this outside shock came at the most difficult of times and thus may further reinforce the ongoing downward trend of income growth in China, although its relative catch-up with the US is a different matter and depends on the performance of the US economy, especially after the pandemic.

In the 2000s, when the Chinese economy was maintaining strong growth (Figure 1.2 in Chapter 1), the popular term used to explain the growth was "Beijing Consensus," which declares that China is different not only from the Washington Consensus but also from the East Asian model pioneered by Japan, followed by the Asian Tigers South Korea and Taiwan. However, as discussed in Chapter 5, China still shares several common weaknesses of East Asian capitalism, because the country is also a developmental state that combines political authoritarianism and mercantilist operation of the economy (Johnson 1982; Whittacker et al. 2000). Neighboring East Asian economies, such as Japan, Korea, and Taiwan, all tended to suffer weaknesses of varying degrees, such as from a weak financial sector, vulnerability to exogenous shocks, or cronyism associated with the tension between political authoritarianism and independent and sound private sector growth. The symptoms in China, such as rising corporate debts and non-performing loans in government-controlled financial resources, look very similar to the 1990s Korea before the outbreak of the Asian financial crisis. Although one of the differences in China is the closed nature of its capital market, financial turmoil would always be a possibility. Of course, the state-controlled financial resources would work as a buffer for a moment and to a certain extent. It can be said that a possibility of financial crisis or at least some forms of turmoil is increasing because the Chinese economy has been on track of financial liberalization, which is also favored by some economists inside China.

If we follow Milanovic (2019: 91–96) and consider China as a state-led, political capitalism defined as a system with efficient bureaucracy, weak rule of law (discretionary control), and autonomy of the state, China would also suffer from several problems associated with its two intrinsic contradictions—the first one between the need for rule-based management of affairs required for a good bureaucracy and discretionary application of law, and the second one between the possibility of inequality-increasing corruption associated with weak rule of law and the maintenance of economic performance (for political legitimacy) of high growth and less inequality. Response to these contractions were different across the leadership in China; while Hu Jintao tried to reinforce the rule of law, Xi

Jinping tried to control corruption while keeping the principle of discretion in decision-making (Milanovic 2019: 95). Whether either approach has been or is succeeding is uncertain, given the fundamentality of the contradiction. One way for China to handle the contradiction has been to keep a certain degree of elite competition associated with collective leadership and the rule of one 10-year-long tenure for every leader. Given that this tradition has now become uncertain under the current leadership, the Chinese version of state capitalism can be said to be always in precarious equilibrium if we borrow the term of Milanovic (2019: 95).

10.5 Concluding Remarks: Will China Overcome the Triple Traps by Leapfrogging?

Until the mid-2010s, or before the Trump government, China was navigating steadily to grow beyond the MIT, building its China-led GVC and localizing formerly imported goods into domestic production. Further the so-called 4th Industrial Revolution has been serving as a critical window of opportunity for China to leapfrog into the next generations of technologies ahead of many Western nations. Such leapfrogging has been spearheaded by the three platform giants called BAT (Baidu, Alibaba, and Tencent) and other high-tech firms dealing in electric cars, drones, and artificial intelligence. The Belt and Road Initiative was to scale up and globalize the China-led GVC.

However, China suddenly faced the trap of Thucydides because of the US measures for containing the further rise of China as a superpower that threatens American hegemony. The US–China trade war and other measures against China are expected to slow down China's catch-up with the US in terms of economic power, although the sudden onset of Covid-19 came as a shock but helped China speed up the catch-up at least for a while; it is the only country that has shown signs of a V-shaped recovery, with 3–4 percent growth in 2020, whereas the US record was minus 6–8 percent growth. In the meantime, China will not collapse unless the US dares to go into an all-out war by taking drastic measures across various fronts of confrontation, which has become less likely under the Biden administration. A new forecast after Covid-19 is that China would be able to catch up in size with the US by the early 2030s. Not an collapse but a partial decoupling is most likely scenario in the future.

The sudden emergence of the Thucydides trap disrupted the China-led GVC formed around Asia, which still relies on the West for key high-tech goods. Such disruption would have further repercussions on the prospect of China's growth beyond the MIT because China now has to reallocate resources away from economic competitiveness and "Made in China 2025" to socio-economic stabilization and job creation, which became important as response to exogenous shocks (including the pandemic) and external challenges. This rebalancing, including that in the GVC, implies additional fiscal burden, which tends to increase deficits of the government and debts of the corporate sector.

China wants to be different from its neighboring Asian economies in terms of economic system. However, it is still a developmental state. Thus, it shares several weaknesses of the East Asian-style state-led capitalism, such as a weak financial sector, vulnerability to exogenous shocks, or cronyism associated with the tension between political authoritarianism and independent and sound private sector growth. Although China does not necessarily have to adopt Western-style liberal democracy, the country has yet to find a viable alternative that is compatible with the people's increasing demand for political democracy and basic human rights. Political democracy has become an issue through the Hong Kong Crisis in 2019 and again some mishandling of the coronavirus eruption at its initial stage in Wuhan in 2020. Although its Asian neighbors have gone through their own path of political democratization, China is now facing the challenge of crossing this unknown territory. It needs political innovation to leapfrog into a new form of political democracy. Seeing the weakness of Western capitalism during the global financial crisis, China dismissed it as its role model and instead decided to go for its own version of the system under the slogan of the so-called "new normal" (*xin changtai*) and declared that it will strive to "institutionalize" socialism with Chinese characteristics.

This situation may be a more challenging trap than the MIT and Thucydides trap. Thus, China is now facing triple traps. Also, the US–China hegemony struggle or the Thucydides trap situation is now forcing China to seek a different technological, economic, and political path from that led by Western countries, which means nothing other than leapfrogging or path creation in diverse dimensions. It is risky and China might fail. But if it succeeds, it will forge ahead as a new superpower capable of its own indigenous innovation and a model of state capitalism. Overcoming the triple trap really requires multidimensional leapfrogging, which involves China seeking and creating its own path of technological, economic, and political development. Such leapfrogging is inevitable for China if it really wants to catch up with the US. The so-called "catch-up paradox" implies that you cannot catch up if you just keep catching up, where the latter catch up means imitation and the former means overtaking (Lee 2019: 9). In a sense, it is not a paradox because the so-called "catch-up effect" in learning or productivity enhancing is to decrease as you get close to the frontier. Japan and Germany were close to the US in income levels and economic sizes in the 1990s but they failed to catch up with the US because they have become too similar to, rather than different from, the US in economic systems; David cannot beat Goliath if he plays the same way that Goliath used to play. The triple traps are pushing China toward some kind of a crisis but it could be an opportunity. The word "crisis" in Chinese (*weiji*) is a combination of two characters, signifying danger and opportunity.

Bibliography

Abramovitz, M. (1986). "Catching Up, Forging Ahead, and Falling Behind," *The Journal of Economic History*, 46(2), 385–406.

Acemoglu, D., S. Johnson, and J.A. Robinson (2001). "The Colonial Origins of Comparative Development: An Empirical Investigation," *American Economic Review*, 91(5), 1369–401.

Acemoglu, D., S. Johnson, and J.A. Robinson (2002). "Reversal of Fortune: Geography and Institutions in the Making of the Modern World Income Distribution," *The Quarterly Journal of Economics*, 117(4), 1231–94.

Aiyar, S., R. Duval, D. Puy, Y. Wu, and L. Zhang (2013). "Growth Slowdowns and the Middle-Income Trap," *IMF Working Paper*, No. 13/71, International Monetary Fund.

Albert, M.B., D. Avery, F. Narin, and P. McAllister (1991). "Direct Validation of Citation Counts as Indicators of Industrially Important Patents," *Research Policy*, 20(3), 251–9.

Alcatel Bell Telephone (1992). *Report on the Cooperation between Belgium and the People's Republic of China in the Field of Telecommunications*, Antwerp: Bell Telephone Manufacturing Company.

Alesina, A. and R. Perotti (1996). "Income Distribution, Political Instability, and Investment," *European Economic Review*, 40(6), 1203–28.

Alesina, A. and D. Rodrik (1994). "Distributive Politics and Economic Growth," *The Quarterly Journal of Economics*, 109(2), 465–90.

Alesina, A., E. Spolaore, and R. Wacziarg (2005). "Trade, Growth and the Size of Countries," in: P. Aghion and S. Durlauf (Eds.), *Handbook of Economic Growth*, Amsterdam: Elsevier, 1499–542.

Allen, T.J. (1984). *Managing the Flow of Technology: Technology Transfer and the Dissemination of Technological Information within the R&D Organization*, Cambridge: MIT Press.

Allison, G. (2018). *Destined for War: Can America and China Escape Thucydides's Trap?*, Boston: Houghton Mifflin Harcourt.

Amsden, A. (1989). *Asia's Next Giant: South Korea and Late Industrialization*, New York and Oxford: Oxford University Press.

Amsden, A. (2001). *The Rise of the Rest: Late Industrialization Outside the North Atlantic Region*, New York and Oxford: Oxford University Press.

Amsden, A. and W. Chu (2003). *Beyond Late Development: Taiwan's Upgrading Policies*, Cambridge: MIT Press.

Athreye, S. and W. Chen (2010). "Go West for Fame and Fortune? The Role of Internationalization in the Growth of Chinese Telecom Firms," *Proceedings of the 3rd China Goes Global Conference*, Sep. 30–Oct. 2, 2009 held in Harvard Kennedy School, Cambridge, USA.

Bai, M.-K. (1982). "The Turning Point in the Korean Economy," *The Developing Economies*, 20(2), 117–40.

Baldwin, R. (2011). "Trade and Industrialisation after Globalisation's 2nd Unbundling: How Building and Joining A Supply Chain Are Different and Why It Matters," *NBER Working Paper*, No. 17716, National Bureau of Economic Research.

Baldwin, R. (2016). *The Great Convergence*, Cambridge and London: Harvard University Press.

Banerjee, A.V. and A.F. Newman (1993). "Occupational Choice and the Process of Development," *Journal of Political Economy*, 101(2), 274–98.

Beck, T., A. Demirguc-Kunt, and R. Levine (2005). "SMEs, Growth, and Poverty: Cross-Country Evidence," *Journal of Economic Growth*, 10(3), 199–229.

Berry, S. and J. Waldfogel (2010). "Product Quality and Market Size," *The Journal of Industrial Economics*, 58(1), 1–31.

Berthélemy, J.-C. and S. Démurger (2000). "Foreign Direct Investment and Economic Growth: Theory and Application to China," *Review of Development Economics*, 4(2), 140–55.

Best, M.H. (2018). *How Growth Really Happens: The Making of Economic Miracles through Production, Governance, and Skills*, Princeton: Princeton University Press.

Blodgett, L.L. (1991). "Partner Contributions as Predictors of Equity Share in International Joint Ventures," *Journal of International Business Studies*, 22(1), 63–78.

Bolton, P. and G. Roland (1997). "The Breakup of Nations: A Political Economy Analysis," *The Quarterly Journal of Economics*, 112(4), 1057–90.

Brenner, M.D. (2001). "Re-Examining the Distribution of Wealth in Rural China," in: C. Riskin, R. Zhao, and S. Li (Eds.), *China's Retreat from Equality: Income Distribution and Economic Transition*, Armonk: M.E. Sharpe, 245–75.

Breschi, S., F. Malerba, and L. Orsenigo (2000). "Technological Regimes and Schumpeterian Patterns of Innovation," *The Economic Journal*, 110(463), 388–410.

Bresser-Pereira, L.C., E.C. Araújo, and S.C. Peres (2020). "An Alternative to the Middle-Income Trap," *Structural Change and Economic Dynamics*, 52, 294–312.

Brester, G.W. and J.B. Penn (1999). "Strategic Business Management Principles for the Agricultural Production Sector in a Changing Global Food System," *Policy Issues Paper*, No. 11, Trade Research Center, Department of Agricultural Economics and Economics, Montana State University.

Breznitz, D. and M. Murphree (2011). *Run of the Red Queen: Government, Innovation, Globalization, and Economic Growth in China*, New Haven: Yale University Press.

Brouthers, K.D. and G.J. Bamossy (1997). "The Role of Key Stakeholders in the International Joint Venture Negotiations: Case Studies from Eastern Europe," *Journal of International Business Studies*, 28(2), 285–308.

BusinessWeek (2010). "Huawei 'Open' to Opportunities in North America, Executive Says," April 15, 2010, www.businessweek.com/technology/content/apr2010/tc20100414_543829.htm.

Cai, F. (2010). "Demographic Transition, Demographic Dividend, and Lewis Turning Point in China," *China Economic Journal*, 3(2), 107–19.

Callon, M. (1992). "The Dynamics of Techno-Economic Networks," in: R. Coombs, P. Saviotti, and V. Walsh (Eds.), *Technical Change and Company Strategies*, London: Harcourt Brace Jovanovich, 72–102.

Carlsson, B. and R. Stankiewicz (1991). "On the Nature, Function and Composition of Technological Systems," *Journal of Evolutionary Economics*, 1(2), 93–118.

CCID (China Center for Information Industry Development) (2001). *Analysis of China's Enterprise Management Software Industry* (in Chinese). Accessed at: https://www.ccidgroup.com/

CCID (2001–2007). *Report of China's Software Industry* (in Chinese). Accessed at: https://www.ccidgroup.com/

CCID (2006–2009). *Embedded Software Development in China* (in Chinese). Accessed at: https://www.ccidgroup.com/

CCID (2009). *2009 China's Software Industry Annual Report* (in Chinese).

Chakravarthy, B. and D. Yau (2017). "Becoming Global Leaders: Innovation Challenges for Five Large Chinese Firms," *Strategy & Leadership*, 45(2), 19–24.

Chandler, A.D. (1959). "The Beginning of Big Business in American Industry," Business History Review, 33 (1), 1–31.

Chandler, A.D. (1977). *The Visible Hand: Managerial Revolution in American Business*, Cambridge, MA: Harvard University Press.

Chandler, A.D. (1990). *Scale and Scope: The Dynamics of Industrial Capitalism*, Cambridge, MA: Harvard University Press.

Chandra, V. (Ed.) (2006). *Technology, Adaptation, and Exports: How Some Developing Countries Got It Right*, Washington, DC: The World Bank.

Chen, B. and Y. Feng (2000). "Determinants of Economic Growth in China: Private Enterprise, Education, and Openness," *China Economic Review*, 11(1), 1–15.

Chen, L. (2005). *Institution, Elite and Consensus: The Policy Process of China's Semiconductor Industrial Policies* (in Chinese), Dissertation Submitted to Tsinghua University in partial fulfillment of the requirement for the degree of Doctor of Management.

Chen, L. and B. Naughton (2016). "An Institutionalized Policy-Making Mechanism: China's Return to Techno-Industrial Policy," *Research Policy*, 45(10), 2138–52.

Chen, M. and J. Yue (2002). "Exchange Market Share for Technology? An Analysis of China's Strategy in Absorbing FDI," *Dangdai Zhongguo Yanjiu* [Modern China Studies] (in Chinese), 4, 93–100.

Chen, X. (2014). "Current Status and Future Development of Chinese IC Industry," *Zhongguo dianxin shichang* [China Electronics Market] (in Chinese), 1/2, 14–18.

Cheng, S. (1999). *Jiedu Minzu Xinxi Chanye* [Analysis on National Information Industries], Beijing: Huawen Press.

China Center of Information Industry Development Consulting (2015). *Chinese Mobile Phone Market 2011–2012* (in Chinese), http://znzd.cena.com.cn/2015-02/03/content_260933.htm.

Cho, D.S. and J. Mathew. (2000). *Tiger Technology: The Creation of a Semiconductor Industry in East Asia*, Singapore: Cambridge University Press.

Cho, D.-S., D.-J. Kim, and D.K. Rhee (1998). "Latecomer Strategies: Evidence from the Semiconductor Industry in Japan and Korea," *Organization Science*, 9(4), 489–505.

Choi, Y. (1996). *Dynamic Techno-Management Capability: The Case of Samsung Semiconductor Sector in Korea*, Aldershot: Avebury.

Choo, K., K. Lee, K. Ryu, and J. Yoon (2009). "Changing Performance of Business Groups over Two Decades: Technological Capabilities and Investment Inefficiency in Korean Chaebols," *Economic Development and Cultural Change*, 57(2), 359–86.

Chosun Ilbo, (2009). A report at this newspaper site, Oct. 6, 2009, http://news.chosun.com/site/data/html_dir/2009/10/05/2009100501369.html.

Chu, W.-W. (2011). "How the Chinese Government Promoted a Global Automobile Industry," *Industrial and Corporate Change*, 20(5), 1235–76.

Chung, J.H. (2016). *Centrifugal Empire: Central–Local Relations in China*, New York: Columbia University Press.

Chung, J.H. (2019). "International Politics of the US-China Relations," Presented at *the Conference on US-China Conflicts and Technological Rising of China*, October 29, 2019, Seoul.

Cline, R.S. (1975). *World Power Assessment: A Calculus of Strategic Drift*, Boulder: Westview Press.

Cyhn, J.W. (2002). *Technology Transfer and International Production: The Development of the Electronics Industry in Korea*, Cheltenham and Northampton: Edward Elgar.

Czepiel, J.A. (1974). "Word-of-Mouth Processes in the Diffusion of a Major Technological Innovation," *Journal of Marketing Research*, 11(2), 172–80.

D'Costa, A.P. (2014). "Compressed Capitalism and Development: Primitive Accumulation, Petty Commodity Production, and Capitalist Maturity in India and China," *Critical Asian Studies*, 46(2), 317–44.

Das, M. and P. N'Diaye (2013). "Chronicle of a Decline Foretold: Has China Reached the Lewis Turning Point?," *IMF Working Paper*, No. 13–26, International Monetary Fund.

Deininger, K. and L. Squire (1998). "New Ways of Looking at Old Issues: Inequality and Growth," *Journal of Development Economics*, 57(2), 259–87.

Dittberner, D.L. (1977). "Telephone Switching–Technologies in Conflict," in: P. Polishuk and M.A. O'Bryan (Eds.), *Telecommunications and Economic Development*, Norwood: Horizon House International.

Dollar, D., Y. Huang, and Y. Yao (Eds.) (2020). *China 2049: Economic Challenges of a Rising Global Power*, Washington, DC: Brookings Institution Press.

Dosi, G., C. Freeman, R.R. Nelson, G. Silverberg, and L. Soete (Eds.) (1988). *Technical Change and Economic Theory*, London: Pinter.

Dunning, J.H., R. Van Hoesel, and R. Narula (1996). "Explaining the 'new' wave of Outward FDI from Developing Countries: The Case of Taiwan and Korea," *MERIT Working Paper*, No. 2/96-013, UNU-MERIT.

Duysters, G. (1996). *The Dynamics of Technical Innovation: The Evolution and Development of Information Technology*, Cheltenham: Edward Elgar.

Editing Committee (2008). *Big Leap Forward* [Da Kuayue] (in Chinese), Beijing: Renmin Press.

Edquist, C. (1997). *Systems of Innovation: Technologies, Institutions, and Organizations*, London: Cassel.

Eichengreen, B., D. Park, and K. Shin (2013). "Growth Slowdowns Redux: New Evidence on the Middle-Income Trap," *NBER Working Paper*, No. 18673, National Bureau of Economic Research.

Enterprise Research Institute in Development Research Center of the State Council (2007). *Annual Report on the Development of China's Large Enterprise Groups*, Beijing: Zhongguo fazhan chubanshe.

Ericsson (1989). *Ericsson Annual Report 1988*. Available at company home page: *https://www.ericsson.com/en/investors*

Ericsson (2014). "Nine Decade of Innovation," *Ericsson Review*, 91, 11.

Erken, H., B. Giesbergen, and L. Nauta (2019). "US-China Trade War: Which Sectors Are More Vulnerable in the GVC," *RaboBank Research Paper*.

Ernst, D. and L. Kim (2002). "Global Production Networks, Knowledge Diffusion, and Local Capability Formation," *Research Policy*, 31(8), 1417–29.

Eun, J.-H. and K. Lee (2002). "Is an Industrial Policy Possible in China? The Case of the Automobile Industry," *Journal of International and Area Studies*, 9(2), 1–21.

Eun, J.-H., K. Lee, and G. Wu (2006). "Explaining the 'University-Run Enterprises' in China: A Theoretical Framework for University–Industry Relationship in Developing Countries and Its Application to China," *Research Policy*, 35(9), 1329–46.

Fagerberg, J. and M.M. Godinho (2006). "Innovation and Catching-Up," in: J. Fagerberg, D.C. Mowery, and R.R. Nelson (Eds.), *The Oxford Handbook of Innovation*, New York: Oxford University Press, 514–42.

Fagre, N. and L.T. Wells (1982). "Bargaining Power of Multinationals and Host Governments," *Journal of International Business Studies*, 13(2), 9–23.

Fan, G. (1996). "Lun Zichan Chongzu" [Studies on Asset's Reorganization], in: M. Hong (Ed.), *Qiye Gaigezhongde Zichanchongzu: Anli Yanjiu yu Lilun Fenxi* [Asset's Reorganization in Enterprises' Reform: Case Studies and Theoretical Analysis], Beijing: Jingji Guanli Chubanshe [Economic Management Publishing House], 125–32.

Fan, P. (2006). "Catching up through Developing Innovation Capability: Evidence from China's Telecom-Equipment Industry," *Technovation*, 26(3), 359–68.

Fan, P. (2010a). "Developing Innovation-Oriented Strategies: Lessons from Chinese Mobile Phone Firms," *International Journal of Technology Management*, 51(2–4), 168–93.

Fan, P. (2010b). "From a Latecomer to a Global Telecom Giant: The Development Pathway of Huawei," *International Journal of Business and Systems Research*, 4(5–6), 691–719.

Farrell, H. and A.L. Newman (2020). "Chained to Globalization: Why It Is Too Late to Decouple," *Foreign Affairs*, Jan./Feb., 70–80.

Feenstra, R.C., M. Yang, and G.G. Hamilton (1997). "Business Groups and Trade in East Asia: Part 2, Product Variety," *NBER Working Paper*, No. 5887, National Bureau of Economic Research.

Fishman, A. and A. Simhon (2002). "The Division of Labor, Inequality and Growth," *Journal of Economic Growth*, 7(2), 117–36.

Flood, J.E. (1994). *Telecommunications Switching, Traffic and Networks*, New York: Prentice Hall.

Franco, A.M. and D. Filson (2000). "Affiliation, Knowledge Diffusion through Employee Mobility," *Federal Reserve Bank of Minneapolis Staff Report*, No. 272.

Freeman, C. (1987). *Technology, Policy, and Economic Performance: Lessons from Japan*, London: Pinter.

Fridlund, M. (2000). "Switching Relations: The Government Development Procurement of a Swedish Computerized Electronic Telephone Switching Technology," in: C. Edquist, L. Hommen, and L. Tsipouri (Eds.), *Public Technology Procurement and Innovation*, Norwell and Dordrecht: Kluwer Academic, 143–66.

Fu, X. (2015). *China's Path to Innovation*, New York: Cambridge University Press.

Fuller, D.B. (2016). *Paper Tigers, Hidden Dragons: Firms and the Political Economy of China's Technological Development*, Oxford: Oxford University Press.

Galor, O. and D.N. Weil (2000). "Population, Technology, and Growth: From Malthusian Stagnation to the Demographic Transition and Beyond," *American Economic Review*, 90(4), 806–28.

Gao, X. (2011). "Effective Strategies to Catch up in the Era of Globalization: Experiences of Local Chinese Telecom Equipment Firms," *Research-Technology Management*, 54(1), 42–9.

Gao, X. (2014). "A Latecomer's Strategy to Promote a Technology Standard: The Case of Datang and TD-SCDMA," *Research Policy*, 43(3), 597–607.

Gao, X. and J. Liu (2012). "Catching up through the Development of Technology Standard: The Case of TD-SCDMA in China," *Telecommunications Policy*, 36(7), 531–45.

Gartner (2001). *Worldwide Telecommunications Equipment Overview*. Accessed at: https://www.gartner.com/en/documents

Gartner (2005). *Forecast: Global Telecommunications Market Take*. Accessed at https://www.gartner.com/en/documents

Gartner (2006). *Top 20 Telecom Equipment Vendors, Worldwide*. Accessed at https://www.gartner.com/en/documents

Gartner (2007). *Dataquest Insight: Top 20 Telecom Equipment Vendors, Worldwide*. Accessed at https://www.gartner.com/en/documents

Gartner (2010). *Market Insight: A Snapshot Review of the Top Telecom Equipment Vendors, Worldwide*. Available at: https://www.gartner.com/en/documents

Gereffi, G. (1999). "International Trade and Industrial Upgrading in the Apparel Commodity Chain," *Journal of International Economics*, 48(1), 37–70.

Gereffi, G. (2014). "Global Value Chains in a Post-Washington Consensus World," *Review of International Political Economy*, 21(1), 9–37.

Gerschenkron, A. (1962). *Economic Backwardness in Historical Perspective*, Cambridge, Harvard University Press.

Glaeser, E.L., R. La Porta, F. Lopez-de-Silanes, and A. Shleifer (2004). "Do Institutions Cause Growth?," *Journal of Economic Growth*, 9(3), 271–303.

Goto, A. (1982). "Business Groups in a Market Economy," *European Economic Review*, 19(1), 53–70.

Griliches, Z. (1990). "Patent Statistics as Economic Indicators: A Survey," *Journal of Economic Literature*, 28(4), 1661–707.

Grossman, G.M. and E. Helpman (1994). "Protection for Sale," *The American Economic Review*, 84(4), 833–50.

Gu, S. (1999). *China's Industrial Technology: Market Reform and Organisational Change*, London: Routledge.

Gu, S. and B.-Å. Lundvall (2006a). "Introduction: China's Innovation System and the Move towards Harmonious Growth and Endogenous Innovation," *Innovation: Management, Policy & Practice*, 8(1–2), 1–26.

Gu, S. and B.-Å. Lundvall (2006b). "Policy Learning as a Key Process in the Transformation of the Chinese Innovation Systems," in: B.-Å. Lundvall, P. Intarakumnerd, and J. Vang (Eds.), *Asia's Innovation Systems in Transition*, Cheltenham: Edward Elgar, 293–312.

Gu, S., B.-Å. Lundvall, J. Liu, F. Malerba, and S.S. Serger (2009). "China's System and Vision of Innovation: An Analysis in Relation to the Strategic Adjustment and the Medium- to Long-Term S&T Development Plan (2006–20)," *Industry and Innovation*, 16(4–5), 369–88.

Guillén, M.F. (2001). *The Limits of Convergence: Globalization and Organizational Change in Argentina, South Korea, and Spain*, Princeton: Princeton University Press.

Gustafsson, B., S. Li, and T. Sicular (Eds.) (2008). *Inequality and Public Policy in China*, Cambridge: Cambridge University Press.

Hahn, D. and K. Lee (2006). "Chinese Business Groups: Their Origins and. Development," in: S. Chang (Ed.), *Business Groups in East Asia: Financial Crisis, Restructuring, and New Growth*, Oxford and New York: Oxford University Press, 207–231.

Hall, B.H., A. Jaffe, and M. Trajtenberg (2005). "Market Value and Patent Citations," *The RAND Journal of Economics*, 36(1), 16–38.

Han, H. (2001). "Large Firms' Growth and Market Competition in China: Case of Household Appliances Industry" (in Korean), Presented at *Annual Conference of Academy of Contemporary China Studies: Korea and China in the 21 Century: Re-explanation of the Implication*, Nov. 30, 2001, Seoul.

Hess, W. (2006). "Going Outside, Round-Tripping and Dollar Diplomacy: An Introduction to Chinese Outward Direct Investment," *World Market Analysis*, January, www.globalinsight.com.

Hidalgo, C.A., B. Klinger, A.-L. Barabási, and R. Hausmann (2007). "The Product Space Conditions the Development of Nations," *Science*, 317(5837), 482–7.

Hiratsuka, D. (Ed.) (2006). *East Asia's De Facto Economic Integration*, New York: Palgrave Macmillan and IDE-JETRO.

Hobday, M. (1995). *Innovation in East Asia: The Challenge to Japan*, London: Edward Elgar.

Hobday, M. (2000). "East versus Southeast Asian Innovation Systems: Comparing OEM- and TNC-Led Growth in Electronics," in: L. Kim and R.R. Nelson (Eds.), *Technology, Learning and Innovation*, Cambridge: Cambridge University Press, 129–169.

Hu, A. (2009). "Quantitative Assessment of China's Power in Economy, Science and Technology," in: K. Lee, J. Kim, and W. Woo (Eds.), *Power and Sustainability of the Chinese State*, London: Routledge, 31–46.

Hu, Q. (2006). *Xinlulicheng: 909 Chaodaguimo Jichengdianlu Gongcheng Jishi* (in Chinese), Beijing: Publishing House of Electronics Industry.

Huang, J.S. (2000). "1997nina shangshi gongsi jianbing feishangshi gongsi anli fenxi" [Analysis of the M&A of Non-Listed Firms by Listed Firms in 1997] (in Chinese), http://www.mergers-china.com/redianjujiao/bzsddetail.asp?id=169.

Huang, W. (2006). "Internationalization of Chinese Firms: A Case Study of Huawei Technologies Ltd.," Master's thesis, Nottingham University.

Huang, Y., G. Qin, and W. Xun (2013). Institutions and the Middle-income Trap. *Paper at the International Conference on the Inequality and the Middle-income Trap in China*, hosted by the CCER of the Peking University.

Huawei (2001, 2004, 2006, 2007, 2008, 2011, 2012). *Huawei Annual Report*. Accessed at https://www.huawei.com/us/annual-report

Hubbard, G. and T. Kane (2013). *Balance: The Economics of Great Powers from Ancient Rome to Modern America*, New York: Simon & Schuster Paperbacks.

Hughes, T. (1984). "The Evolution of Large Technological Systems," in: W. Bijker, T. Hughes, and T. Pinch (Eds.), *The Social Construction of Technological Systems*, Cambridge: MIT Press, 51–82.

Hussain, A., P. Lanjouw, and N. Stern (1994). "Income Inequalities in China: Evidence from Household Survey Data," *World Development*, 22(12), 1947–57.

IC Insights (2015). "IDMs Could Top Fabless Semiconductor Company Growth for Only the Second Time in History," *Online Research Bulletin*, https://www.icinsights.com/news/bulletins/IDMs-Could-Top-Fabless-Semiconductor-Company-Growth-For-Only-The-Second-Time-In-History.

iResearch (2006, 2007, 2008). *China Online Game Report* . Accessed at: https://www.iresearchchina.com/index.html

Jaffe, A.B. (1986). "Technological Opportunity and Spillovers of R&D," *NBER Working Paper*, No.1815, National Bureau of Economic Research.

Jaffe, A.B. (1989). "Characterizing the 'Technological Position' of Firms, with Application to Quantifying Technological Opportunity and Research Spillovers," *Research Policy*, 18(2), 87–97.

Jaffe, A.B. and M. Trajtenberg (2002). *Patents, Citations, and Innovations: A Window on the Knowledge Economy*, Cambridge, MA: MIT Press.

Jankowska, A., A. Nagengast, and J.R. Perea (2012). "The Product Space and the Middle-Income Trap: Comparing Asian and Latin American Experiences," *Working Paper*, No. 311, OECD Development Center.

Jee, M., E. Choi, N. Lee, S. Kim, and G. Baek. (2005). *Development of China's Firms and Industries: The Impacts on Korea* (in Korean), Seoul: Korea Institute for International Economic Policy. Accessed at https://www.kiep.go.kr/gallery.es?mid=a10101010000&bid=0001&list_no=792&act=view

Jia, K., M. Kenney, J. Mattila, and T. Seppala (2018). "The Application of Artificial Intelligence at Chinese Digital Platform Giants: Baidu, Alibaba and Tencent," *ETLA Reports*, No. 81.

Jin, F. (2010). "Changing Mechanisms of Economic Growth and Urban-Rural Inequality in China," PhD thesis in economics, Seoul National University.

Jin, F. and K. Lee (2017). "Dynamics of the Growth–Inequality Nexus in China: Roles of Surplus Labor, Openness, Education, and Technical Change in Province-Panel Analysis," *Journal of Economic Policy Reform*, 20(1), 1–25.

Jin, F., K. Lee, and Y.-K. Kim (2008). "Changing Engines of Growth in China: From Exports, FDI and Marketization to Innovation and Exports," *China & World Economy*, 16(2), 31–49.

Johnson, C. (1982). *MITI and the Japanese Miracle*, Stanford: Stanford University Press.

Joo, D.Y. (2004). *A Study on the Growth Patterns and National R&D Strategy in the Semiconductor Industry* (in Korean), Seoul: KIET.

Joo, S.H. and K. Lee (2010). "Samsung's Catch-up with Sony: An Analysis Using US Patent Data," *Journal of the Asia Pacific Economy*, 15(3), 271–87.

Joo, S.H., C. Oh, and K. Lee (2016). "Catch-up Strategy of an Emerging Firm in an Emerging Country: Analysing the Case of Huawei vs. Ericsson with Patent Data," *International Journal of Technology Management*, 72(1–3), 19–42.

Jung, M. and K. Lee (2010). "Sectoral Systems of Innovation and Productivity Catch-up: Determinants of the Productivity Gap between Korean and Japanese Firms," *Industrial and Corporate Change*, 19(4), 1037–69.

Kaldor, N. (1955). "Alternative Theories of Distribution," *The Review of Economic Studies*, 23(2), 83–100.

Kanbur, R. and X. Zhang (1999). "Which Regional Inequality? The Evolution of Rural–Urban and Inland–Coastal Inequality in China from 1983 to 1995," *Journal of Comparative Economics*, 27(4), 686–701.

Kang, B. (2014). "The Innovation Process of Huawei and ZTE: Patent Data Analysis," *China Economic Review*, 36, 378–93.

Kang, R. and Y. Ke (1999a). *Qiye Duoyuanhua Jingying* [Corporate Diversification], Beijing: Jijing Kexue Chubanshe [Economic Science Press].

Kang, R. and Y. Ke (1999b), *Zhongguo Qiye Pinglun: Zhanlue yu Shijian* [Chinese Enterprise Review: Strategy and Practice], Beijing: Qiye Guanli Chubanshe [Corporate Management Press].

Kang, Y.-S. and K. Lee (2008). "Performance and Growth of Large Firms in China," *Seoul Journal of Economics*, 21(1), 229–59.

Kawakami, T. (2004). "Structural Changes in China's Economic Growth during the Reform Period," *Review of Urban & Regional Development Studies*, 16(2), 133–53.

Keister, L.A. (2000). *Chinese Business Groups: The Structure and Impact of Interfirm Relations during Economic Development*, Oxford and New York: Oxford University Press.

Kennedy, P. (1987). *The Rise and Fall of the Great Powers*, New York: Random House.

Khan, A.R. and C. Riskin (1998). "Income and Inequality in China: Composition, Distribution and Growth of Household Income, 1988 to 1995," *The China Quarterly*, 154, 221–53.

Kim, C. and K. Lee (2003). "Innovation, Technological Regimes and Organizational Selection in Industry Evolution: A "History Friendly Model" of the DRAM Industry," *Industrial and Corporate Change*, 12(6), 1195–221.

Kim, J.-Y., T.-Y. Park, and K. Lee (2012). "Technological Catch-up and Governmental Role in Chinese SW Industry" (in Korean), *Hyundai Zung-guk Yeon-gu* [Contemporary China Study], 13(3), 157–202.

Kim, L. (1980). "Stages of Development of Industrial Technology in a Developing Country: A Model," *Research Policy*, 9(3), 254–77.

Kim, L. (1997). *Imitation to Innovation*, Boston, MA: Harvard Business Press.

Kim, Y.-Z. and K. Lee (2008). "Sectoral Innovation System and a Technological Catch-up: The Case of the Capital Goods Industry in Korea," *Global Economic Review*, 37(2), 135–55.

Kindleberger, C.P. (1996). *World Economic Primacy, 1500 to 1990*, New York: Oxford University Press.

King, D.A. (2004). "The Scientific Impact of Nations," *Nature*, 430(6997), 311–16.

KingDee (2001~2007). *Annual Business Report* (in Chinese), www.kingdee.com.cn/en.

KISA (Korea Information Security Agency) (2006). *China Information Security Market Analysis*, www.kisa.or.kr. (in Korean).

Knight J. and L. Song (1999). *The Urban-Rural Divide: Economic Disparities and Interactions in China*, New York: Oxford University Press.

Knight, J., S. Li, and H. WAN, 2016. "The Increasing Inequality of Wealth in China, 2002–2013," Economics Series Working Papers No.816, University of Oxford, Department of Economics.

KOCCA (2009). *Online Game White Paper* (in Korean), 642–57. Accessed at: https://www.kocca.kr/cop/bbs/

Korea Industrial Technology Foundation (2003). *China's Industrial Technology Report: Semiconductor* (in Korean), Seoul: KOTEF.

Kotler, M. (2001). "Distribution in China," *Kotler Marketing Brief*, Kotler Marketing Group. Accessed at: https://www.kotlermarketing.com/

KT Business Research Center (2008). *Digico Issue Report: Current Status of Chinese Online Game Market* (in Korean).

Kuznets, S. (1955). "Economic Growth and Income Inequality," *The American Economic Review*, 45(1), 1–28.

Kwak, J. (2000). "Technological Catch up and Development Strategies in China: In the Case of the Telecommunication Industry," Master's thesis, Seoul National University.

La Porta, R., F. Lopez-De-Silanes, and A. Shleifer (1999). "Corporate Ownership around the World," *The Journal of Finance*, 54(2), 471–517.

Lall, S. (1992). "Technological Capabilities and Industrialization," *World Development*, 20(2), 165–86.

Lall, S. (2000). "The Technological Structure and Performance of Developing Country Manufactured Exports, 1985-98," *Oxford Development Studies*, 28(3), 337–69.

Lecraw, D.J. (1984). "Bargaining Power, Ownership, and Profitability of Transnational Corporations in Developing Countries," *Journal of International Business Studies*, 15(1), 27–43.

Lee, J. and J. Lee (1992). "Technological Development Process and Technological Innovation Strategy of Telecommunication Industry in Korea: Case of Electronic Switches' Development" (in Korean), *Telecommunication Review*, 2(11), 18–43.

Lee, K. (1991). *Chinese Firms and the State in Transition: Property Rights and Agency Problems in the Reform Era*, New York: M.E. Sharpe.

Lee, K. (1996). "Economic Reform, Structural Changes, and Regional Economic Growth in China: Cross-Province Regressions," *Asian Economic Journal*, 10(3), 225–37.

Lee, K. (2005). "Making a Technological Catch-up: Barriers and Opportunities," *Asian Journal of Technology Innovation*, 13(2), 97–131.

Lee, K. (2006a). "Business Groups as an Organizational Device for Catch-up," in: J. Nakagawa (Ed.), *Managing Development: Globalization, Economic Restructuring and Social Policy*, London: Routledge, 217–33.

Lee, K. (2006b). "The Washington Consensus and East Asian Sequencing: Understanding Reform in East and South Asia," in: J. Fanelli and G. McMahon (Eds.), *Understanding Market Reforms Volume 2: Motivation, Implementation and Sustainability*, New York: Palgrave Macmillan, 99–140.

Lee, K. (2011). "Thirty Years of Catch-up in China, Compared with Korea," in: H.-M. Wu and Y. Yao (Eds.), *Reform and Development in China*, London: Routledge, 224–42.

Lee, K. (2013). *Schumpeterian Analysis of Economic Catch-up: Knowledge, Path-Creation, and the Middle-Income Trap*, Cambridge: Cambridge University Press.

Lee, K. (2019a). *The Art of Economic Catch-up: Barriers, Detours and Leapfrogging in innovation systems*, Cambridge: Cambridge University Press.

Lee, K. (2019b). "Economics of Technological Leapfrogging." Inclusive and Sustainable Industrial Development, Working Paper series, no 17. Geneva: UNIDO.

Lee, K. and D. Hahn (2004). "From Insider-Outside Collusion to Insider Control in China's SOEs," *Issue and Studies* (English Edition), 40(2), 1–45.

Lee, K. and D. Hahn (2007). "Market Competition, Plan Constraints, and the Hybrid Business Groups: Explaining the Business Groups in China," *Seoul Journal of Economics*, 20(4), 481–504.

Lee, K. and X. Jin (2009). "The Origins of Business Groups in China: An Empirical Testing of the Three Paths and the Three Theories," *Business History*, 51(1), 77–99.

Lee, K. and J. Ki (2017). "Rise of the Latecomers and Catch-Up Cycles in the World Steel Industry," *Research Policy*, 46(2), 365–75.

Lee, K. and B.-Y. Kim (2009). "Both Institutions and Policies Matter but Differently for Different Income Groups of Countries: Determinants of Long-Run Economic Growth Revisited," *World Development*, 37(3), 533–49.

Lee, K. and Y.-K. Kim (2010). "IPR and Technological Catch-up in Korea," in: H. Odagiri, A. Goto, A. Sunami, and R.R. Nelson (Eds.), *Intellectual Property Rights, Development, and Catch up*, Oxford: Oxford University Press, 133–67.

Lee, K. and J. Lee (2019). "National Innovation Systems, Economic Complexity, and Economic Growth: Country Panel Analysis Using the US Patent Data," *Journal of Evolutionary Economics*, 30, 897–928.

Lee, K. and S. Li (2014). "Possibility of a Middle Income Trap in China: Assessment in Terms of the Literature on Innovation, Big Business and Inequality," *Frontiers of Economics in China*, 9(3), 370–97.

Lee, K. and C. Lim (2001). "Technological Regimes, Catching-up and Leapfrogging: Findings from the Korean Industries," *Research Policy*, 30(3), 459–83.

Lee, K. and F. Malerba (2017). "Catch-up Cycles and Changes in Industrial Leadership: Windows of Opportunity and Responses of Firms and Countries in the Evolution of Sectoral Systems," *Research Policy*, 46(2), 338–51.

Lee, K. and F. Malerba (2018). "Economic Catch-up by Latecomers as an Evolutionary Process," in: R.R. Nelson, G. Dosi, C. Helfat, A. Pyka, P. Saviotti, K. Lee, K. Dopfter, F. Malerba, and S. Winter (Eds.), *Modern Evolutionary Economics: An Overview*, Cambridge: Cambridge University Press, 172–207.

Lee, K. and J.A. Mathews (2010). "From Washington Consensus to BeST Consensus for World Development," *Asian-Pacific Economic Literature*, 24(1), 86–103.

Lee, K. and W.T. Woo (2002). "Business Groups in China Compared with Korean Chaebols," in: J. Dutta (Ed.), *Post-crisis Challenges for Asian Industrialization*, Oxford: Elsevier Science Press, 252–280.

Lee, K., S.-J. Cho, and J. Jin (2009). "Dynamics of Catch-up in Mobile Phones and Automobiles in China: Sectoral Systems of Innovation Perspective," *China Economic Journal*, 2(1), 25–53.

Lee, K., X. Gao, and X. Li (2016). "Industrial Catch-up in China: A Sectoral Systems of Innovation Perspective," *Cambridge Journal of Regions, Economy and Society*, 10(1), 59–76.

Lee, K., D. Hahn, and J. Lin (2002). "Is China Following the East Asian Model? A 'Comparative Institutional Analysis' Perspective," *China Review*, 2(1), 85–120.

Lee, K., M. Jee, and J.-H. Eun (2011). "Assessing China's Economic Catch-up at the Firm Level and Beyond: Washington Consensus, East Asian Consensus and the Beijing Model," *Industry and Innovation*, 18(5), 487–507.

Lee, K., C. Lim, and W. Song (2005). "Emerging Digital Technology as a Window of Opportunity and Technological Leapfrogging: Catch-up in Digital TV by the Korean Firms," *International Journal of Technology Management*, 29(1–2), 40–63.

Lee, K., J.Y. Lin, and H.-J. Chang (2005). "Late Marketisation versus Late Industrialisation in East Asia," *Asian-Pacific Economic Literature*, 19(1), 42–59.

Lee, K., S. Mani, and Q. Mu (2012). "Explaining Divergent Stories of Catch-up in the Telecommunication Equipment Industry in Brazil, China, India and Korea," in: F. Malerba and R.R. Nelson (Eds.), *Economic Development as a Learning Process: Variation across Sectoral Systems*, Cheltenham and Northampton: Edward Elgar, 21–71.

Lee, K., T.Y. Park, and R.T. Krishnan (2014). "Catching-up or Leapfrogging in the Indian IT Service Sector: Windows of Opportunity, Path-Creating, and Moving up the Value Chain," *Development Policy Review*, 32(4), 495–518.

Lee, K., D. Qu, and Z. Mao (2021). "Global Value Chains, Industrial Policy, and Industrial Upgrading: Automotive Sectors in Malaysia, Thailand, and China in Comparison with Korea," *The European Journal of Development Research*, 33(2), 275–303.

Lee, K., M. Szapiro, and Z. Mao (2018). "From Global Value Chains (GVC) to Innovation Systems for Local Value Chains and Knowledge Creation," *The European Journal of Development Research*, 30(3), 424–41.

Lee, K., B.-Y. Kim, Y.-Y. Park, and E. Sanidas (2013). "Big Businesses and Economic Growth: Identifying a Binding Constraint for Growth with Country Panel Analysis," *Journal of Comparative Economics*, 41(2), 561–82.

Lee, K., T. Miyagawa, Y. Kim, and K. Edamura (2016). "Comparing the Management Practices and Productive Efficiency of Korean and Japanese Firms: An Interview Survey Approach," *Seoul Journal of Economics*, 29(1), 1–41.

Lewis, W.A. (1954). "Economic Development with Unlimited Supplies of Labour," *The Manchester School*, 22(2), 139–91.

Li, J. (2000). *Yidong Tongxin 100 Nian* [100 Years for Mobile Communication], www.chinatelecom.com.cn.

Li, J. and X. Pu (2009). "Technology Evolution in China's Color TV Industry," *Industry and Innovation*, 16(4–5), 479–97.

Li, S. (2018). "Four Decades of China's Income Distribution Reform," *China Economist*, 13(4), 2–33.

Li, S. and P. Lian (1999). "Decentralization and Coordination: China's Credible Commitment to Preserve the Market under Authoritarianism," *China Economic Review*, 10(2), 161–90.

Li, S. and C. Luo (2008). "Growth Pattern, Employment, and Income Inequality: What the Experience of Republic of Korea and Taipei, China Reveals to the People's Republic of China," *Asian Development Review*, 25(1/2), 100–18.

Li, S. and X. Yue (2004). "A Survey of the Income Gap between Urban and Rural Areas in China," *Caijing* [Finance and Economics] (in Chinese), 3, 30–8.

Li, S. and R. Zhao (2008). "Changes in the Distribution of Wealth in China, 1995–2002," in: J.B. Davies (Ed.), *Personal Wealth from a Global Perspective*, Oxford: Oxford University Press, 42–63.

Li, S., S. Li, and W. Zhang (2000). "The Road to Capitalism: Competition and Institutional Change in China," *Journal of Comparative Economics*, 28(2), 269–92.

Li, S., H. Sato, and T. Sicular (2013). *Rising Income Inequality in China*, Cambridge: Cambridge University Press.

Li, Z. (1995). *Modern Chinese Business Groups (Zhongguo Xiandai Qiye Jituan)*, Beijing: Zhongguo Shangye Ban.

Lim, C. (2007). "Catch-up Failure in Core IT Components: The Case of Numerical Controllers," *Asian Journal of Technology Innovation*, 15(2), 101–24.

Lin, C. (2009). *Chanye yu Zhengce: Liangan Xianghu Yilai de Shidai* (in Chinese), Beijing: Shijie Zhishi Chubanshe.

Lin, J.Y. (2003). "Development Strategy, Viability, and Economic Convergence," *Economic Development and Cultural Change*, 51(2), 277–308.

Lin, J.Y. (2012a). *Demystifying the Chinese Economy*, Cambridge: Cambridge University Press.

Lin, J.Y. (2012b). *The Quest for Prosperity: How Developing Economies Can Take off*, Princeton: Princeton University Press.

Lin, J.Y. (2011). "New Structural Economics: A Framework for Rethinking Development." *World Bank Research Observer*, 26(2), 193–221.

Lin, J.Y., F. Cai, and Z. Li (1996). *China Miracle*, Hong Kong: Chinese University Press.

Lissoni, F. (2001). "Knowledge Codification and the Geography of Innovation: The Case of Brescia Mechanical Cluster," *Research Policy*, 30(9), 1479–500.

Liu, C. (2000). *Zhongguo Dianxinye Gaige yu Fazhan* [Reform and Development of Telecommunication in China], http://cn-telecom.com.

Liu, C. (2001). *Dui Woguo Yidongtongxin Shebei Zhizaoye Fazhan Zhanlue de Sikao*]Thinking about the Development Strategy of Manufacturing Industry for Mobile Telecommunication Equipment], http://www.drcnet.com.cn.

Liu, H. and Y. Jiang (2001). "Technology Transfer from Higher Education Institutions to Industry in China: Nature and Implications," *Technovation*, 21(3), 175–88.

Liu, T. and K.-W. Li (2001). "Impact of Liberalization of Financial Resources in China's Economic Growth: Evidence from Provinces," *Journal of Asian Economics*, 12(2), 245–62.

Liu, T. and W.T. Woo (2018). "Understanding the U.S.-China Trade War," *China Economic Journal*, 11(3), 319–40.

Liu, X. (2010). "China's Catch-up and Innovation Model in IT Industry," *International Journal of Technology Management*, 51(2–4), 194–216.

Liu, X. and B. Dalum (2009). "Path-Following or Leapfrogging in Catching-up: The Case of the Chinese Telecommunications Equipment Industry," *Proceedings of 1st International Conference on Wireless Communication, Vehicular Technology, Information Theory and Aerospace & Electronic Systems Technology (Wireless VITAE)*, May 17–20, Aalborg, 446–70.

Liu, X. and S. White (2000). "China's National Innovation System in Transition: An Activity-Based Analysis," Presented at *the US-China Conference on Technical Innovation Management*, Apr. 24–27, Beijing.

Liu, X. and S. White (2001). "Comparing Innovation Systems: A Framework and Application to China's Transitional Context," *Research Policy*, 30(7), 1091–114.

Lu, Q. (2000). *China's Leap into the Information Age: Innovation and Organization in the Computer Industry*, Oxford: Oxford University Press.

Lu, Q. and W. Lazonick (2001). "The Organization of Innovation in a Transitional Economy: Business and Government in Chinese Electronic Publishing," *Research Policy*, 30(1), 55–77.

Lucas, R.E. (2002). *Lectures on Economic Growth*, Harvard: Harvard University Press.

Lundvall, B.Å. (Ed.) (1992). *National System of Innovation towards a Theory of Innovation and Interactive Learning*, London: Pinter.

Luo, J. (2006). "The Impact of Government Policies on Industrial Evolution: China's Automotive Industry," PhD thesis, Engineering Systems Division, MIT.

Ma, R. and X. Ye (2013). "Effect of Purchase Restriction on Chinese Automobile Market," *Qiye Daobao* (in Chinese), 2, 16–17.

Ma, X. and J. Lu (2005). "The Critical Role of Business Groups in China," *Ivey Business Journal*, 69(5), 1–12.

Malerba, F. (2001). "Sectoral Systems of Innovation and Production: Concepts, Analytical Framework and Empirical Evidence," Presented at *the Conference on The Future of Innovation Studies*, Eindhoven University of Technology, the Netherlands, 2001.

Malerba, F. (2002). "Sectoral Systems of Innovation and Production," *Research Policy*, 31(2), 247–64.

Malerba, F. (2003). "Sectoral Systems and Innovation and Technology Policy," *Revista Brasileira de Inovação*, 2(2), 329–75.

Malerba, F. (Ed.) (2004a). *Sectoral Systems of Innovation: Concepts, Issues and Analysis of Six Major Sections in Europe*, Cambridge: Cambridge University Press.

Malerba, F. (2004b). "Sectoral Systems: How and Why Innovation Differs across Sectors" in: J. Fagerberg, D.C. Mowery, and R.R. Nelson (Eds.), *The Oxford Handbook of Innovation*, New York: Oxford University Press, 380–406.

Malerba, F. and S. Mani (2009). *Sectoral Systems of Innovation and Production in Developing Countries, Actors, Structure and Evolution*, Cheltenham: Edward Elgar.

Malerba, F. and R.R. Nelson (2012). *Economic Development as a Learning Process: Variation across Sectoral Systems*, Cheltenham and Northampton: Edward Elgar.

Malerba, F. and L. Orsenigo (1996). "The Dynamics and Evolution of Industries," *Industrial and Corporate Change*, 5(1), 51–87.

Malerba, F. and L. Orsenigo (1997). "Technological Regimes and Sectoral Patterns of Innovative Activities," *Industrial and Corporate Change*, 6(1), 83–118.

Mani, S. (1999). *Public Innovation Policies and Developing Countries in a Phase of Economic Liberalisation*, Maastricht, United Nations University, Institute for New Technologies.

March, J.G. (1991). "Exploration and Exploitation in Organizational Learning," *Organization Science*, 2(1), 71–87.

Martilla, J.A. (1971). "Word-of-Mouth Communication in the Industrial Adoption Process," *Journal of Marketing Research*, 8(2), 173–8.

Mathews, J.A. (2002a). "Competitive Advantages of the Latecomer Firm: A Resource-Based Account of Industrial Catch-up Strategies," *Asia Pacific Journal of Management*, 19(4), 467–88.

Mathews, J.A. (2002b). "The Origins and Dynamics of Taiwan's R&D Consortia," *Research Policy*, 31(4), 633–51.

Mathews, J.A. (2005). "Strategy and the Crystal Cycle," *California Management Review*, 47(2), 6–32.

Mathews, J.A. (2006). "Electronics in Taiwan: A Case of Technological Learning," in: V. Chandra (Ed.), *Technology, Adaptation, and Exports: How Some Developing Countries Got It Right*, Washington, DC: The World Bank, 83–126.

Mathews, J.A. (2008a). "China, India and Brazil: Tiger Technologies, Dragon Multinationals and the Building of National Systems of Economic Learning," *Asian Business & Management*, 8(1), 5–32.

Mathews, J.A. (2008b). "Energizing Industrial Development," *Transnational Corporations*, 17(3): 59–83.

Mathews, J.A. and D.-S. Cho (2000). *Tiger Technology: The Creation of a Semiconductor Industry in East Asia*, New York: Cambridge University Press.

Mazzoleni, R. and R.R. Nelson (2007). "Public Research Institutions and Economic Catch-up," *Research Policy*, 36(10), 1512–28.

Meng, Z., M. Zuo, and J. Fu (2008). "Why Google Cannot Beat Baidu in China Search Engine Market," Presented at *2008 International Symposium on Ubiquitous Multimedia Computing*, October 15, 190–4.

Meyer, M.W. and X. Lu (2005). "Managing Indefinite Boundaries: The Strategy and Structure of a Chinese Business Firm," *Management and Organization Review*, 1(1), 57–86.

MII (Ministry of Information Industry, China) (1997). *China Posts and Telecommunications Annual Report*. Accessed at: https://www.miit.gov.cn/

MII (Ministry of Information Industry, China) (2001). *China Posts and Telecommunications Statistical Publication Report*. Accessed at: https://www.miit.gov.cn/

Milanovic, B. (2019). *Capitalism, Alone: The Future of the System that Rules the World*, Cambridge: Belknap Press of the Harvard University Press.

Ministry of Commerce (MOC) (2004, 2005). *China Outbound Investment Statistics Report*. Accessed at: https://mofcom.gov.cn

Ministry of Education (Ed.) (2004, 2006). *Statistical Report of University-run Industry in China*, Chengdu: Xinan Jiaotong Daxue Chubanshe.

Mody, A. and R. Sherman (1990). "Leapfrogging in Switching Systems," *Technological Forecasting and Social Change*, 37(1), 77–83.

Mowery, D.C., J.E. Oxley, and B.S. Silverman (1998). "Technological Overlap and Interfirm Cooperation: Implications for the Resource-Based View of the Firm," *Research Policy*, 27(5), 507–23.

Mu, Q. (2002). "Market Segmentation, Knowledge Diffusion and Technological Leapfrogging in China: The Case of Telephone Switch," PhD thesis, Seoul National University.

Mu, Q. and K. Lee (2005). "Knowledge Diffusion, Market Segmentation and Technological Catch-up: The Case of the Telecommunication Industry in China," *Research Policy*, 34(6), 759–83.

Narin, F., E. Noma, and R. Perry (1987). "Patents as Indicators of Corporate Technological Strength," *Research Policy*, 16(2), 143–55.

National Bureau of Statistics (2012). *China Statistics Abstract*, Beijing: China Statistics Press.

National Bureau of Statistics, China (2002). *Zhongguo daqiyejituan* [Chinese Big Business Group] *2001*, Beijing: China Statistics Press.

National Bureau of Statistics, China (2006a; 2004). *China Statistical Abstract* (in Chinese), Beijing: China Statistical Press.

National Bureau of Statistics, China (2006b). *China Statistical Yearbook 2005*, Beijing: China Statistics Press.

National Bureau of Statistics, China (2006c). *Zhongguo daqiyejituan* [Chinese Big Business Group] *2005*, Beijing: China Statistics Press.

National Bureau of Statistics, China (2008a). *China Statistical Yearbook 2007*, Beijing: China Statistics Press.

National Bureau of Statistics, China (2008b). *Zhongguo daqiyejituan* [Chinese Big Business Group], Beijing: China Statistics Press.

Naughton, B. (2008). "China's Institutional Catch-up: Achievement and Challenges," Presented at *2008 SNU-NEAR International Conference: "China's Economic Catch-up: Assessment and Prospects,"* held in 2008, Seoul, Korea.

Naughton, B. (2007; revised edition in 2018). *The Chinese Economy: Transitions and Growth*, Cambridge: The MIT Press.

Naughton, B. and Y. Qi (2000). "Inward Technology Transfer and the Chinese National Innovation System," Presented at *the US-China Conference on Technical Innovation Management*, Apr. 24–27, Beijing.

Nelson, R.R. (1993). *National Systems of Innovation: A Comparative Study*, New York: Oxford University Press.

Nelson, R.R. (1995). "Recent Evolutionary Theorizing about Economic Change," *Journal of Economic Literature*, 33(1), 48–90.

Nelson, R.R. (2008a). "Economic Development from the Perspective of Evolutionary Economic Theory," *Oxford Development Studies*, 36(1), 9–21.

Nelson, R.R. (2008b). "What Enables Rapid Economic Progress: What Are the Needed Institutions?," *Research Policy*, 37(1), 1–11.

Nelson, R.R. and H. Pack (1999). "The Asian Miracle and Modern Growth Theory," *The Economic Journal*, 109(457), 416–36.

Nelson, R.R. and S. Winter (1982). *An Evolutionary Theory of Economic Change*, Harvard: Harvard University Press.

NIPA (2002, 2003, 2004, 2005, 2006, 2007, 2008, 2009). *Software Industry White Paper* (in Korean). Accessed at https://www.nipa.kr/main/index.do

Nolan, P. (2001). *China and the Global Economy*, Hampshire and New York: Palgrave Macmillan.

Nolan, P. (2002). "China and the Global Business Revolution," *Cambridge Journal of Economics*, 26(1), 119–37.

Ocampo, J.A. (Ed.) (2005). *Beyond Reforms: Structural Dynamics and Macroeconomic Vulnerability*, Palo Alto: Stanford University Press.

OECD (2013). *OECD Telecommunication Outlook 2013*, Paris, OECD.

Park, J. and K. Lee (2015). "Do Latecomer Firms Rely on 'Recent' and 'Scientific' Knowledge More than Incumbent Firms Do? Convergence or Divergence in Knowledge Sourcing," *Asian Journal of Technology Innovation*, 23(sup1), 129–45.

Park, J., D. Ryu, and K. Lee (2019). "What Determines the Economic Size of a Nation in the World: Determinants of a Nation's Share in World GDP vs. per Capita GDP," *Structural Change and Economic Dynamics*, 51, 203–14.

Park, K.-H. and K. Lee (2006). "Linking the Technological Regime to the Technological Catch-up: Analyzing Korea and Taiwan Using the US Patent Data," *Industrial and Corporate Change*, 15(4), 715–53.

Patel, P. and K. Pavitt (1997). "The Technological Competencies of the World's Largest Firms: Complex and Path-Dependent, but Not Much Variety," *Research Policy*, 26(2), 141–56.

Pause, E. (2009). "Latin America's Middle Income Trap," *Americas Quarterly*. http://www.americasquarterly.org/node/2142.

Perez, C. and L. Soete (1988). "Catching up in Technology: Entry Barriers and Windows of Opportunity," in: G. Dosi, C. Freeman, R.R. Nelson, G. Silverberg, and L. Soete (Eds.), *Technical Change and Economic Theory*, London: Pinter, 458–79.

Perotti, R. (1996). "Growth, Income Distribution, and Democracy: What the Data Say," *Journal of Economic Growth*, 1(2), 149–87.

Persson, T. and G. Tabellini (1994). "Is Inequality Harmful for Growth?," *The American Economic Review*, 84(3), 600–21.

Phillips, K.L. and K. Shen (2005). "What Effect Does the Size of the State-Owned Sector Have on Regional Growth in China?," *Journal of Asian Economics*, 15(6), 1079–102.

Piketty, T. (2014). *Capital in the Twenty-First Century*, Cambridge: Belknap Press of Harvard University Press.

Podolny, J.M., T.E. Stuart, and M.T. Hannan (1996). "Networks, Knowledge, and Niches: Competition in the Worldwide Semiconductor Industry, 1984–1991," *American Journal of Sociology*, 102(3), 659–89.

Porter, M. (1990). *The Competitive Advantage of Nations*, New York: Free Press.

Porter, M. (2003). "The Economic Performance of Regions," *Regional Studies*, 37(6–7), 549–78.

PWC (2009). *China's Impact on Semiconductor Industry: 2008 Update*, Pricewater houseCoopers.

PWC (2013). *Continuing to Grow: China's Impact on the Semiconductor Industry: 2013 Update*, www.pwc.com/gx/en/technology/chinas-impact-on-semiconductor-industry/assets/china-semicon-2013.pdf.

PWC (2014). *China's Impact on Semiconductor Industry: 2013 Update*, Pricewater houseCoopers.

PWC (2016). *China's Impact on the Semiconductor Industry*, www.pwc.com/gx/en/technology/pdf/china-semicon-2015-report-1-5.pdf.

Pyramid (1996). *Telecom Markets in China*, Cambridge: Pyramid Research.

Qian, Y. and B.R. Weingast (1996). "China's Transition to Markets: Market-Preserving Federalism, Chinese Style," *The Journal of Policy Reform*, 1(2), 149–85.

Ramani, S.V. and S. Guennif (2012). "Catching up in the Pharmaceutical Sector: Lessons from Case Studies of India and Brazil," in: F. Malerba and R.R. Nelson (Eds.), *Economic Development as a Learning Process: Variation across Sectoral Systems*, Cheltenham and Northampton: Edward Elgar, 157–93.

Ramo, J. (2004). *Beijing Consensus*, London: Foreign Policy Center.

Rasiah, R. (2006). "Electronics in Malaysia: Export Expansion but Slow Technical Change," in: V. Chandra (Ed.), *Technology, Adaptation, and Exports*, Washington, DC: The World Bank, 127–62.

Ravallion, M. and S. Chen (2007). "China's (Uneven) Progress against Poverty," *Journal of Development Economics*, 82(1), 1–42.

Rho, S.H. (2008). "Comparative Study on the Chinese IC Manufacturing Firm and Korean IC Manufacturing Firm" (in Chinese), Dissertation submitted to Tsinghua University in partial fulfillment of the requirement for the degree of Master of Management.

Rho, S.H., K. Lee, and S.H. Kim (2015). "Limited Catch-up in China's Semiconductor Industry: A Sectoral Innovation System Perspective," *Millennial Asia*, 6(2), 147–75.

Riskin, C., R. Zhao, and S. Li (Eds.) (2001). *China's Retreat from Equality: Income Distribution and Economic Transition*, Armonk: M.E. Sharpe.

Rodrik, D. (1996). "Understanding Economic Policy Reform," *Journal of Economic Literature*, 34(1), 9–41.

Rodrik, D., A. Subramanian, and F. Trebbi (2004). "Institutions Rule: The Primacy of Institutions over Geography and Integration in Economic Development," *Journal of Economic Growth*, 9(2), 131–65.

Rogers, E.M. (1982). "Information Exchange and Technological Innovation," in: D. Sahal (Ed.), *The Transfer and Utilization of Technical Knowledge*, Lexington: Lexington Books, 105–23.

Rosenberg, N. and R.R. Nelson (1994). "American Universities and Technical Advance in Industry," *Research Policy*, 23(3), 323–48.

Rothaermel, F.T. and W. Boeker (2008). "Old Technology Meets New Technology: Complementarities, Similarities, and Alliance Formation," *Strategic Management Journal*, 29(1), 47–77.

Sanidas, E. (2007). "The Impact of Large Firms in Promoting Economic Growth, Exports, and Regional Integration: A Chandlerian Perspective," *Middle East Business and Economic Review*, 19(2), 61–75.

Saxenian, A. and J. Hsu (2001). "The Silicon Valley–Hsinchu Connection: Technical Communities and Industrial Upgrading," *Industrial and Corporate Change*, 10(4), 893–920.

Schmitt, B. (1997). "Who Is the Chinese Consumer? Segmentation in the People's Republic of China," *European Management Journal*, 15(2), 191–4.

Schoenecker, T. and L. Swanson (2002). "Indicators of Firm Technological Capability: Validity and Performance Implications," *IEEE Transactions on Engineering Management*, 49(1), 36–44.

Schrader, S. (1991). "Informal Technology Transfer between Firms: Cooperation through Information Trading," *Research Policy*, 20(2), 153–70.

Schumpeter, J.A. (1934). *Theory of Economic Development: An Inquiry into Profits, Capital, Credit, Interest, and the Business Cycle*, Cambridge, MA: Harvard University Press.

Schumpeter, J.A. (1942). *Capitalism, Socialism and Democracy*, New York: George Allen & Unwin.

Seo, B.-K., K. Lee, and X. Wang (2006). "Explaining Performance Changes in the Business Groups: Three Hypotheses in the Case of China," Presented at *the 2006 Convention of the East Asian Economic Association (EAEA)*, November, 18–19, Beijing.

Shang, J. and P. He (2016). "Advice on Indigenous Innovation of Chinese Automobile Industry," *Automobile Industry Study* (in Chinese), 3, 15–19.

Shanghaishi Xinxihua Weiyuanhui (2007). *Nian Shanghai Jichengdianlu Chanye Fazhan Yanjiu Baogao* (in Chinese), Shanghai: Shanghai Educational Publishing House.

Shen, X. (1999). *The Chinese Road to High Technology: A Study of Telecommunications Switching Technology in the Economic Transition*, London: Macmillan; New York: St. Martin's.

Shi, P. (1999). *Houfa Youshi: Mofang Chuangxin de Lilun yu Shizheng Yanjiu* [Latemover's Advantages: Theory and Empirical Study on Imitative Innovation], Beijing: Tsinghua University Press.

Shin, H. and K. Lee (2012). "Asymmetric Trade Protection Leading not to Productivity but to Export Share Change," *Economics of Transition and Institutional Change*, 20(4), 745–85.

Shin, H. and K. Lee (2019). "Impact of Financialization and Financial Development on Inequality: Panel Cointegration Results Using OECD Data," *Asian Economic Papers*, 18(1), 69–90.

Sino Link Securities (2007). Report on Firm Study. http://www.gjzq.com.cn. 2007.2.14. (in Chinese)

Smith, W.R. (1956). "Product Differentiation and Market Segmentation as Alternative Marketing Strategies," *Journal of Marketing*, 21(1), 3–8.

Steinbock, D. (2018). "U.S.-China Trade War and Its Global Impacts," *China Quarterly of International Strategic Studies*, 4(4), 515–42.

Stewart, K. and H.P. Choi (2003). "PC-Bang (Room) Culture: A Study of Korean College Students' Private and Public Use of Computers and the Internet," *Trends in Communication*, 11(1), 63–79.

Sun, L.S. (2009). "Internationalization Strategy of MNEs from Emerging Economies: The Case of Huawei," *Multinational Business Review*, 17(2), 129–56.

Swart, G. (2015). "Innovation Lessons Learned from the Joule EV Development," *IAMOT 2015 Conference Proceedings*, June 8–11, Cape Town.

Sylwester, K. (2000). "Income Inequality, Education Expenditures, and Growth," *Journal of Development Economics*, 63(2), 379–98.

Tan, Z. (1994). "Challenges to the MPT's Monopoly," *Telecommunications Policy*, 18(3), 174–81.

Tan, Z.A. (2002). "Product Cycle Theory and Telecommunications Industry—Foreign Direct Investment, Government Policy, and Indigenous Manufacturing in China," *Telecommunications Policy*, 26(1), 17–30.

Tenev, S., C. Zhang, and L. Brefort (2002). *Corporate Governance and Enterprise Reform in China*, Washington, DC: The World Bank and the International Finance Corporation.

Thun, E. (2006). *Changing Lanes in China: Foreign Direct Investment, Local Governments, and Auto Sector Development*, Cambridge: Cambridge University Press.

Tian, L. (2001). "Government shareholding and the value of China's modern firms," William Davidson Working Paper Number 395.

Tian, X., S. Lin, and V.I. Lo (2004). "Foreign Direct Investment and Economic Performance in Transition Economies: Evidence from China," *Post-Communist Economies*, 16(4), 497–510.

Todo, Y. and K. Miyamoto (2002). "The Revival of Scale Effects," *Topics in Macroeconomics*, 2(1), 1058–8.

Treacy, M. and F. Wiersema (1995). *The Discipline of Market Leaders*, Cambridge, MA: Perseus Books.

Tsui, K. (1993). "Decomposition of China's Regional Inequalities," *Journal of Comparative Economics*, 17(3), 600–27.

UFIDA (2002~2007). *Annual Business Report* (in Chinese), www.ufida.com.cn/en.

UNCTAD (2005). *Linkages, Value Chains and Outward Investment: Internationalization of Developing Countries' SMEs*, New York and Geneva: United Nations Conference on Trade and Development.

UNCTAD (2013). *World Investment Report 2013, Global Value Chains: Investment and Trade for Development*, New York and Geneva: United Nations Conference on Trade and Development.

Utterback, J.M. and W.J. Abernathy (1975). "A Dynamic Model of Process and Product Innovation," *Omega*, 3(6), 639–56.

Vernon, R. (1966). "International Investment and International Trade in the Product Cycle," *The Quarterly Journal of Economics*, 80(2), 190–207.

Verspagen, B. (1991). "A New Empirical Approach to Catching up or Falling Behind," *Structural Change and Economic Dynamics*, 2(2), 359–80.

Voigtländer, N. and H.-J. Voth (2006). "Why England? Demographic Factors, Structural Change and Physical Capital Accumulation during the Industrial Revolution," *Journal of Economic Growth*, 11(4), 319–61.

Von Hippel, E. (1987). "Cooperation between Rivals: Informal Know-How Trading," *Research Policy*, 16(6), 291–302.

Von Hörnigk, P.W. (1684). *Österreich über Alles, wenn es nur will*, G. Otruba (Ed.), Vienna: Bergland Verlag.

Wang, S. and F. Lai (2013). "State of the Art of China's IC Industry and Strategies for Its Leapfrog Development," *Microelectronics* (in Chinese), 43(4), 572–6.

Wang, X. (1998). "Zhongguo Dianxunye Fazhan Zhanlue" [Development Strategy in Telecommunication Industry in China], *Chanye Luntan* [Industrial Forum], March 1998, Beijing, China.

Wang, X., L. Xu and T. Zhu. (2004). "State-Owned Enterprises Going Public: The Case of China," *Economics of Transition*, 12(3), 467–87.

Wang, X. (2012). "Foreign Direct Investment and Innovation in China's E-commerce Sector," *Journal of Asian Economics*, 23(3), 288–301.

Wang, Z. (2009). "Zhongxin Guoji Jiushulu," *Caijing*, 251, 128–30.

Wang, Z. and J. Yang, (2019). "The Impact of Sino-US Trade Conflicts on Global Value Chain Activities." Presented at *the GReCEST Annual Conference*, Nov. 7, 2019, Peking University.

Wen, J. and S. Kobayashi (2002). "Impacts of Government High-tech Policy: A Case Study of CAD Technology in China," *Journal of Engineering and Technology Management*, 19(3), 321–42.

Westphal, L.E., L. Kim, and C.J. Dahlman (1985). "Reflections on the Republic of Korea's Acquisition of Technological Capability," in: N. Rosenberg and C. Frischtak (Eds.), *International Technology Transfer: Concepts, Measures, and Comparisons*, New York: Praeger, 167–221.

Whittaker, H., T. Sturgeon, T. Okita, and T. Zhu (2020). *Compressed Development*, Oxford: Oxford University Press.

Williamson, J. (1990). "What Washington Means by Policy Reform," in: J. Williamson (Ed.), *Latin American Adjustment: How Much Has Happened*, Washington: Institute for International Economics, 90–120.

Williamson, J. (2012). "Some Basic Disagreements on Development," Presented at *High-Level. Knowledge Forum on Expanding the Frontiers in Development Policy*, Oct 15–16, hosted by the KDI, held in Seoul.

Wong, C. (2016). "Budget Reform in China: Progress and Prospects in the Xi Jinping Era," *OECD Journal on Budgeting*, 2015(3), 1–10.

Woo, W.T. (2012). "China Meets the Middle-Income Trap: The Large Potholes in the Road to Catching-up," *Journal of Chinese Economic and Business Studies*, 10(4), 313–36.

Woo, Y.P. and K. Zhang (2006). "China Goes Global: The Implications of Chinese Outward Direct Investment for Canada," *Horizons*, 2(9), 34–9.

World Bank (1993). *East Asian Miracle*, Oxford: Oxford University Press.

World Bank (1997). *Sharing Rising Incomes: Disparities in China*, Washington, DC: The World Bank.

World Bank (2002, 2004). *Review of Small Business Activities*. Washington, DC: World Bank.

World Bank (2005). *Economic Growth in the 1990s: Learning from a Decade of Reform*, Washington, DC: The World Bank.

World Bank (2010). *World Bank East Asia Pacific Economic Update 2010, Volume 2: Robust Recovery, Rising Risks*, Washington, DC: The World Bank.

World Bank (2012). *China 2030: Building a Modern, Harmonious, and Creative High-Income Society*, Washington, DC: The World Bank.

Wrigley, E.A. and R.S. Schofield (1989). *The Population History of England 1541–1871*, Cambridge: Cambridge University Press.

Wu, J. (Ed.) (1997). *Zhongguo Tongxin Fazhan Zhilu* [The Development Road of Telecommunication in China], Beijing: Xinhua Press.

Wu, X., R. Ma, Y. Shi, and K. Rong (2009). "Secondary Innovation: The Path of Catch-up with 'Made in China,'" *China Economic Journal*, 2(1), 93–104.

Xie, W. (2004). "Technological Learning in China's Colour TV (CTV) Industry," *Technovation*, 24(6), 499–512.

Xie, W. and G. Wu (2003). "Differences between Learning Processes in Small Tigers and Large Dragons: Learning Processes of Two Color TV (CTV) Firms within China," *Research Policy*, 32(8), 1463–79.

Xin, X. and Y. Wang (2000). *Kuayue Shikong: Zhongguo Tongxin Chanye Fazhan Qishilu* [Crossing Time and Space: Revelation from the Development of Telecommunication Industry of China], Beijing: Beijing Youdian daxue Chubanshe [Beijing University of Post and Telecommunication Press].

Xing, Y. (2019). "Global Value Chains and the Innovation of the Chinese Mobile Phone Industry," *GRIPS Discussion Paper*, No. 19–14.

Xiong, Q. and J. Long (2006). "Impact of Auto-Part Localization Policy on Automobile Industry," *Annals of Shanghai Economic Society* (in Chinese), 2006, 242–53.

Xu, C. (2011). "The Fundamental Institutions of China's Reforms and Development," *Journal of Economic Literature*, 49(4), 1076–151.

Xu, J. and R.H. Girling (2004). *Huawei Technologies Co., Ltd.*, Sonoma: Sonoma State University.

Xu, R. and J. Fu, (1997). "Huawei Became the largest Supplier of Indigenous SPC Switching" [Huawei Chengwei Guochan jiaohuanji Zuida Gongyingshang], *Sehnzhen Tequ Bao* [Shenzhen Special Zone Daily].

Xu, X. and Y. Wang (1999). "Ownership Structure and Corporate Governance in Chinese Stock Companies," *China Economic Review*, 10(1), 75–98.

Yam, R.C.M., J.C. Guan, K.F. Pun, and E.P.Y. Tang (2004). "An Audit of Technological Innovation Capabilities in Chinese Firms: Some Empirical Findings in Beijing, China," *Research Policy*, 33(8), 1123–40.

Yan, A. and B. Gray (1994). "Bargaining Power, Management Control, and Performance in United States-China Joint Ventures: A Comparative Case Study," *The Academy of Management Journal*, 37(6), 1478–517.

Yan, A. and B. Gray (2018). "Linking Management Control and Interpartner Relationships with Performance in US-Chinese Joint Ventures," in: J. Child and Y. Lu (Eds.), *Management Issues in China (Vol.2): International Enterprises*, London: Routledge, 106–27.

Yang, D.T. (1999). "Urban-Biased Policies and Rising Income Inequality in China," *American Economic Review*, 89(2), 306–10.

Yao, Y. (2010). "The End of the Beijing Consensus: Can China's Model of Authoritarian Growth Survive?," *Foreign Affairs Online*, 2, 2–5.

Yao, Y. and K. Zhang (2010). "Has China Passed the Lewis Turning Point? A Structural Estimation Based on Provincial Data," *China Economic Journal*, 3(2), 155–62.

Yeung, A. (2005). "How Can Chinese Companies Go Global More Successfully," *CEIBS The Link*, 2005(Fall), 18–21.

Yiping, H., G. Qin, and W. Xun (2013). "Institutions and the Middle-income Trap: Implications of cross-country experiences for China," Presented at *the International Conference on the Inequality and the Middle-Income Trap in China*, July 1–2, hosted by the CCER, Peking University, 2013.

Yu, J. (2006). "Local State Corporatism, Rent-Seeking, and the Failure of Chinese Automobile Industrial Policy," *China Public Administration Review* (in Chinese), 2, 75–94.

Yu, J. (2011). "From 3G to 4G: Technology Evolution and Path Dynamics in China's Mobile Telecommunication Sector," *Technology Analysis & Strategic Management*, 23(10), 1079–93.

Yu, J., Y.J. Shi, and X. Fang (2004). "Building Technological Capability by Latecomer Firms in Developing Countries," *2004 IEEE International Engineering Management Conference*, 1, 387–91.

Yu, X.K. (2008). "Improving Industry Policy to Promote the Development of Chinese IC Industry," *Zhongguo Dianzi Shangqing* (in Chinese), 9, 16–22.

Yusuf, S. and K. Nabeshima (2009). "Can Malaysia Escape Middle Income Trap? A Strategy for Penang," *Policy Research Working Paper*, No. 4971, Washington, DC: The World Bank.

Zaghah, R. and G.T. Nankani (Eds.) (2005). *Economic Growth in the 1990s: Learning from a Decade of Reform*, Washington, DC: The World Bank.

Zeng, M. and P.J. Williamson (2007). *Dragons at Your Door: How Chinese Cost Innovation Is Disrupting Global Competition*, Boston, MA: Harvard Business School Press.

Zhang, K. (2005). "Going Global: The Why, When, Where and How of Chinese Companies' Outward Investment Intentions," Presentation at seminar, *Canada in Asia*, Vancouver: Asia Pacific Foundation. Accessed at: https://www.asiapacific.ca

Zhang, M. (1999). "Chronicle of Events in Telecommunication Industry in China" [Zhongguo Tongxin Chanye Fazhan Dashiji], www.electron.cetin.net.cn/w1999/nrxs. php3?lsh =5134.

Zhang, Q. (2000). *PUTIAN: Zhongguo Zhizao* [PTIC: Made in China], Beijing: Zhongguo Yanshi.

Zhang, W. and B. Igel (2001). "Managing the Product Development of China's SPC Switch Industry as an Example of CoPS," *Technovation*, 21(6), 361–8.

Zhang, X., J. Yang, and S. Wang (2011). "China Has Reached the Lewis Turning Point," *China Economic Review*, 22(4), 542–54.

Zhang, X.P. (Ed.) (2000). *Dianxin Yewu Shiyong Quanshu* [The Complete Knowledge of Telecommunication], Beijing: Taihai Chubanshe [Taihai Press].

Zhang, Y. (2009). "Alliance-Based Network View on Chinese Firms' Catching-up: Case Study of Huawei Technologies Co. Ltd.," *UNU-MERIT Working Paper*, No.2009–039.

Zhao, X. (2010). "Some Theoretical Issues on Lewis Turning Point," *Economist*, 5, 75–80.

Zhou, H.S. and M. Kerkhofs (1987). "System 12 Technology Transfer to the Peoples Republic of China," *Electrical Communication*, 61(2), 186–93.

Zhou, P. and L. Leydesdorff (2006). "The Emergence of China as a Leading Nation in Science," *Research Policy*, 35(1), 83–104.

Zhou, Q. (1998). "Compounding Three Networks and Digital Network Competition: Concurrently Discussing the Policy Environment for the Development of China's Telecom Industry," *Dianzi zhangwang yu zuici* [Electronic Prospects and Decision] (in Chinese), 6, 25–39.

Zhu, B. (2008). "Internationalization of Chinese MNEs and Dunning's Eclectic (OLI) Paradigm: A Case Study of Huawei Technologies Corporation's Internationalization Strategy," Master's thesis, Lund University.

Zhu, F., L. Xiao, and S. Li (2009). "The Strategic Role of Indigenous Innovation for Global Competition—The Case Study of Mobile and Telecom Equipment Industry in China," *Proceedings of the 2009 First International Workshop on Database Technology and Applications*, April 26, 123–7.

Zhu, G. (2000). "Zhongguo Dianxin Jishude Fazhanyu Zahnwang" [Development and Prospect of Telecommunication Technology in China], *Beijing dianxin* [Beijing Electronics] (in Chinese), (12), 2–5.

Zhu, H. (2005). "A Research on the Effects of Inter-firm Product Modularity on Industrial Development" (in Chinese), PhD thesis, Tsinghua University.

Zhu, H., Y. Yang, M.T. Tintchev, and G. Wu (2006). "The Interaction between Regulation and Market and Technology Opportunities: A Case Study of the Chinese Mobile Phone Industry," *Innovation: Organization & Management*, 8(1–2), 102–12.

Zhu, R. and J. Lu (Eds.) (1999). *Zhongguo Tielu Tongxinshi* [The History of Communication Railway in China], Beijing: Zhongguo Tiedao Chubanshe [China Railway Press].

Zhu, S. (1999). *Chengkong Shuzi Jiaohuanji Yuanli Yu Yingyong* [Principle and Application of SPC Switching], Xi'an: Xi'an Jiaotong University Press.

Zhu, S. and Y. Shi (2010). "Shanzhai Manufacturing – An Alternative Innovation Phenomenon in China: Its Value Chain and Implications for Chinese Science and Technology Policies," *Journal of Science and Technology Policy in China*, 1(1), 29–49.

Zhu, Y. (2006). *Zhongguo Jichengdianlu Chanye Fazhan Lunshu Wenji* (in Chinese), Beijing: Xinshidai Chubanshe.

Index